Best Practices, Case Studies and Management of Content, Information and Knowledge in LIS Profession

Best Practices, Case Studies and Management of Content, Information and Knowledge in LIS Profession

Editor-in-Chief

Nagappa V Bakkannanavar

Organizers:

Tata Consultancy Services (TCS), Bangalore

Special Library Association (SLA)– Asian Chapter

Karnataka State Library Association (KALA), Bangalore

Ess Ess Publications

New Delhi

Best Practices, Case Studies and Management of Content, Information and Knowledge in LIS Profession

ISBN: 978-81-7000-675-6

Rs.825/-

First Published 2012

Published by:
Ess Ess Publications
4831/24, Ansari Road,
Darya Ganj,
New Delhi-110 002.
INDIA
Phones: 23260807, 41563444
Fax: 41563334
E-mail: info@essessreference.com
www.essessreference.com

Cover Design by *Patch Creative Unit*

Printed and bound in India at Salasar Imaging Systems.

SoFerence Kit Sponsors:
McGraw Hill, New Delhi

Chief Patrons:

Mr. BP Prakash, President, SLA Asian Chapter and Global IRC Head, TCS, Mumbai

Mr. Nagaraj Ijari, Head, TCS Bangalore Operations

Mr. P Y Rajendra Kumar, President, KALA, Bangalore

COMMITTEES

Advisory Committee

Dr. SK Patil, University Librarian, Symbiosis International University , Pune

Mr. NV Satyanarayana, MD & Chairman, Informatics Ltd., Bangalore

Dr. Shalini Urs, Executive Director, ISiM, Mysore

Dr. SL Sangam, Professor & Chairman, DLIS, Karnatak University, Dharwad

Dr. PV Konnur, University Librarian, Bangalore University, Bangalore

Dr. TD Kemparaju, Professor & Chairman, DLIS, Bangalore University, Bangalore

Dr. Mallinath Kumbar, Professor & Chairman, DLIS, University of Mysore

Dr. B S Biradar, Kuvempu Professor & Chairman, DLIS, University, Shimoga

Dr. B S Maheswarappa, Professor, DLIS, Gulbarga University, Gulbarga

Dr. AK Baradol, Professor & Chairman, DLIS, Mangalore University, Mangalore

Dr. P Sadashivamurthy, Professor & Chairman, DLIS, Tumkur University, Tumkur

Dr. PG Tadasad, Reader & Chairman, DLIS, KSWU, Bijapur

Dr. Francis Jayakanth, Scientific Staff, NCSI, Bangalore

ORGANIZING COMMITTEE

Mr. Kishore Ingale, Chair– Events Committee, SLA Asian Chapter and Branch IRC Head, TCS, Pune

Ms. M. Manjula, Manager, TCS, Bangalore

Mr. Rajendra Babu, Manager, Wipro Technologies, Bangalore

Mr. Anand Byrappa, Manager, General Electric, Bangalore

Mr. Manish Mankad, Manager, Hindustan Unilever Limited, Bangalore

Mr. M Nandeesha, KM Consultant, SAP, Bangalore

Mr. Raghavendra Patil, Executive, TCS, Bangalore

Mr. Iranna Shettar, Executive, TCS, Bangalore

ORGANIZING SECRETARY

Dr. Nagappa V. Bakkannanavar, Member - SLA Asian Chapter Membership Committee and Branch IRC Head, TCS, Bangalore

Contents

FOREWORD

In the age of information explosion, our knowledge is doubling at very fast pace due to advancements in ICT technologies and shift in socioeconomic factors. In such a scenario; TCS, SLA, and KALA came together to organize an inclusive social conference or SoFerence. The target of the conference was Library and Information Science professionals, the managers of world's information. The event aptly attracted a wide range of papers to examine some of the best practices and some steps forward in future.

"Every paper selected for publication in the SoFerence-2011 proceedings has been checked for originality and plagiarism. Editorial Committee's evaluation and live ratings by the SoFerence-2011 participants during the stage presentation provided additional criteria for selection. I am sure these papers would be useful & topical for the LIS community.

The paper, 'Applying Psychometrics in Managing Library Customers' focuses on the management of library customers while 'Wow Me – Soft Skills Required for LIS Professional' looks inward to better manager self to serve the customers better. Through papers like 'Developing a Cost Effective E-Library, 'Success Vs Best Practices in Academic Libraries', 'Library and Information Centre @ Tata Consulting Engineers – A Case Study', and 'Some Best Practices Adopted in the College Libraries and Information Centres – An Overview' the authors share experiences that can benefit the end users as well as library managers.

I appreciate the innovative efforts of TCS, SLA and KALA in organizing SoFerence-2011, which has created a new benchmark and a role model in conducting events & seminars. The SoFerence format was truly democratic right from the selection of the papers for presentation to the selection of papers for publication. This experiment has created lot of excitement and I wish it's tried at higher levels and eventually attract experts of international repute.

The book will be immensely useful for the knowledge seekers in the library community. I congratulate the editors and also thank the authors for sharing their thoughts.

Wish the organizing committee a great success for their future such endeavours.

Chief Patrons

Mr. BP Prakash, President, SLA Asian Chapter and Global IRC Head, TCS, Mumbai, Mr. Nagaraj Ijari, Head, TCS Bangalore Operations, Bangalore, Mr. P Y Rajendra Kumar, President, KALA, Bangalore

PREAMBLE

In this age of information explosion, professionals hardly get the time to meet each other personally and share their professional experience and knowledge with fellow professionals as every movement new tools, queries, problems, etc., (which are challenging our skill sets) are coming into our professional life in the field. It's the responsibility of each one of us to accept them with enthusiasm to deliver the best out of it. Present generation of LIS fraternity is very much dynamic and working towards addressing the raising day to day issues, which are taking place in the field through different modes.

We learn many things from the student life to manage our present professional life. Recent advancements in ICT helped LIS professionals to enhance their skill sets to achieve the best in the industry. However, there are many issues, which are still unanswered. That's where the social conferences or forums like SoFerence play a vital role in finding out solutions to such issues.

SoFerence, is novel concept and a social platform, which allows professionals to share their experiences in the form of best practices, processes improvements, new initiatives, success stories, case studies, etc., which will help other co-professionals to know and implement them at their workplace. SoFerence will empower every author & participant to play a vital role by acting as a moderator to choose the best set of papers, which will eventually bringing this publication. (SoFerence Souvenir, a CD and Book with ISBN Number).

We received a marvellous response for this SoFerence for the entire LIS fraternity and related industry from across India, which was quite encouraging and placed huge responsibilities on us to make the event very victorious and to live up to the expectations of participants, authors and other supports. Though, the registration was restricted to only 80, many professional come forward and requested to increase the number and finally we forced to increase the seats to 125 participants. More than 50 papers were submitted by different authors; however editorial committee has selected only 41 and 3 papers for presentation and poster presentations respectively. Based on the plagiarism report, online ratings, editorial ratings and ratings given during the presentation, 22 papers were selected for publication as a part of SoFerence Proceedings.

Our Heartfelt gratitude to Mr. Nagaraj Ijari, Operations Head, Tata Consultancy Services, Bangalore for providing all necessary support to host this event in premises of TCS, Bangalore. We are also grateful Mr. BP Prakash, President SLA-Asian Chapter & Global IRC Head, Tata Consultancy Services and P Y Rajendra Kumar, President, KALA, Bangalore for accepting invitation to patronage and inaugurate the SoFerence.

Our special Thanks to Social Discussion moderator Ms. Geetha V, IRC Head (Rtd.), TCS Bangalore and members Dr. B. M. Meera, Raman Research Institute, Bangalore, Dr. Ramesha, Bangalore University, Bangalore, Mr. M. Nandeesha, SAP, Bangalore, Mr. Madhuresh, Advinus, Bangalore, Dr. K Prakash, Azim Premji University, Bangalore and Ms. M Manjula, TCS Bangalore for making the event more meaningful and memorable.

We sincerely appreciate Dr. Chowadappa N, Chief Librarian, BMS College of Engineering, & President, AKELPA, Bangalore, Mr. Giridhar Kunkur, Librarian, Welingkar Institute of Management Development and Research, Mumbai, Ms. Asha Balaji, Manager, British Council Library, Chennai and Dr. AY Asundi, Professor & Chairman (Rtd.) DLIS, Bangalore University, Bangalore, who have successfully facilitated technical sessions.

We also thank Mr. Manish Mankad, Manager, Hindustan Unilever Limited, Bangalore, who delivered the Spotlight Lecture on "Better Customer Connect through Process Improvement in Information Services".

Without authors contribution and LIS professionals active participation, no one can organize any such event in the field. Therefore, it's our moral duty to acknowledge and appreciate their contribution and participation.

Last but not the least; we thank each and every member of Advisory Committee, Organizing Committee, TCS (Information Resource Centre, Admin and IS), Bangalore for their wonderful and timely advice, support and efforts made towards this successful and memorable event. This SoFerence wouldn't have taken place, without the great support by all the above professional friends. Hope this event has created a new milestone in the history of learning and sharing of knowledge in the field of LIS and related areas. Below is a brief feedback on the SoFerence 2011.

Feedback on	Rating (1-low & 10-high)
SoFerence Concept	8.6
Content	7.7
Registration Process	8.3
Ambience	8.4
Food	7.9
Hospitality	8.6
Overall	**8.3**

Have a great Experience and Knowledge Sharing!

Dr. Nagappa V Bakkannanavar,
Organizing Secretary, SoFerence, 2011 and
Branch Head – Information Resource Centre,
Tata Consultancy Services, Bangalore, Karnataka, India

Section – I
SPOTLIGHT LECTURES

1

Better Customer Connect Through Process Improvement in Information Services

Mankad Manish
Shanthi P
Hindustan Unilever Limited, 64 Main Road, Whitefield, Bangalore 560066, Karnataka, India

ABSTRACT

This paper presents a case study of enhancing customer connect by introducing a series of process improvement measures. It takes a historical perspective of the information services rendered using traditional methods and traces the subsequent developments which were ushered in by various factors. The paper also showcases select areas in which the proactive steps were introduced including various methods of collecting and evaluating customer feedback, portal development, user empowerment, services performance evaluation metrics and the use of the latest information technology options.

Key words: *Information services, portal development, user feedback, e-surveys, share point services, user empowerment.*

Preamble: Enabled by the digitization of research and development (R&D) workflows, the drive to accelerate both innovation and time to market, plus the technological capability to collaborate globally, is changing the way industrial organizations manage R&D[1].

INTRODUCTION

Established in 1890's, Unilever's mission is to add vitality to life. We meet everyday needs for nutrition; hygiene and personal care with brands that help people feel good, look good and get more out of life. With more than 400 brands focused on health and wellbeing, no company touches so many people's lives in so many different ways.

Our portfolio ranges from nutritionally balanced foods to indulgent ice creams, affordable soaps, luxurious shampoos and everyday household care products. We produce world-leading brands including Lipton, Knorr, Dove, Axe, Hellmann's and Omo, alongside trusted local names such as Blue Band, Pureit and Suave[2]

OVERVIEW OF RESEARCH & DEVELOPMENT IN UNILEVER

The R&D function at Unilever employs over 6,000 professionals located in 20 countries spanning the globe from Mexico to Australia. Successful collaboration ensures our experts' collective minds are brought together as one R&D organization to help create the products for which we're so well-known. We do this through our six strategic R&D laboratories that focus on delivering ground-breaking technologies and our 31 major development centers that develop and implement product innovations. Additionally, throughout 92 locations around the globe we have R&D teams implementing innovations in countries and our factories.[2]

ROLE OF INFORMATION SERVICES

R&D and information services always co-existed at Unilever. The senior leadership of the company believed and practiced 'joining hands', support setting up and nurturing new information services. As the research activities grew so did the

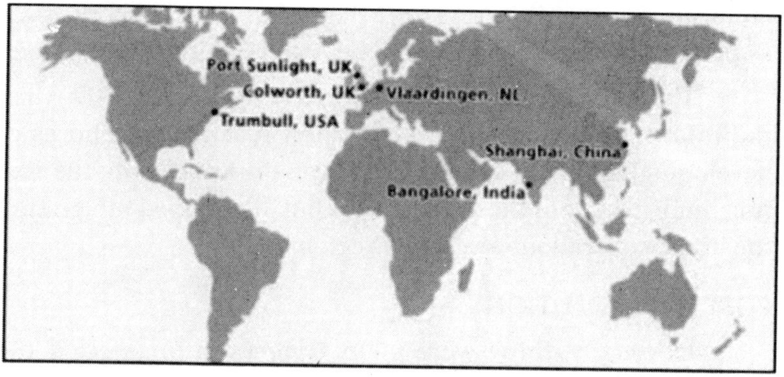

Fig. 1. Unilever R&D locations

information services. The role of information services was therefore to: support research and development by proactively extending timely and precise information services to the scientists by using modern information management techniques.

HISTORICAL PERSPECTIVE: PRE-IT REVOLUTION

The library services (as it was called that time) in Unilever started off as early as in 1930's in the US and Europe laboratories. Subsequently, in 1967, in India, a first ever private sector research centre came up in Mumbai which also had a library services division. All these libraries were large, each of them catering to about 300 to 1500 scientists working on the site.

These libraries offered standard library services such as books and journals management, current awareness service, documentation of internal knowledge. All these material were in the physical form; access was limited by the specific site. The resource sharing was limited due to the distances hence the resource duplication was inevitable.

This scenario changed to some extent during the late 70's and 80's when the western labs ushered in the automation. The important databases were made available on the floppies and subsequently on the local servers. The internal scientific documentation, books and journals management also underwent e-transformation. These measures had the positive impact on the quality of services, the users were happy but other concerns such as poor resource sharing and duplication remained unresolved.

The second phase of change was during 90's and 00's when the information technology revolution reached the shores of developing countries as well. This brought in not only the real time information to the western labs but also helped integrating the library operations across the regions.

POST IT-REVOLUTION

Externally, there were many triggers in this period-the pricing of the personal computers and other hardware peripherals becoming competitive; every big corporate initiated having a separate policy on the implementation of information technology across their various functions, the operating systems turning more robust, user friendly, and most importantly the internet was becoming an essential part of every communication strategy.

These triggers made many processes and businesses either redundant or made them to change completely-the financial markets, information management, entertainment, travel, education and training, science and technology, administration to name a few.

Unilever have always been a pro-active in embracing new technologies to enhance productivity and to deliver value to its shareholders and investors.

WHY PROCESS IMPROVEMENT?

The growing pace of business and R&D at Unilever necessitated another trigger for the information management team to re-look at the current ways of working and to come out with a long term, strategic plan to deliver information effectively and efficiently. This called for a complete re-look at the existing processes, carry out gap analysis and come out with a plan to fill these gaps in the process.

Let us first understand the theme 'Process'- the Wikipedia[3] defines it as:

Process or processing typically describes the action of taking something through an established and usually routine set of procedures or steps to convert it from one form to another, such as processing paperwork to grant a mortgage loan, processing milk into cheese, or converting computer data from one form to another. A process involves steps and decisions in the way work is accomplished, and may involve a sequence of events.

The process that one follows is as important as the results that are produced by the process. Without understanding the underlying process, it is difficult to know how a certain set of results were achieved, or why they were good or bad. So, if results are viewed as the "destination", then process can be viewed as the "vehicle" that gets you there (and ideally, you should be able to use the same "vehicle" for many trips...with a few modifications based on the desired destination!)

The information management teams across the regions took up this challenge to re-align the information delivery process towards supporting the core business strategies of Unilever. Hence it was important for us to understand the existing processes, evaluate the results and work towards optimizing these results.

Broadly, the following represents a typical information access flowchart within a traditional library setup:

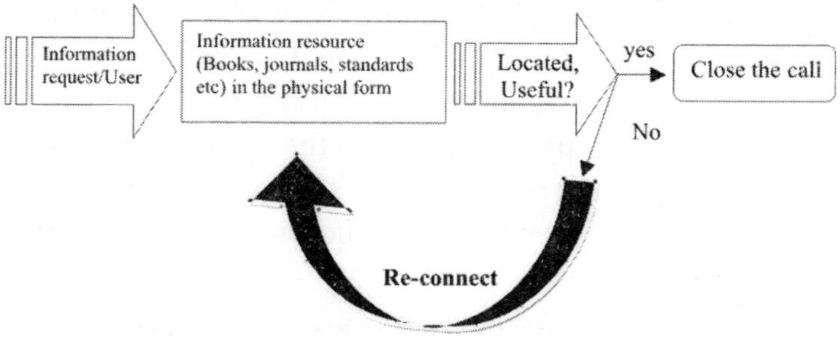

Fig. 2. Typical Information access flow chart

The 'Re-connect' is a vital and critical component in this entire process of accessing and using information. This provides the library personnel an opportunity to keep improving their services which includes the resources.

PROCESS IMPROVEMENT BEGINS

The very first step in improving any process is to have a realization that the existing process has outlived its utility and hence needs to change/improve. Our global teams across the information centers discussed, shared ideas and facilitated the leveraging of the emerging IT trends to our advantage.

A combined analysis of existing ways of working was the first step across all the information centers. It clearly showed up the following areas which needed an overhaul:

- customer connect/feedback analysis
- access to subscribed information sources
- cost optimization and spend analysis
- expanding the footprints of our services
- enlarging the scope of our services
- skills analysis of information center teams
- customer empowerment

TAKING IT FORWARD

As is the case with most of the improvement plans, there are times when one needs to take tough and challenging decisions to make the process improvement work. These include staff realignment, restructuring of information sources portfolio, redefining vendors' relationships, centralization of budgets for tighter and better controls, lastly even the customer will have to be convinced to accept the newer ways of working i.e. web based instead of face to face interaction, self-help instead of hand holding all the time.

Fortunately, for us, the senior leadership of our company shared and supported our line of thinking on our process improvement plans. We listed out our priorities and drew up a timeline for its execution. Next was to set up a strong core team capable of creating the plan and delivering it on time.

The team was truly global having its members across all the centers driving a common agenda of process improvement. They had the full independence of building their teams and talent pool, capable of reaching the agreed goals. This included local recruitment, training and induction, periodic performance assessment and working out their career aspirations. Although this exercise was global, it was agreed to respect site/regional norms on HR management.

CASE STUDIES: SERVICE TRANSFORMATION

Although, we have made a complete change over in all the areas, we will list out some of them where we took some noticeable and impactful steps towards process improvements:

- customer connect/feedback → e-survey
- access to subscribed information sources → e-resources and portal development
- customer empowerment → direct ordering of reprints.

FUNDAMENTAL SHIFT

An exploratory study by Hustaad Eli [(4)], investigating how MNCs are leveraging Web 2.0 applications to improve knowledge sharing and creation within and across their boundaries categorizes the multinational companies into 4 quadrants according to their maturity of how they are utilizing Web 2.0 and social networking either within their intra-organizational boundaries or in an extended inter-organizational context.

Interestingly, all the multinationals under investigation demonstrate curiosity towards experimenting with new social networking tools through pilot studies or other initiatives of different scales. Examples are 1) utilizing MS SharePoint platforms internally to take advantage of collaboration and knowledge sharing through wikis, blogs, and social tagging, 2) using social networking sites for recruiting purposes that may cause considerable savings, 3) using Facebook for connecting geographically dispersed employees, and 4) utilizing virtual worlds such as Second Life to support collaboration as well as co-creation and innovation across academic and public researcher groups through facilitating a rich collaborative space.

Unilever started moving in towards using Microsoft Sharepoint Server (MOSS) technology [5] for managing its data. Taking clues from various case studies like University of Mississippi Libraries using Sharepoint for their various library functions [6]; we also initiated making use of collaborative space.

CUSTOMER CONNECT/FEEDBACK

We realized that before embarking any change in the basic information services, we must ensure alignment to users' requirements and their expectations. There are many methods available to gauge the users' expectations. In the past, we had employed manual survey methods i.e. physical questionnaire based and then used SPSS statistical package to get the insight. However, with the user community spread across the globe, it was not feasible to employ traditional survey methods.

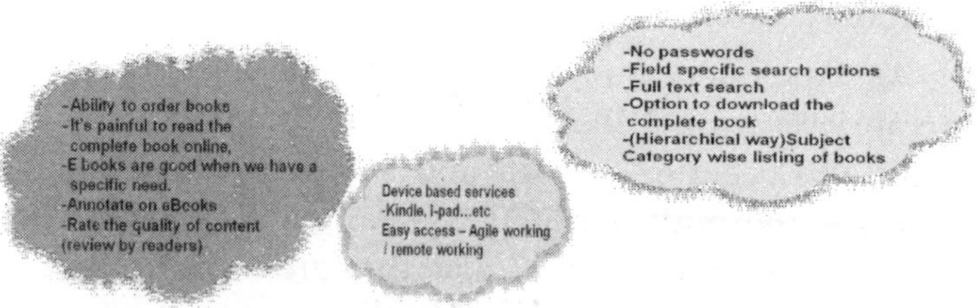

Fig. 3. Survey comments, wishes

Hence, we created number of surveys under MOSS : user expectations on the e-books, making use of current awareness service, knowledge retention methods, quality assessment of searches are some of the surveys. The survey invitations were created in an HTML format and sent as an email.

The insights helped us in refining our choices of our e-resources, creating robust vendor agreements; collating a users' wish list for replacement of existing tools, on knowing how people find, use, and store and share the technical & scientific information that is used within projects to drive the innovation process.

PORTAL DEVELOPMENT

One of the major shifts was moving away from the physical library space so that the access to various resources is not limited by the proximity to a library. This opened up another challenge to develop a portal which can host all the useful, technical resources and subsequently become a brand for our information services. We had to ensure simplicity of the design, adherence to MOSS guidelines, fulfill users' requirements, capture all the tools, resources and services and finally create a long lasting image for the user so that there is a recall for a repeat visit.

The Technical Information Service (TIS) portal, as it is better known, was conceptualized and developed by our information services team members incorporating all the current requirements. As this is a global portal, we also created a common mail box email whereby all the queries across all the regions get resolved within 24 hours by our teams situated at India and UK.

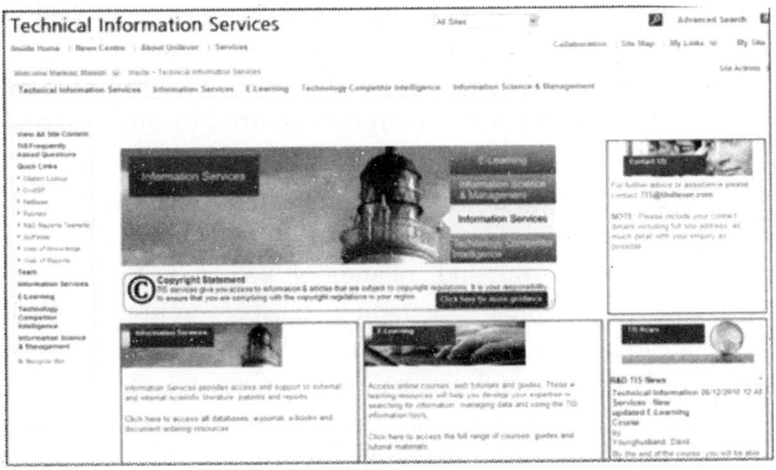

Fig. 4. TIS portal

The portal has sub-parts as follows:

- e-resources like books, journals, databases, patents
- e-training resources like animated tutorials (internally produced and from the various publishers)
- document ordering tool – for unsubscribed journals
- Internal knowledge retention system including templates and animated user guides
- Links to other important, internal portals
- Competitors' technology information
- RSS feeds of externally published scientific output by Unilever scientists
- e-bulletin board and 'contact us' email.

The footfalls on this site have been encouraging since it was launched last year. This is also apparent from the increased use of e-resources, more number of article ordering and less number of routine queries. We attribute these positive changes towards aggressive promotion, presence of our portal on other intranet portal, training and induction.

E-RESOURCES

Once we were out of physical library space, we had to immediately work out an alternative plan.. Our main collection-books and journals- must get equivalent if not better replacement. Keeping in mind our users' wish list captured by one of the e-survey, we decided to go fully electronic.

The challenges in deployment of e-resources were many: budgetary provision, licensing agreement, global spread of user base, usage monitoring and collation of 'Return on Investment' (ROI) data. Before embarking upon final list of resources, we had an exhaustive usage analysis of existing resources across all the sites. This helped us eliminate a number of redundant, duplicate resources. Of course, we did work out an alternative access mechanism for the least used resources.

Currently we have e-journals, e-books and various databases subscribed and made available on our portal. These are all IP (internet protocol) address enabled so as to take care of unauthorized access.

The Outsell study [7] identified five imperatives for librarians to consider as they rethink their approach to measuring and communicating value and ROI:

1. Libraries should measure their impact on the enterprise and on business performance and communicate it to management and key stakeholders.
2. A structured approach to aligning investment decisions with business goals and to confirming value and ROI data will provide stronger and more sustainable results than will ad hoc measures.
3. Librarians should develop a model for discussion.
4. Librarians should find the right partner(s) with whom to create ROI evaluations.
5. Information managers must not allow the value of the library to be underestimated.

We connect to the respective publishers to access usage statistics for each e-resource. This is further analysed to take various decisions on next year allocations and selection; market the value of the information services.

USER EMPOWERMENT

In the traditional information services, most of the user requests are handled and resolved by the information personnel. These include, book orders, journal reprint requests, translation request, interlibrary loan request etc. Typically the requests are either sent in via email or handed over in person. This system has its share of pros and cons. The pros include a personal touch and may be a quick action if there is possibility of knowing a requester. The cons would be a delay if the person handling the requests is absent, mail box is full, the request is copied/interpreted incorrectly, the response time is long because the person is busy etc.

In the current system, we have empowered the users to take their own decisions and activate the order mechanism themselves. The unsubscribed journals reprints now can be ordered directly using WorldCat link manager. The order goes directly to the British Library for document supply. The journal reprint arrives in the respective users' mailbox in the secured Adobe® format. One needs to have special reader software to access the same. It is copyright protected so cannot be circulated further. Our users have appreciated this process improvement as there is no time delay and they have a complete freedom of their choice.

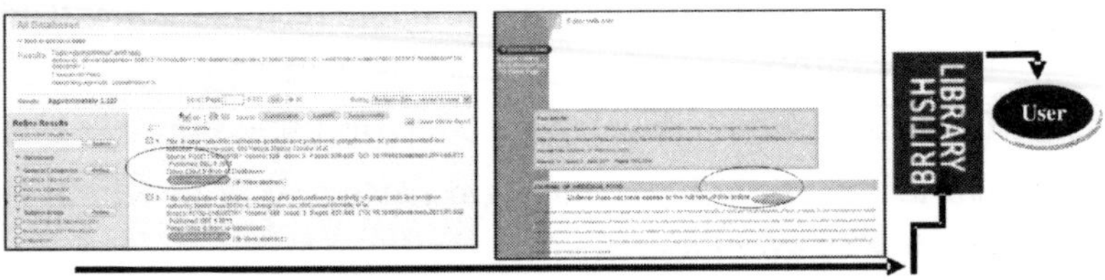

Fig. 5. Direct document ordering system

Even for the books which are not available on any of the e-books platforms, the user can request to get specific parts/chapters which would then arrive from the British library.

As suggested by O'Neill[(8)], when the overall ordering data is analyzed, it provides valuable insights into the emerging subject areas, additional journals which might be added, research interest areas, gaps in the core collection etc. Additionally, the site specific ordering pattern helps us build credibility for the collection and provide further clarity on the future training and promotional efforts for the information services.

PROMOTION AND TRAINING

Although, the information services are considered to be essential and critical for R&D community, the overall awareness about the services and capability is generally found to be low. This is more so in the electronic, virtual space where the personal, face-to-face interactions are either less or simply absent. Using various market research techniques including surveys, focus groups and analysis of suggestions, libraries can understand the needs and design appropriate services and facilities (*Sharma, Bhardwaj*) (9).

We initiated promotion of our virtual information services – portal- even before we had it up and running. This was done to create excitement, anticipation and expectations for the promoted service. When we launched our portal, we observed immediate impact on its browsing data. However, it was a challenge to create wide spread awareness about the availability of scientific information tools and also to inculcate a culture of moving away from public search engines such as Yahoo, Google etc.

The promotion was done in various formats, electronic (Telepresence, email, screen savers, slide show) as well as physical (face to face, poster, flyer). We took help from site Human Relation (HR) department to include the information training module in their induction programme. This helped new recruits to connect to the portal services quickly and also to enroll for any further training. We also contacted all the research divisions for sharing our promotional material and the response was fairly high. The remote sites were connected thru' IT communication tools such as livemeetings' or Telepresence.

The tools training was the next phase once the scientists had settled in their new roles. This training was imparted again in two ways- the first, in person or via remote connectivity. We also had the webinar based training options from the vendors from time to time. We informed our users well in advance so that they can join these short learning sessions from their laptops or PCs. Our observation so far has been that there is a far less participation in the web-based training session compared to the ones conducted face to face. However, that could be the passing phenomenon as the participation would surely go up once more and more people are comfortable with new training technologies.

We have also tied up with the central training department

to upload e-training modules which user can enroll and learn.

CONCLUSION

Every fundamental change needs a process change. We have ensured that customers get the best of the information services by placing necessary workflows and right processes at the right places. The journey will be ongoing with the continuous reviewing of new processes using customer feedback. The challenge is to reach out to newer groups, explore IT-enabled ways to provide the existing services in a differentiated manner like mobile telephony, remote access, single sign-on for multiple resource access and higher level of user empowerment.

REFERENCES

1. Joanne Lustig; David Bousfield; **http.//www.outsellinc.com/store/products/980-how-industrial-r-d-trends-are-impacting-stm-information-overview-for-information-managers** (accessed on 24/08/2011).
2. **http.//www.unilever.com** (accessed on 24/08/2011).
3. **http.//en.wikipedia.org/wiki/Process** (accessed on 01/09/2011).
4. Hustaad Eli, PROCEEDINGS OF THE 9TH EUROPEAN CONFERENCE ON KNOWLEDGE MANAGEMENT, **Pages.** 323-331 **Published.** 2008.
5. **http.//sharepoint.microsoft.com/en-us/Pages/default.aspx** (accessed on 27/08/2011).
6. Kevin Herrera, (2008) "From static files to collaborative workspace with SharePoint", Library Hi Tech, Vol. 26 Iss. 1, pp.80 – 94.
7. Scotti, George J., THE IMPACT OF E-ESOURCES; Special Libraries Association; June 2010 (accessed on 24/08/2011).
8. O'Neil, JOURNAL OF THE AMERICAN SOCIETY FOR INFORMATION SCIENCE AND TECHNOLOGY **Volume.** 59 **Issue.** 13 **Pages.** 2042-2050 **Published.** NOV 2008.
9. Ajay Sharma, Sapna Bhardwaj, **Marketing and Promotion of Library Services** (accessed on 27/08/2011).

Section – II
BEST PAPERS

2

Knowledge Manifestations in Creative Hobbies: *A Study of Numismatics and Philately*

Dr. A.Y. Asundi
Professor and Chairman (Ret.),
Department of Library & Information Science,
and Officer-in-charge, IT Centre,
Bangalore University, Bangalore – 560 056

Dr. Ramesha
Associate Professor, Department of Library and Information Science,
Bangalore University, Bangalore – 560 056,

ABSTRACT

The knowledge extraction from different domains of human activity would be a creative passion and an innovative idea. Knowledge that rests in human mind termed as mentefact is transformed into some creative vocation, and/or occupation which is denoted as the artifacts. There are numerous creative hobbies practiced by human beings since centuries, as a pastime, as lifetime vocation, as part of preservation of historical and cultural relics and tradition and also sometimes as a business proposition - antiques business. The hobbyists inherently have some of their own and some borrowed ideas to profess their hobby and which are tacit and also implicit within the subject domain. So the paper, utilizing two very popular creative hobbies, Numismatics and Philately has attempted to manifest their knowledge content, and that would serve to organize the information related to such and other related hobbies.

Keywords: Creativity, Creative Occupations Hobbies, Knowledge Creation, Knowledge Management, Metadata, Numismatics, Philately.

INTRODUCTION

Knowledge has many residents. It lies in human mind, which is expressionless; it is manifested as intangible and which is termed as mentefact. The artifacts are resulted out of mentefacts and which though tangible, but the knowledge is implicit and it is a tacit knowledge. The expressions are manifold. It is a creative manifestation of individuals, who put their expressions into the artifacts and are exclusive creations of an individual. The instances the paintings, musical compositions can be given here as examples. Similarly there are other intellectual occupations which are termed as hobbies and pastimes, which manifest characteristics of hidden knowledge or implicit knowledge. The paper has used two creative hobbies, numismatics and philately to manifest their knowledge content which is expressed in their hobbyist vocation.

HOBBIES AND THEIR CREATIVE NATURE

It is well known fact that human being are social animals and always engaged in some gregarious occupations. The occupations (one who is occupied) as such are many, for the purpose of earning a livelihood, for a social cause, as a family responsibility, for leisure and fun and or an urge to be creative. Hobbies as one of the creative occupations have manifold objectives – for fun, as a pastime, as a creative and fine art, as part of the preservation of heritage and cultural tradition, or sometimes as an antique business.

The hobbies are not about doing something just for the sake of it, but it has become a passion for someone as part of their life.. Another reason to choose a hobby is that it gives a sense of being in charge of ones life and career. Thus, a hobby allows an individual to find his/her hidden talent, creativity or maybe just discover the hidden insights into its elements and characteristics. A hobby becomes as meaningful as a creative work as, it also adds a new meaning to ones life. There are hobbies as strange as collection of bottles,

Sometimes, when a person feels helpless of not doing anything, hobby is the best pastime and it could turn out to be a great morale and confidence booster in one's lonely life. So, going on an adventurous trip to the mountains, rock climbing or simply taking a nature walk, which can boost thinking and creativity, is a good idea. Such an environment definitely teaches the importance of appreciating nature. The world around us becomes a beautiful place, and that can also makes one to be creative to accumulate thoughts and knowledge of – rock climbing, appreciation of nature and so on. The bird watching or Ornithology, as appreciation of birds has turned "Salim Ali" as one of the greatest Ornithologist and naturalist in the world and known as a "Birdman of India" who incidentally has created enormous wealth of knowledge on the subject, otherwise it would be dormant. So a hobby when incubated, nurtured and assimilated can turn out to be an intellectual occupations and can lead to generation of new ideas, and a body of new knowledge.

There is a case of another incident of person turning out to be a traveloguer, who has added meaning to his life by following his heart, and taking up a hobby. It is narrated so; "I remember, my brother loved collecting stamps and currencies of different countries. He grew up admiring those places and dreamt of visiting these countries some day. And he realised his dream by the age of 30. So, for him, a childhood hobby turned into a full-fledged career as a travel writer". Knowledge manifested in hobbies might be an innovation and would lead to creativity.

NUMISMATICS AND PHILATELY

It is well said, "after all, money is ubiquitous in our daily life. We can't possibly survive in a social setting without money for any length of time". That is the power of money. ***Money is as old as civilization and it is considered to be one of the relics and traits of cultures.*** The study of coinage leads to the study of history as evident from the incident of Muhammad **Bin Tughlaq** who was one of the most remarkable and interesting ruler of the Tughlaq dynasty. Muhammad took a very modern step in introducing bronze coins as the token currency, the feature of "coinage" fantasies of Tughlag is extensively presented in Wikipedia (Wikipedia)

What is after all money has to do with numismatics? Coins and currencies of many dimensions and values are the representations of money and are exchanged towards the value of material. Numismatics is the art or hobby of collecting coins and currencies of different countries, times, values, etc. It is one of the most popular hobbies practiced all over the world. The world of "Plastic Money" may be endangering this hobby.

The Philately is a hobby of collecting and organising stamps and also making veritable presentations. It is another interesting and yet the most popular hobby taken up by young and old alike. It has an international reputation, as philatelic exhibitions and fairs are organised at different levels – national, regional and international. Philatelic exhibitions are also held by subjects. For more descriptive account of philately, one can refer to any encyclopaedia. The National Book Trust of India brought out a dossier in 1973. Similar to coinage the, stamps may become irrelevant with the growth of electronic mail and franking devises gradually replacing affixing a postage stamp.

KNOWLEDGE MANIFESTATIONS OF NUMISMATICS.

The birth of Coins and Coinage

The study of coins and collection of coins is part of the

history. They are non-conventional sources of information. The study and notion of information and information sources in recent years is widening due to the advent of digital technology, which is facilitated with simple data capture technologies. It has thus become one of the important and interesting aspects of collection of information from non-conventional sources information. In the digital information organisation, the metadata plays a key role and the knowledge implicit in such non-conventional sources has to be manifested to identify the basic and related concepts and ideas.

Among the types of historical sources, the archeological sources – inscriptions, coins and monuments are the core and from which the historical documentation can be devised. It is said, the discovery of metals led man invent coins. These metals, which replace cows as exchange items in early ages, were used in exchange of materials. The first coins were struck about 700 B.C. in Lydia, a Greek province. So thus the Coinage was born. Though the coins today all over the world are round in shape, but early coins were of different shapes – oval, square, oblong, hexagonal, rectangular, knife like, shirt like and so on

Knowledge Components of Coins

From the study of coins of different periods, countries and cultures, the following are the generic components of coins, which the numismatists would normal consider in organizing them.

i) Chronology of the Coins (Date)
ii) Currency (Face Value)
iii) Areas
iv) Dynasty – Political Situation and Conditions
v) Symbols and Emblems
vi) Gods and Goddesses on the coins
vii) Type of Metal – Gold, Silver, Bronze, Copper, Lead, Alloy
viii) Size and shape of the coin, Designs
ix) Animals depicted on the coins

x) Technology – Alloy, Minting

xi) Commemoration, Anniversaries

xii) Personalities

Each one of the above can be further divided by the Gods and Goddesses depicted in different periods of history and by dynasties. The categorisation also can be attempted by the Animals Depicted on them. Sreenivas has made an extensive study of historical non-conventional sources of information with particular reference to Coins and coinage of Vijayanagar Empire. The coins of Vijayanagar Empire are very important historical sources and the hobbyists would find the knowledge of coins very interesting and useful. The coins used, Gold Silver and Copper metals. They had a very interesting names – *Gadayana, Varaha, Pana, Pogaada, Pratabha, Kati, Chinnam, Madahaga, Visa, Bele Ruka and Kasu.*

KNOWLEDGE MANIFESTATIONS OF PHILATELY:

Birth of a Stamp

The history of postage stamp is not so old as coin. The history of postage stamps is associated with the story of postal service. It is very interesting to note that the present popular 'Courier' service is older than the postal service. The postal services were pre-paid in early years, and due to loss of revenue, the postage stamp was brought into use on 6th May 1840, and was named as "Penny Black".

The knowledge of Postage Stamp

It is reported that 'a one-cent' stamp had been insured at Rs.36,00,000 and was brought out by a 'body guard'. This implies the importance of Stamp by its special trait that 4-Cent Stamp had been printed with the value of 'one-cent". So this was the 'Collectors' treasure.

Philately is the hobby of stamp collection. Stamp-collecting is now far from just a hobby, it is a subject of serious study. The study of stamps leads its enthusiasts to the study of "geography, history, and the natural life of various countries". An album of stamps can, therefore be a book of Knowledge as well as a book of original research. Some of the components of the stamps are:

i) Value
ii) Colour and Design
iii) Size
iv) Official Insignia (Indian Postage)
v) Themes – Animals, Birds, Technology (can be further divided)
vi) Commemoration and Anniversaries
vii) Subjects (Topical Collection)
viii) Culture and Heritage
ix) Personalities – Statesman, Religious Leaders and so on with dates
x) Trade and Industries
xi) Art and Craft
xii) Events – Olympic Games, Asian Games
xiii) Errors and Defects in Stamps – There are some specific terminologies for the errors and defects in stamps – Tete Bece, Double, "Kiss", Reentry, Re-touches, Change in shape, Flaws
xiv) Philately Terminology – Philately has its own terminology- First day cover, Killer, Watermark, Cachet etc.
xv) Mounting of Stamps.

CONCLUSION

In this paper an attempt is made to explore new areas of information organisation and the need for the harvesting metadata in several unexplored areas of knowledge. It is just an attempt to demonstrate through the two very popular hobbies that are well very well known. It also demonstrates the mode of harvesting metadata from some unconventional sources of information which are increasingly becoming available for building information systems on the web.

REFERENCES

1. Wikipedia Retrieved from ***http.//en.wikipedia.org/wiki/Muhammad_bin_Tughluq***. Accessed on 20th September 2011.
2. Sreenivasa, G.(2001). Study of historical evidences as non-conventional sources of information with special reference to Vijayanagar Dynasty – Hampi.MLISc Dissertation, Bangalore University, Bangalore. Guide Dr. A.Y. Asundi.
3. Chatterjee, S.P.(1973). Romance of postage stamps. New Delhi, National Book Trust, India, (Nehru Bala Pustakalaya-24. Nehru Library for Children.)

3

Plagiarism: A Bane to the Research Productivity

Rajendra Babu H
Manager, Wipro Technologies, Bangalore – 560100,
Chandrashekara M
Associate Professor, Dept. of Studies in Library and Information Science, Manasagangotri, University of Mysore, Mysore-06

ABSTRACT

Plagiarism has become a Cultural, social and economical issue today. In today's past paced information/ knowledge world, gathering information is not a humongous task anymore as compared to few years ago. Today everything is available in internet (at least snippets enough to satisfy the Information/ knowing thirsty). This phenomenon has led to interesting transformation into both a boon as well as a bane. The reading and thus in-questing habits are getting diminished with the availability of information at anyone's fingertips. With the free/ easy availability of information, the usage of the information has considerably gone up, there by increased utility of the information for critical need basis with much less fuss. On the other hand, the same free/ easy information availability in the various reusable formats also started posing a lot of threat for the credibility of information on part of the original ideas/ thoughts and so on. This trend not only contributes to the over (re) production of the same information and also contaminating the already available original information/ ideas/ thoughts. The trend has grown many folds with the advent of Internet. This article has provided such trends; credibility aroused out of the alarming trend of over production and also analyzed few probable solutions at countering this trend. There is a mention of few tools in detecting the percentage of plagiarism are discussed.

Keywords : Plagiarism; Information over-production; Copyright; Piracy; Academic dishonesty; Plagiarism detection; and Plagiarism detection tools / software.

INTRODUCTION

The idea of stealing / unauthorised copying others works has been recorded ever since human civilization started. In the great epics of Ramayana and Mahabharatha has also the mention of such undesired acts. With the growth of human intellectual capabilities, this is even more evident that such things prevail at all the ages, geographies, cultures and races. The reasons may vary from Getting the job done (using short-cuts), self satisfaction, to causing harm (destruction) to others works/ ideas and so on. With the advent of Internet in the late 1980s and 1990s has given a more sophisticated structure (of easy search, finding, copying and pasting of e-version of original information/ ideas) to this already decayed trend of plagiarism. This also supported by the growth of internet, according to an estimate, in 1993 the Internet carried only 1% of the information flowing through two-way telecommunication, by 2000 this figure had grown to 51%, and by 2007 more than 97% of all telecommunicated information was carried over the Internet1.

DEFINITION OF PLAGIARISM

In the 1st century, the use of the Latin word plagiarius (kidnapper), to denote someone stealing someone else's work, was pioneered by Roman poet „Martial , who complained that another poet had "kidnapped his verses." This use of the word was introduced into English in 1601 by dramatist Ben Jonson, to describe as a plagiary someone guilt of literary theft. The derived form, plagiarism was introduced into English around 16202.

- According to Random House and Oxford English Dictionaries
  - Plagiarism is defined as the "wrongful appropriation," "close imitation," or "purloining and publication" of another author's "language, thoughts, ideas, or expressions," and the representation of them as one's own original work2
- Word Web dictionary defines Plagiarism as
  - "A piece of writing that has been copied from someone else and is presented as being your own work"
  - The act of plagiarizing; taking someone's words or ideas as if they were your own

WHAT IS PLAGIARISM?

It is the misinterpretation of attribution towards authorship. It is the state of an idea/ article/report conceived/ authored by the one author is being credited to another author. It is the form of an intellectual theft of original works (Music, ideas, quotes, words, and some one s understanding). This kind of an activity, undervalues the currency and nascency of original idea/ thought and weakens the whole generation of human thought process and there by society.

The most common form of plagiarism is in the form of; the words from one author are inserted as same as in the works of a second author, with no quotation, no acknowledgement, or attribution towards the original author s work/ article.

Anyone is allowed to borrow ideas or works from other sources, provided, one should furnish a proper citation/ acknowledgement on the use of such works/ ideas. This is allowed and one should abide by the guidelines set by the fair use doctrine. Fair use practice consists of the elements such as;

- The nature of one s use of the original idea/ work
- The amount of the original work/ idea borrowed

- The resulting effect/ impact on the creditability of the original work by the borrowing

As a rule, one must be careful in borrowing too liberally from the original works/ ideas, even though the sufficient acknowledgements/ citations are provided by the borrower4.

PLAGIARISM AND COPYRIGHT

Plagiarism and copyright are not same, they are totally difference concepts. But, both terms may be applied to a particular act/ misdeed. An infringement of copyright is a violation of the rights of a copyright holder, when a copyrighted material is used without the consent of the copyright holder. Whereas, plagiarism is the unearned increment to the author who does plagiariee, and the reputation that the plagiarizing author is achieved through false claims of authorship.

PUNISHABLE OFFENCE

As with any plagiarism issue, the degree of intent must be determined to see the nature of committed offense level. The punishment varies based on the amount of malpractice. If the plagiarism occurs in the academic setup, it may be handled by the academic institution involved. Most of the academic institutions today have zero tolerance for plagiarists in place. Setups such as public sector, Private Sector and other multinational organizations have stringent policies on plagiarism and copyright violations. If found guilty, may result in minor reprimand, Denial of higher positions and Job expulsion based on the magnitude of the offense. If the offense involves money, prize, Job, then it calls for a criminal offense and punishable in the court of law.

PREVENTING PLAGIARISM

The first and foremost important step in preventing plagiarism is finding and addressing its cause[5].

Few of the strategies in this direction are;

- Be aware of the reasons, why/where plagiarism occurs

- Student assignments
- Project/ work deadline
- Pressure to innovate

- Different forms of plagiarism
  - Intentional
    - Searching v/s Researching
    - Poor planning/ execution
    - But their words are better
    - Making it to the grade/ deadline
    - Everyone does it, so do I
    - Lack of reading and comprehending skills
  - Unintentional
    - Citation confusion
    - Plagiarism vs. Paraphrasing
    - Confusion about expectations
- Integrating techniques into preventing plagiarism
  - Awareness courses offered at all higher learning environments
  - Employee Induction
  - Make it a criteria of performance evaluation
  - Training sessions on the implications (Local/ organizational and Legal)

TOOLS TO DETECT PLAGIARISM

Plagiarism has become a Cultural, social and economical issue today. Plagiarism detection is the process of finding out the occurrences of plagiarism within a work or document. The advent of computers and Internet has created a great ease in plagiarism. Today, plagiarism can be found in all the fields, such as scientific papers, art designs, diagrams, music and software code.

There have been a lot of efforts gone into countering

plagiarism. Once such efforts are building tools and techniques to effectively find out the research/ academic productivity and help plagiarism free works such as academic literature, journalism, research output and so on.

MANUAL DETECTION

This required a great effort and calls for an substantial memory on part of a person who is involved in plagiarism detection. The task is, humongous and impossible to compare various documents in different formats. Most of the times it take a lot of time in collating a lot of original articles and costs a lot and time consuming effort.

The other semi-automated way to detect plagiarism is to copy and paste each and every phrase/ paragraph of the article into available search engines to see if the content is plagiarized. This in turn also a time consuming effort and a simple mistake can derail the whole process.

COMPUTER/ SOFTWARE ASSISTED DETECTION

Computer-assisted detection allows vast collections of documents to be compared to each other, making successful detection much more likely.

Key features of typical Automated Plagiarism detection (Online and Offline) tool consists;

- Capability to all forms/ formats of the documents
- Detect Plagiarism
- Provide Detailed Reports (DOC(X) & HTML) for further analysis

Few of the Plagiarism detecting software/ tools are enumerated below—

- DOC CopTM: is a plagiarism, cryptomnesia and collusion detection tool.
- Viper: Free Plagiarism Detection tool
  — 10 billion resources scanned

- — Checks the Unlimited document length/ resubmitting
- — Side by Side comparison
- — Provide links to plagiarized works

- Plagiarism Detect.com
  - — No restriction on number of pages
  - — Original Multi-Layered technology with SMART scanning
  - — Parts of texts that contain plagiarism are highlighted
- TurnItIn: The global leader in addressing plagiarism and delivering rich feedback
  - — Products:
    - TurnItIn: for Educators
    - WriteCheck: for Students
    - TurnItIn: for Admissions
    - iThenticate: for Researchers & Publishers.
  - — Features:
    - 150+ million archived student papers
    - 90,000+ journals, periodicals & books
    - 1+ million active instructors
    - 14+ billion web pages crawled
    - 10,000 educational institutions covered
    - 20+ million licensed students community
    - 126 countries covered
- Dupli-Checker: Free Online Plagiarism detection tool
  - — No need to register
  - — Can check articles, web content and blogs for detecting plagiarism.
  - — Provides the Writing Process
  - — Provides General academic writing tips
- Plagiarism Detector: Proprietary Plagiarism Detecting tool

— Checks >7 billion sources
— Uses Google, Bing and AltaVista
— Works fast - less than 1 minute
— Supports Multiple Formats Support (MFS): pdf, doc, docx, html, txt, rtf
— References Detection
— Multiple document processing
— 97% effective
— Compatible with all MS Office versions
— State-of-art Advanced Report Generation and view

Snap shots of the Plagiarism Detector report is provided below;

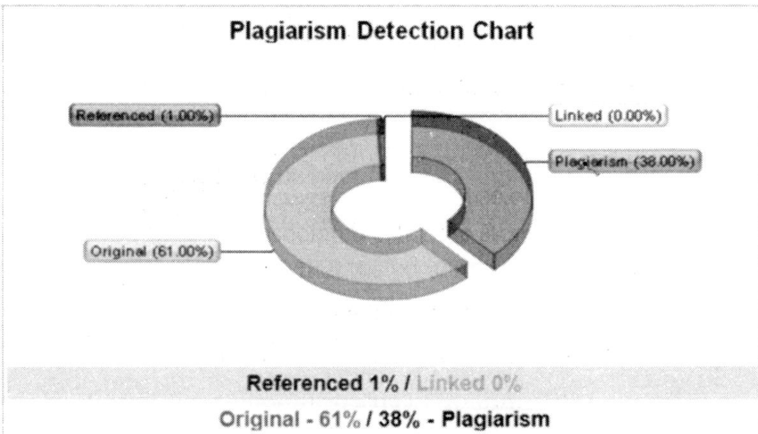

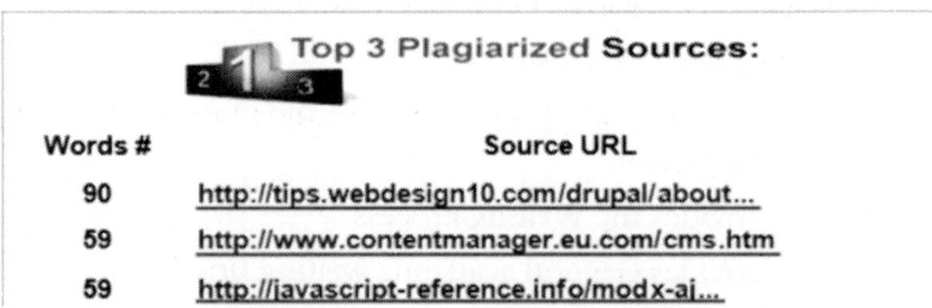
Top 3 Plagiarized Sources:

Words #	Source URL
90	http://tips.webdesign10.com/drupal/about...
59	http://www.contentmanager.eu.com/cms.htm
59	http://javascript-reference.info/modx-aj...

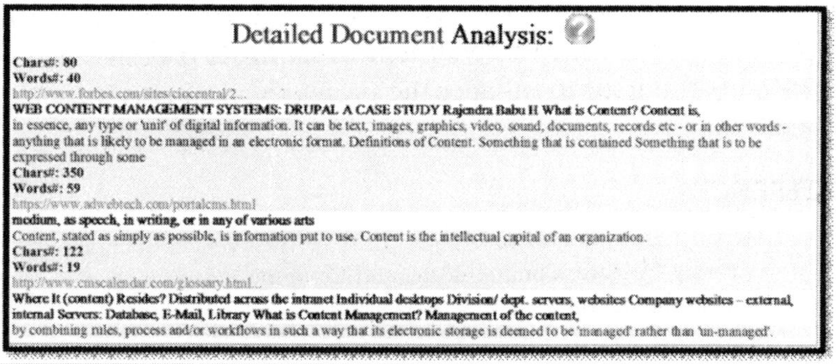

Detailed Document Analysis:

Chars#: 80
Words#: 40
http://www.forbes.com/sites/ciocentral/2...
WEB CONTENT MANAGEMENT SYSTEMS: DRUPAL A CASE STUDY Rajendra Babu H What is Content? Content is,
in essence, any type or 'unit' of digital information. It can be text, images, graphics, video, sound, documents, records etc - or in other words - anything that is likely to be managed in an electronic format. Definitions of Content. Something that is contained Something that is to be expressed through some
Chars#: 350
Words#: 59
https://www.adwebtech.com/portalcms.html
medium, as speech, in writing, or in any of various arts
Content, stated as simply as possible, is information put to use. Content is the intellectual capital of an organization.
Chars#: 122
Words#: 19
http://www.cmscalendar.com/glossary.html...
Where It (content) Resides? Distributed across the intranet Individual desktops Division/ dept. servers, websites Company websites – external, internal Servers: Database, E-Mail, Library What is Content Management? Management of the content,
by combining rules, process and/or workflows in such a way that its electronic storage is deemed to be 'managed' rather than 'un-managed'.

CONCLUSION

Plagiarism has way all along the history of human civilization. Thought it got formal notice since 16th century. It was only in the 18th century; new morals have been institutionalised and enforced prominently in the sectors of academia, Public/ Private sector and journalism. Plagiarism is now considered as a social sin, also considered as academic dishonesty and a breach of journalistic ethics. This is subject to sanctions withholding growth opportunities, expulsion from work and other severe career damage. This may not be the same case in the arts, which not only have resisted in their long-established tradition of copying as a fundamental practice of the creative process, but with the boom of the modernist and post-modern movements in the 20th century. It is agony that, Plagiarism remains tolerated even by 21st century artists. Plagiarism is not a crime per se but is disapproved more on the grounds of moral offence, and cases of plagiarism can involve liability for copyright infringement and much more.

It is the need of the hour and responsibility on part of Library and Information Science/ services professionals to start thinking in the direction of educating oneself and library users about plagiarism and its implications, organizing constructive activities/ awareness to prevent plagiarism, strategies for detecting/ preventing plagiarism, implementing effective system in all the organizations publications and learn to deal with administrative and institutional issues relating to plagiarism and countering this issue to enhance the professional and institutional image.

REFERENCES

1. Martin Hilbert and Priscila L´pez. (2011). The World's Technological Capacity to Store, Communicate, and Compute Information. Science, 332(6025), 60-65.
2. Plagiarism. Accessed from http://en.wikipedia.org/wiki/Plagiarism on 15th Sep 2011
3. "Random House Compact Unabridged Dictionary" and "Oxford English Dictionary"
4. Plagiarism. Accessed from http://www.plagiarism.org/ on 15th Sep 2011
5. Educational tips on plagiarism prevention. http://www.plagiarism.org/plag_article_educational_tips_on_plagiarism_prevention.html. Accessed on 15th Sep 2011

Section – III
THEME PAPERS

4

"Wow Me": Soft Skills Required for LIS Professional – A User Perspective

Raju Tiwary
Team Leader, Tata Consultancy Services Ltd, Pioneer Building, International Tech Park, Padandhur Agrahara, Whitefield Road, Bangalore - 560066, Karnataka, India

ABSTRACT

The article discusses the soft skills required for LIS professionals from a user perspective. Author had surveyed the soft skills literature from EBSCO database, discussed with other library users and depended on the personal experience of using university, public and corporate libraries cum information system.

Author believes LIS Professionals will benefit from acquiring skills in soft skills. Further academic researches and discussion is required.

Keywords: LIS Professionals, LIS and Soft Skills, LIS Professionals and users, Users perspective.

INTRODUCTION

In recent years soft skills has attracted a lot of attention. Different professional bodies like the accounting bodies across the world are stressing the need for development of generic skills among the future professionals. In the Information Technology and Information Technology Enabled Services area discussions on soft skills are omnipresent. Same is the case with professionals in Library and Information Science (LIS). This paper adds to the discussion by adding users' perspective.

DECONSTRUCTING LIBRARY USERS

Deconstructing modern library users is not easy. They are academic researcher; serious readers; business researchers; subject matter experts trying to build as well as be on the top of developments in their domain; fun readers; young library users and many more. These users are very different in their socio-economic and demographic profiles. Their personalities and needs are different.

Millennials also use library : Millennials[1] are motivated and self-confident users. They work well in the teams for their share of sky with can-do attitude. They are less tolerant for poor quality and not willing to compromise besides they equally hate non-transparency. In short, they are a bit more demanding.

LIS Professionals needs to deal with the users myriad and diverse needs. Obviously, the available information resources are important but equally crucial is the disposition of library staff.

Problem of users : Whatever is the profile of the users; they face the following common challenges in a library:

- Not conversant with the library classification system and organization
- Not able to find information easily
- In-cooperative staff or staff with poor ability to communicate
- No grievances resolution mechanism

- May be emotionally and time stressed, etc

It is frustrating if one does not get the information quickly.

User Expectations:

"Wow Me" : Library users are with mission. They are motivated to learn. The users want access to resources fast or quick resolution of their issues and in a friendlier manner. Library staff can delight them by facilitating their reading by making relevant information resources available to them quickly. Each book should get a reader likewise each reader should get a book.

Communicate and fill in the information gap : Library users are not always forthcoming; they don't seek help at times. A willing library staff can approach and help such people to find resources. Library professionals are experts in the way resources are organized in the library, users are not.

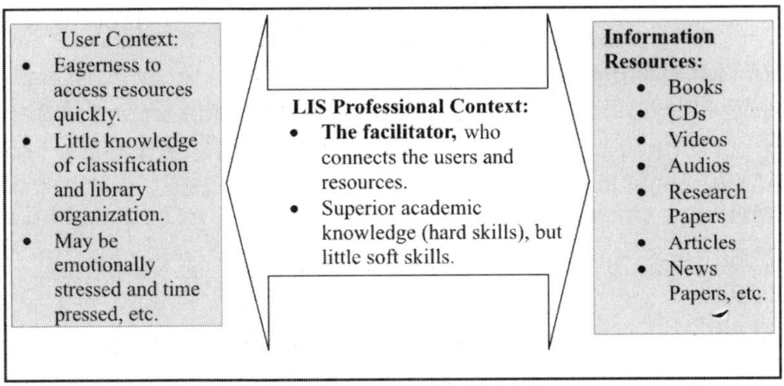

Illustration – Library Professionals, the Facilitator

Soft skills - A Functional Understanding:

In the flat world, competition is redefining service standards. Libraries in the new age need to constantly enhance their customer orientation and realign with the evolving user demands. In the knowledge society, library plays a crucial role in ongoing knowledge acquisition and creation.

LIS professionals, who facilitate the interaction of knowledge seekers and creators with the existing information resources, are the focus of this paper from the perspective of users. The focus is soft skills.

"Soft skills" has been defined as "the cluster of personality traits, social graces, language skills, friendliness, and optimism that mark each of us in varying degrees" (Career Opportunities News, 2002).

"Generic skills, sometimes referred to as 'soft skills', are the range of general education skills that are not domain- or practice-specific, which include communication and interpersonal skills, problem-solving skills, conceptual/analytical and critical skills, visual, oral and aural skills, and judgment and synthesis skills." (Boyce et al)

Soft skills enable professionals to produce results at the workplace in conjunction with their hard skills, which refer to a professional's knowledge and occupational skills.

"Soft skills are personal attributes that enhance an individual's interactions, job performance and career prospects. Unlike hard skills, which are about a person's skill set and ability to perform a certain type of task or activity, soft skills are interpersonal and broadly applicable." (Wikipedia)

Almost every competency and skill required by the LIS professionals is listed by the researchers. Based on the literature survey of 200 papers on the Library and Information Science Abstracts (LISA) database Soo-Guan Khoo enlists a comprehensive set of skills in his paper "Competencies for New Era Librarians and Information Professionals" (Soo-Guan Khoo, C.). However, the present paper focuses to provide some of the essential soft skills from the users' perspective.

The traditional library has professional staff, semi-professional staff, and support staff (Krishnakumar and Smitha)[2]. The skills enumerated here are required by all library staff with different levels of expertise.

REQUIRED SOFT SKILLS – USERS' VIEW

Communication Skills : Communication skill is the most essential and crucial among the soft skills required for the LIS professionals. They should have the skills to clearly understand the users and to be understood by them properly. "...good communication skills are essential for library professionals of all levels. One has to interact and send written communication to faculty members, students, publishers/suppliers, external agencies, etc. S/he should also have etiquettes for communication." (Kumar, 2010)

"LIS professionals have to be effective in oral, written, and electronic communication with users, colleagues, and supervisors. They have to be effective in promoting and marketing their services, as well as promoting the value of their service to the parent organisation." (Kumar, 2010)

An important dimension of communication skills from the part of library professionals can be to encourage two way communications by soliciting feedback and suggestions for providing better services. However, the users should not confuse the right to suggest, provide feedbacks, with the right of determination of forcing their views on their terms. Libraries may decide to design a feedback form to capture the "Things Gone Wrong" to improvise on user services.

Time Management : Efficiency is the only way forward in the global trend of downsizing and desk-killing. The LIS professionals are expected to manage increasing workload and multitask. They would require managing their time wisely and smartly, as time is a highly perishable resource. They will have to finish their routine work as well as attend to the user requests for help. In time management terminology, they will have to effectively manage the interruptions.

Service Orientation and High Self-Esteem : A library professional with healthy self-esteem, motivation and commitment may find it easy to cope with the stress of work overload and of handling difficult users. A motivated and engaged

BASIC NEEDS OF EMPLOYEES

Employee feels:

- Rightly compensated
- Praised
- Appropriately Designated
- Noticed
- Appreciated, etc.

LIS professional spends discretionary energy, the extra effort that people voluntarily invest in work, to provide quality services to library users with motivation and commitment. This improves performance and may create a superior user experience and satisfaction.

Meeting the basic needs of LIS professionals encourages them to give their discretionary energy to the functioning of library. The professional staff members, who provide leadership, will have to ensure that library staff does not feel under-compensated, under-praised, under-titled for the responsibilities they undertake, under-noticed, and underappreciated.

Teamwork : The ability to work effectively with the team will enhance the ability of the LIS professionals to cater to the needs of the users. A user, not aware of the organizational set up of a particular library, may wrongly request a resource available in other department. LIS help desk can direct the user or wow the user by providing the resources leveraging his/her rapport with the department concerned.

Interpersonal Skills : The skill facilitates working together, manage one's behavior and emotions better, assert and persuade others better to get the results, which are best for the stakeholders involved.

Conflict Management : In general, this skill helps one to understand and handle conflict situations, and to solve and manage the relation with the users. Often, the users and LP have conflicting interests (**Refer to the Exhibit 1**). The amicable resolution of such situations by handling conflict effectively would

EXHIBIT 1:
A MAN IN NEED OF INFORMATION – A SHORT STORY

A man emotionally stressed but nicely dressed, time stressed comes to the library at 5:00 pm. You, a library professional, is about to close. He has to meet a deadline. His world is falling apart, and on the other side you are about to miss your shuttle to home. Your spouse is eagerly waiting for you to celebrate your only daughter's first birthday. What will you do?

be a win-win for the user as well as the library staff.

Negotiation Skills : A thorough appreciation of negotiation process - preparation, opening position, bargaining, movement, and closing - and associated evolved skills would be useful for the library professionals.

Stress Management : A proper training in stress management is a must for library professionals. Identification and understanding of stress are keys to develop a personal coping strategy in a stressful situation.

Presenting Skills : Many a times, library professionals engage with the user community to increase the awareness of the resources available in the library. The skill would be very handy. There may be many other occasions like interacting with the senior managers, making a case for more financial resources, the superior presentation skills would make life easier.

The library professionals may have to master the skills of removing barrier to effective presentations like gestures which can dilute or distract the intended communication. The proper presenter would have to prepare his/her message and modulate his voice appropriately while maintaining right body language and giving appropriate signals with his gestures.

Customer Driven Values / Orientation : Library users are akin to customers, who may or may not pay for the service. However, the LP's focus on catering to the needs of the customers while taking full responsibility may improve the acceptability of the library and the library professional engaged. The LP can act as the brand ambassador by delivering excellent customer services.

Say-Do Ratio and Time Commitment : Do what you say and say what you can do. Neither over commit nor under-commit and deliver what you promise to the users. Adhere to the deadline you give. Inform changes which can impact your commitment at the time you notice it. Give the library users time to manage their stakeholders and dependencies.

LIS PROFESSIONALS – DEVELOP THE SKILLS

The academic trainings like Bachelor and Master degrees in Library and Information Sciences provide LIS Professionals superior technical knowledge, or hard skills in information resources, information access, technology, management and research, but little of soft skills.

While visualizing a solution for the development of soft skills among the LIS professionals, we need to take into consideration the present library staff and the future professionals.

Self-study : The working professionals can look at acquiring skills through online and web-based trainings (WBTs), and distance mode self-paced learning modules.

Mirroring : They can employ the mirroring technique[3] (Wikipedia) of Neuro Linguistic Programming. They can mirror the choice of words, metaphors, and attitude of a person considered possessing excellent soft skills.

Call in Experts : Internal training departments can arrange

> **A CHANGING USER PROFILE**
>
> The number of graduates is increasing in India. Fifty Percent of the population is below the age of 25. The education sector is booming and the Indian economy is increasingly becoming the knowledge hub of the world. In this scenario, the serious knowledge seekers and domain knowledge builders will increase. More people will graduate and research. This new batch is generally more confident and ambitious, and does not seem to adjust. The library users will be more demanding, younger, and intensive; and the library will be more relevant in the days to come.

some training sessions or call in external experts, who could help you quickly.

Get a Mentor : Guidance of a mentor helps you understand the nuances of the skills you want to work on.

Role Play Practice : Form a staff club and practice role plays. It can provide avenues to think about a superior way to handle a difficult situation. Peer discussions will provide ways to improvise.

Further discussions and researches are required to establish the best ways to incorporate the development of these skills in the LIS courses. Whatsoever is included in the syllabus, future professionals should be encouraged to adopt the deep learning approaches to facilitate conclusion-oriented learning outcomes[4].

LIMITATION OF THE PAPER

Library users judge the requirement of the soft skills based on the interactions with the front-end library staff, who interact directly with them. They are the face of the library. You might have rightly observed that the paper is biased towards the front-end library staff.

RECOMMENDATION

The following are suggestion on soft skills for the Library professionals from the users' perspective:

Soft skills will be highly required in the times to come. The academicians should

1. The Library professionals should look out for the ways to acquire soft skills.
2. Further research and discussions are required in the area.
3. The academicians should look out for the ways to introduce soft skills as a compulsory course in syllabus to equip the future professionals better.

CONCLUSION

Go learn more : Today's world is fast changing. Not only the technology is evolving, but the users are also becoming demanding. To be successful and serve the user community better, library professionals will have to develop people skills in addition to their technical academic knowledge related to library management. They would benefit by engaging themselves in the lifelong learning path utilizing deep learning approaches to acquire soft skills, which will help them to respond in every novel situation.

REFERENCE

1. Career Opportunities News (2002). "Soft skills a key to employment today," Career Opportunities News, Volume 20, Number 2. Ferguson Publishing Company.
2. Gordon Boyce, Sarah Williams, Andrea Kelly, Helen Yee (2001). Fostering deep and elaborative learning and generic (soft) skill development: the strategic use of case studies in accounting education, Accounting Education 10 (1), 37–60
3. Soft skills – http://en.wikipedia.org/wiki/Soft_skills#cite_note-0 [Accessed on 05 September 2011].
4. Christopher Soo-Guan Khoo, Competencies for New Era Librarians and Information Professionals. Retrieved from http://www.lib.usm.my/elmu-equip/conference/Documents/ICOL%202005%20Paper%202%20Christopher%20Khoo.pdf [Accessed on 05 September 2011].
5. Krishnakumar S and Smitha P, Skills needed for New LIS Professionals: An assessment (2005),
6. Bharat Kumar, Employability of Library and Information Science Graduates: Competencies Expected versus Taught—A Case Study, DESIDOC Journal of Library & Information Technology, Vol. 30, No. 5, September 2010, pp. 74-82; © 2010.
7. Millennials – http://whatis.techtarget.com/definition/

millennials.html, [Accessed on 10 September 2011].

FOOTNOTES

1. **Types of Library Professionals :** Professional staff - They are the associates with professional qualification and managerial experience who work at higher and middle level management. The nature of job includes identifying the needs, analyzing problems, organizing activities, establishing inter-personal and inter-institutional communication etc. They will also be responsible for setting goals, defining objectives and planning programmes.

   Semi Professional Staff - These associates do not possess professional qualification but can be upgraded to the first category with a professional qualification and certain years of experience. The nature of job includes book ordering, accessioning, technical processing, maintaining catalogue, stock verification, shelving etc.

   Support staff : These associates perform a large number of routine and essential jobs. The nature of job includes binding, reprography, lamination, deacidification etc. The recruitment of these staff should be based on necessary professional and technical skill in their trade. (Ref-Skills needed for New LIS Professionals: An assessment by Krishnakumar S and Smitha P, Executives, Tata Consultancy Services Ltd)

2. Mirroring is the behavior in which one person copies another person usually while in social interaction with them. It may include miming gestures, movements, body language, muscle tensions, expressions, tones, eye movements, breathing, tempo, accent, attitude, choice of words/ metaphors and other aspects of communication. It is often observed among couples or close friends. (Ref. http://en.wikipedia.org/wiki/Mirroring_(psychology) accessed on 15 Sept 2011)

3. Conclusion-oriented outcomes are required of LIS when they learn soft skills. "Conclusion-oriented outcomes are the result of a tendency towards understanding with the use of deep learning approaches. A student adopting a deep approach attempts to make sense of what is learnt, to determine interrelationships and to apply underlying principles." (Boyce40, COO, ~~ Marton and saljo 1976B•)

5

Imprints Collection: *A Cyberscholarship of RRI*

B. M. Meera
Kiran Savanur
M. Manjunath
Librarian, Raman Research Institute,
Sadashivanagar Post, Bangalore – 560080

ABSTRACT

Cyberscholarship is relatively a new phenomenon which is in a way related to digital form of information. Cyberscholarship has opened new avenues of looking at scholarship quite different from print format. This novel method has been adopted to develop a database termed "Imprints Collection" having Digital Repository of Raman Research Institute as base line. This is expected to act as a support service to enhance the creativity and collaboration among the scientists of the Institute and also across different countries. In addition this also brings global visibility to scholarly literature of the Institute.

Keywords : Cyberscholarship, scholarly communication, scientific literature, Imprints collection, information retrieval tool, digital repository.

INTRODUCTION

Scholarly communication is an integral part of the life of scientists. The number of books published, number of scientific journals, number of research articles and the escalating growth in number of web pages of scientific information speak volumes about the compounding growth of scholarly communication in the 21st century. According to Vannevar Bush (Wikiquote), 'Scientific progress is one essential key to our security as a nation, to our better health, to more jobs, to a higher standard of living and to our cultural progress'. Scientific progress is generally associated with the Scholarly literature and Scholarly communication. They both put together have a strategic role to play in unbiased dissemination of knowledge (Jacob, 2011). They are the two phases of a coin complementing each other in the knowledge dissemination process. Cyberscholarship is an offshoot of this scientific endeavor.

Cyberscholarship is relatively a new phenomenon which is in a way related to digital form of information. Steady growth and the availability of scientific information in electronic format have opened new avenues of scholarship that are different from the traditional methods of using scholarly literature in print format. This is called Cyberscholarship. Information scientists and library professionals have to identify, capture, assimilate, manage, preserve and provide information services in an unconventional way and thus supporting cybersholarship (Arms & Larse, 2007). Here is an attempt to share the cybersholarship experience at the Raman Research Institute.

Raman Research Institute was started by Sir C V Raman, the one and only noble laureate of India in science to carry out his personal research soon after his retirement from Indian Institute of Science in 1948. Being an experimental physicists, Sir C V Raman published his first paper in 1906 in "Philosophical Magazine" at the age of barely 18 and not yet out of college. This drive of his to publish is all the more significant because the Presidency College was essentially a teaching college with no inclination towards research and this was the first ever paper published from that institution by a student. As he grew to become a matured and one of the finest physicists of the 20th century, he firmly believed that scientific research is useless unless the results are promptly published. He continued to be an active researcher till his demise in 1970. His last research paper was published in "Current Science" in 1970 and thus spanning active research career of 64 years (Venkatraman, 1988).

Raman Research Institute built on the ideologies of Sir CV Raman is a pioneering Institution in scholarly scientific publishing. There are 50 scientists and 20 technical experts working at RRI. On an average 150 research articles are published every year by the scientific community of the RRI in high impact factor journals. This being the scenario, it is the responsibility of the library to develop new forms of knowledge structure and organize research information of the institute for better global visibility (Vickery, 1999). Off late the most sought after solution is Institutional repositories. Keeping in mind the growing e-science infrastructure (Rao, 2004), RRI library has developed Institutional Digital repository using Dspace, an open source software package that provides the tools for management of digital assets. Keeping the Institutional repository as base line, the cyberscholarship phenomenon is adopted to develop a database called "Imprints Collection".

WHAT IS IMPRINTS COLLECTION?

RRI library has been very thoughtful and found a novel way of appreciating the scientists for their contribution to the world of scientific literature when they superannuate. All the research papers of an individual retired scientist is brought together in the form of collected works both in print and electronic format and it is gifted to him/her at the time of retirement. This information product is named as "Imprints Collection" meaning an Imprint of the research work of scientists in the form of research papers which stand a testimony to their contribution to the world of scientific literature. The scientific productivity in terms of research articles published during their entire research career is made available at one place through this imprints collection (Meera et al., 2011).

This look back effort of compiling the collected works is

hosted on the RRI Library web page. The story does not end here. This structured information product is further improvised to look like a wholesome database of the retired scientists and technical staff. The components that are included in this database in addition to research publications are a brief biographical sketch, a photo gallery, audio/video/text version of the popular lectures delivered by of them (wherever available), news paper clippings (wherever available) announcing the achievements of the scientists and obituary (in case of deceased scientists). A prototype has been developed. This is still an ongoing project which is partially complete.

METHODOLOGY INVOLVED IN DESIGNING IMPRINTS COLLECTION

Imprints Collection is a new type of digital repository supporting links between authors, their persona, their papers, lectures and photographs. Base line for developing this database is the Digital repository of Raman Research Institute. This web based information retrieval tool is designed using Dreamweaver software for web designing. A web page entitled "Imprints Collection" lists the names of scientists and technical staff of RRI retired from service after 1972, since RRI was restructured to become an aided autonomous research institute receiving funds from the Department of Science and Technology of the Government of India. This page links the subsequent pages of this database and also the digital repository of RRI to get access to the research publication. To create photo album, Jalbum.net (**http://jalbum.net**) freeware software has been used.

DESIGN OF IMPRINTS COLLECTION

Imprints collection is an intellectual base of the Raman Research Institute since 1972. There has been a considerable shift in the areas of research focus since the demise of Sir CV Raman. The shift is from fundamental research in physical sciences to the multidisciplinary research. The gradual change over in the direction of research is well depicted in "Imprints collection".

The first web page of this information product entitled "Imprints collection" listing the names of the retired scientists and technical staff appear as is in Fig. 1.

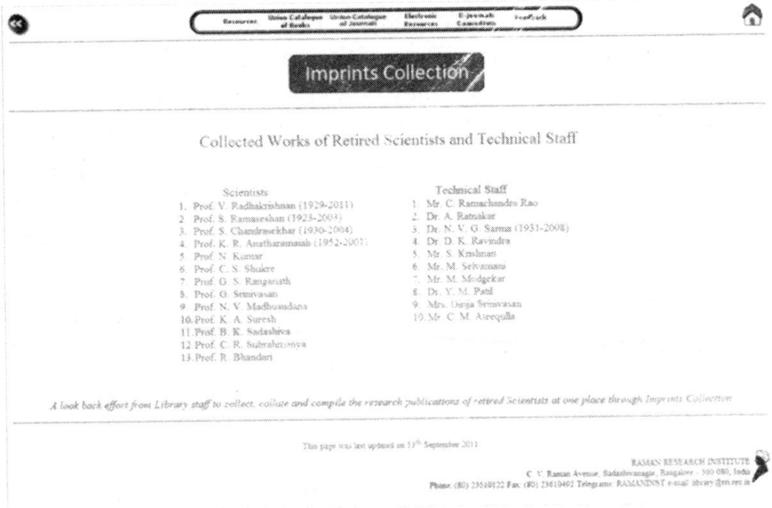

Fig 1. Imprints Collection

Each of the names of the scientists is linked to a second web page. A click on the name of any scientist will take the user to the second page. For example a click on Prof. Radhakrishnan will take the viewer to the next page titled by the name of the scientist. Screenshot of Prof. Radhakrishnan's page is given in Fig. 2.

This second page acts as main page of information for individual scientists providing biographical sketch and further links to their list of publications, photo gallery, lectures, newspaper clippings etc. A click on any of the links, say publications will take the viewer to a subsequent page which gives a list of the research articles published by the respective scientist. Figure 3 below is a webpage giving list of articles published by Prof. Radhakrishnan.

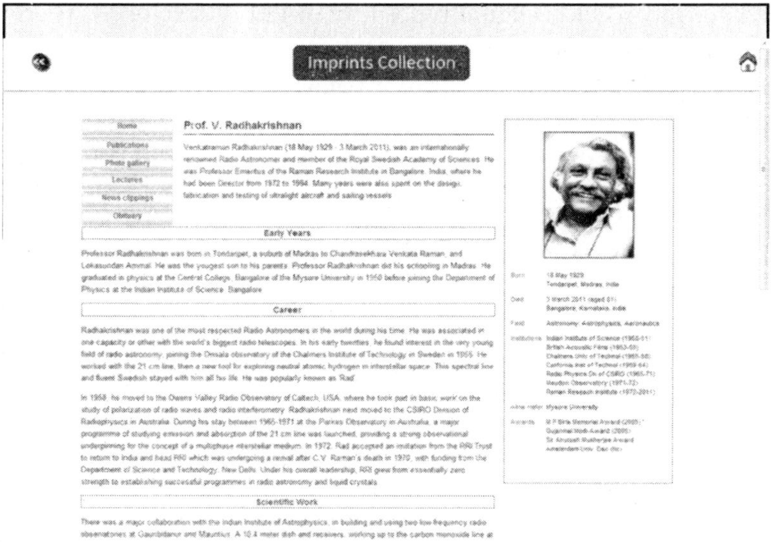

Fig. 2. Scientists Information

Fig. 3. Collected Publications

Further clicks on any article will take the searcher to the digital repository of RRI and from there one can access the full text of the article. Digital repository of RRI is developed strictly adhering to the copyright law and thereby protecting the restricted items from free access. Figure 4 below is the screenshot of the article being accessed through the digital repository. If the article is open source, then it can be accessed anywhere around the globe.

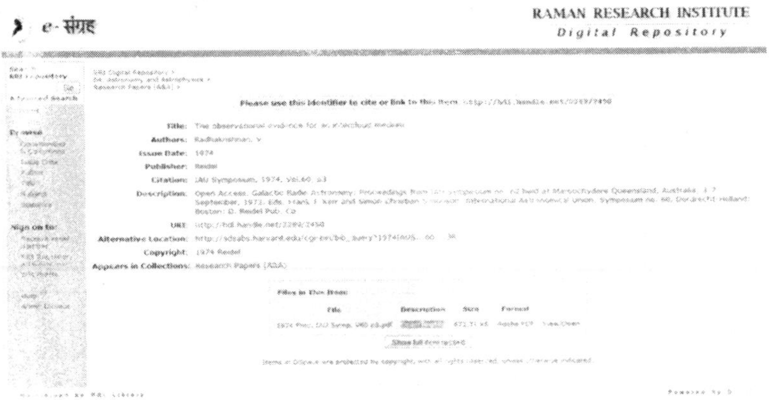

Fig. 4. Article Page Via Digital Repository

Going back to figure 2, one can find links to photo gallery, lectures, new paper clippings etc. Figure 5 gives the photo gallery of Prof. Radhakrishnan; figure 6 gives his lecture in text format, news clippings and obituary note.

MERITS AND DEMERITS:

It is quite certain that this is a new generation information retrieval tool assimilating all the research output of a scientist as one stop-shop, showcasing their life time research accomplishment. On an average the research life span of a scientist is 30-35 years. During this period they grow to become specialists in their own chosen domains of knowledge. A component of this database namely "collected works" encapsulate the evolution and growth of the said knowledge domain and thus providing the holistic picture. Since this database is almost complete in itself, they are a major source for information, if one is trying to collaborate with the scientist for a project or a scientific endeavor.

Fig. 5. Photo Album

Fig. 6. Lectures/ Newspaper Clippings/ Obituary

Research student, a beginner who is trying to identify a problem can use this source as a base to understand the research work of veteran scientists and the culmination of their research work from beginning of the career as a scientist till the end. This is also a tool to showcase the areas of research focus of the Institute across the globe. This can also be used as a source for conducting scientometric studies from different perspectives.

Few of the scientists are still active and pursuing research and continuing to publish papers. This database is constantly updated to include these add-ons as and when they get published.

One of the demerits is that, to build the database in entirety, developers are dependent on the scientists. But for research article for which library has data, authors had to follow up with the scientists for their biographical sketch, photographs etc. This is a time consuming and labor intensive task. Checking up authenticity, copyright clearance are some of the other issues involved in developing this database. To keep this database up-to-date and active, a constant vigilance on the appearance of the research articles of retired scientists is essential. A stream lined mechanism of administration to inform the library about any new publication or any achievement of scientists, if made mandatory, there is no doubt that it becomes one of the useful web based resource.

CONCLUSION

Cyberscholarship approach is a new method of looking at scholarship and presenting them in a novel way for the better utility and visibility. The modern libraries are expected to develop a platform to enhance the visibility of research carried out in the institute by showcasing them through Institutional repositories and such other mechanisms. Cyberscholarship is one such mechanism and it is termed as "Imprints Collection" at Raman Research Institute. This we expect as a support service to enhance the creativity and collaboration among the scientists of the Institutes within and across different countries. This is just a beginning and it is hoped to make it big in the near future.

REFERENCES

1. Arms, W., & Larsen, R. (2007). The future of Scholarly Communication: building the infrastructure for cyberscholarship, Retrieved from http://www.sis.pitt.edu/~repwkshop/NSF-JISC-report.pdf [Accessed on 26th August 2011].
2. Jacob, S. R. (2011). Of science, copyright and open access. *Current Science*, 100(5), 601-601
3. Meera, B. M., Manjunath, M. & Savanur, Kiran. (2011). Digital Information services and products. (In: National seminar on Content Management and Libraries: New Vistas for Harnessing Information organized by Keral Library Association, Thiruvananthapuram, 14-16 July 2011).
4. Rao, M. K. (2001). Scholarly communication and electronic journals: issues and prospects for academic and research libraries, *Library Review*, 50(4), 169-75.
5. Venkataraman, G. (1988). Journey into light: Life and science of C. V. Raman, *Indian Academy of Science and Indian National Science Academy.*
6. Vickery, Brain. (1999). A century of scientific and technical information, *Journal of Documentation*, 55(5), 476-527.
7. wikipedia.Vannevar Bush. Retrieved from http://en.wikiquote.org/wiki/Vannevar_Bush [Accessed on 12th August 2011]

6
Applying Psychometrics in Managing Library Customers

K V Ramaswamy

Senior Consultant, Talent Transformation,
Wipro Technologies, Bangalore

ABSTRACT

One of the challenges faced by librarians is the satisfaction of the library customers or visitors. This satisfaction is a key parameter in determining repeat visits. In today's world, we are bombarded everyday by Gigabytes of information in the form of moving displays, hoardings, cellular phone alerts, television and the like. How then, does a librarian effectively satisfy the intrinsic and unstated needs of the customer? One approach would be to understand the intrinsic needs of the customer by studying the whole person, the words and actions. Some psychometric tools give us insights into these needs. The first step would be to know one's own style of functioning or behaving. Once our own style is known, understanding and satisfying others would be relatively easier. The net result would be satisfaction for all parties, or, in the words of Stephen Covey, Synergy and Win-Win. This paper suggests perspectives as to how Synergy and Win-Win can be enhanced between Librarian and Customer.

Key words : Psychometrics, behaviour, Synergy, Win-Win, reading people, personality traits, Behaviour modelling.

INTRODUCTION

The basic function of a library is to provide information related services. The librarian is a catalyst to provide access to relevant information for the visitor or the customer. This paper tries to explore a different approach to meet the information needs of customers. The approach is to understand the mind, which is the greatest library on earth.

Ref: http://en.wikipedia.org/wiki/Librarian

HOW TO READ PEOPLE?

We have heard of reading books. How about reading people? Is there an observable language that gives us an indication of the behaviour to expect from people? If we are able to have such a language, then it would be very easy to communicate with all people in such a way that they are satisfied. Even though we may speak the same language, we do not. It is a paradox. There is much that is unsaid or said through body language, tone of voice and gestures.

Psychometrics is an attempt to measure the personality traits of individuals or groups. There are many psychometrics available in the Business world today. The great sage Lao Tse has said "*He who knows others is learned. He who knows himself is wise.*"

The first step to know others is to know oneself.

DISC ASSESSMENT

The DISC is a modelling of behaviour based on observable behaviour of people. It is based on the work of Dr. William Moulton Marston (1893-1947). Dr. Marston wrote a book called "Emotions of Normal People" in 1928. He explored human behaviour along few dimensions and these became the Universal Language of behaviour.

Dr. Marston discovered 4 factors which all possess in different proportions. The factors and the interplay among the factors lead to a wide spectrum of behaviours that we observe in people.

The 4 factors of DISC can be explained as under:

- **Dominance** – relating to control, power and assertiveness
- **Influence** – relating to social situations and communication
- **Steadiness** – relating to patience, persistence, and thoughtfulness
- **Compliance** – relating to structure and organization

HISTORY

Some people say that the history of DISC goes back to 400 BC!

Hippocrates (470-360 B.C.), the Greek Philosopher has contributed a lot to the field of medicine. He is considered to be the father of modern medicine. He looked inside of man to explain the differences in people. He believed that behavior was determined by the presence of an excessive amount of one of four fluids or humors: yellow bile (High-D), red bile (High-I), white bile (High-S) and black bile (High-C). The insightful observations of Hippocrates laid the foundation for the temperament model of behavior.

Ref: http://en.wikipedia.org/wiki/Hippocrates

HOW TO RECOGNIZE THE BEHAVIOUR OF A CUSTOMER?

DISC measures observable behaviours and emotions. It is the "How" of your life. How you walk, talk, shop, drive, play and read. It is the language of people watching. You can "read" and know all four factors of a person's behavioral design just through observing or listening.

CHARACTERISTICS OF D–DOMINANCE

The "D" or the dominant persons have a strong, clear and confident voice. They are also fast paced. Their volume is loudest and forceful. They use direct eye contact, are forceful and point a finger at you. The D looks for results.

The prime emotion of the D is anger. They have a high need for control. Their fear is, being taken advantage of.

When your customer is of this nature, then you would do well to be clear, specific and to the point. It is also better to stick to business and avoid all small talk. Talking about irrelevant issues or appearing disorganized can cause tension to a D.

Be quick to service a D. They may not read the full book that you provide but they are interested in books related to power and money.

CHARACTERISTICS OF I – INFLUENCE

The "I" or the influencing persons are very friendly and animated. They may use lot of gestures while asking for something. The volume of voice is fairly loud and casual. They smile a lot and use expressive gestures.

The prime emotion of the I is optimism. They have a high need to verbalize their ideas. They fear social rejection.

For these kinds of customers, you need to provide a warm and friendly environment. Don't give lot of details. Ask feeling questions for their opinions or comments. Being curt and to the point can cause tension to the I. Also do not overwhelm them with too many facts and figures.

Books involving People are what interest the I. Serve them in a friendly manner and keep dropping names of celebrities and who's who. They will enjoy it.

CHARACTERISTICS OF THE S – STEADINESS

The "S" people have a low tone of voice, are warm and detail oriented. The volume is soft and these persons are fairly methodical. The body language involves small hand gestures. These people are generally relaxed and non-emotional. You cannot see any emotions on their face.

The S people would not show their emotions on their face, although they could be internalizing a lot of emotions. The S has a high need to accommodate other people. They are very loyal and will not get angry. If they do get angry, then the world has to watch out! They are the "glue" in any relationship. They value Harmony. Their greatest fear is loss of security.

For customers who display the S behavior, it is better to start with a personal comment to break the ice. Speak to them softly and non-threateningly. Ask questions starting with "How?" to involve them. They like to go step by step. Don't rush into business immediately. Don't be dominating and don't expect quick responses from them.

Typically they are interested in enduring values and people oriented books that show slow and steady winning spirit.

CHARACTERISTICS OF THE C – COMPLIANCE

The "C" people have a monotonous, precise, cool and aloof tone of voice. The volume would be quiet and deliberate. Very few body gestures would be used. They use direct eye contact and the contact is very controlled.

The emotion of the C is fear. They have a high need to follow rules and policies. If you lend a book to a C, you can be sure that it would be returned on or before the due date. The fear of the C is criticism of their work.

For customers who display the C behavior, be well prepared with proper facts and figures. They like facts and figures that are accurate. They would have done their homework in their area. Hence it pays to be extra careful with them on facts and figures. They also expect realistic communication. If you promise to procure a book by a certain date, please ensure that it is done or it would upset a C. Don't be disorganized, unrealistic or casual with them.

The C would be the one who reads all the reports – the latest reports from Gartner, Cutter and similar organizations. They would be interested in magazines that give lots of facts. They would spend more time reading at the library than any other style of people.

TIPS ON PUTTING THE STYLES TOGETHER

DISC is the doorway to communication. The uniqueness of each person extends far beyond the DISC model. Therefore, behavioral models should NOT be referred to as "personality tests." What we have discussed above are "pure" styles. Each person's uniqueness would depend on how the 4 factors get combined to lead to a special style of behavior.

The use of a behavioral model is to create win/win relationships, not in any way to manipulate "pigeonhole" or label a person.

Every person has the potential to be a winner. We all win in different ways. One behavioral design is NOT a better leader than another.

Your behavioral design is the combination of the Highs and Lows of all four factors (D, I, S and C). Every person has the ability and can adapt to any profile. Adapting does require increased energy. How long a person can adapt is unique and different to each person. The DISC model identifies for you, your natural tendencies and gives you the knowledge to CONSCIOUSLY adapt as the situation requires.

As one psychometric expert puts it, *"People don't get up in the morning thinking about how they can make it a bad day for you."*

The key is to find the common ground. The Librarian's own style would influence the interaction as well. From experience, we know that one cannot adopt beyond 20 points of their current style. Yet, when one makes an attempt to speak the real language of the other person, there is a principle of reciprocity that takes place and the other person also tries to look for the common ground.

CONCLUSION

A good starting point for any Library professional to apply the principles mentioned in the above paper would be to get their own profiling done. Once they have done that, they can consciously adapt to the needs of the customers. This would be a more proactive approach that would be appreciated by more people than a reactive approach of doing what we think best, in today's changing environment. This is especially relevant in current times where electronic forms of media and virtualization are providing threats to the attractiveness of libraries. To end, a quote from Peter Drucker would hopefully motivate us to buy into this new perspective:

> ***"Success in the knowledge economy comes to those who know themselves, their strengths, their values, and how they best perform."***

REFERENCES

- DISC assessment. **http://en.wikipedia.org/wiki/DISC_assessment**. Accessed on 9th Sep 2011
- Psychometrics. **http://en.wikipedia.org/wiki/Psychometrics**. Accessed on 9th Sep 2011
- Marston William Moulton (Jul 1999). Emotions of Normal People (International Library of Psychology). Routledge; 1 edition ISBN-10: 0415210763/ ISBN-13: 978-0415210768. For more details: **http://www.amazon.com/Emotions-Normal-International-Library-Psychology/dp/0415210763**

7

Design and Development of Competitive Intelligence Portal using Wordpress – An Open Source Software

Madhuresh Singhal
Maruthu Pandiyan B
Advinus Therapeutics Ltd, 21, 22 Phase – II, Peenya Industrial Area, Bangalore – 560058

ABSTRACT

Companies need competitive intelligence information for staying ahead in the corporate world and for strategic decision making. Competitive intelligence is an ethical and legal business practice. It incorporates collecting information informally from various internal and external sources, such as the Internet, conferences, networking meetings and customers. In this article we discuss about building the competitive intelligence portal designed purely on open source software WORDPRESS with various features. The article focuses on brief overview of competitive intelligence, identification of the problems and finding alternative solutions and implementation of the system against various requirements. This case study will guide others who are working on similar lines.

Keywords. Competitive Intelligence, Wordpress, CI, Open Source Software, Information Organization.

INTRODUCTION

In this highly competitive world, staying ahead of the competition is the primary goal of the corporate world. To achieve this they need to have the competitive intelligence of the companies working on the same domain or the similar domain. Competitive intelligence is an ethical and legal business practice. The term CI is often viewed as synonymous with competitor analysis, but competitive intelligence is more than analyzing competitors — it is about making the organization more competitive relative to its entire environment and stakeholders: customers, competitors, distributors, technologies, macro-economic data etc.

In this article we discuss about building the competitive intelligence portal designed purely on open source software WORDPRESS with various features. The article focuses on brief overview of competitive intelligence, identification of the problems and finding alternative solutions and implementation of the system against various requirements. This case study will guide others who are working on similar lines.

COMPETITIVE INTELLIGENCE

A broad definition of **competitive intelligence** is the action of defining, gathering, analyzing, and distributing intelligence about products, customers, competitors and any aspect of the environment needed to support executives and managers in making strategic decisions for an organization.[1]

Key points of this definition

1. Competitive intelligence is an ethical and legal business practice, as opposed to industrial espionage which is illegal.

2. The focus is on the external business environment.
3. There is a process involved in gathering information, converting it into intelligence and then utilizing this in business decision making. CI professionals erroneously emphasize that if the intelligence gathered is not usable (or actionable) then it is not intelligence.

A more focused definition of CI regards it as the organizational function responsible for the early identification of risks and opportunities in the market before they become obvious. Experts also call this process the early signal analysis. This definition focuses attention on the difference between dissemination of widely available factual information (such as market statistics, financial reports, newspaper clippings) performed by functions such as libraries and information centers, and competitive intelligence which is a perspective on developments and events aimed at yielding a competitive edge.[2]

Why is CI important?

Competitive Intelligence offers a real strategic advantage for many businesses. Some of the largest corporate organizations have a dedicated CI department, while smaller businesses often practice CI on an ad hoc basis by informally collecting information from a variety of internal and external sources, such as the Internet, trade shows or conferences, networking meetings or even customers. Competitive Intelligence is of importance to any business that wishes to make better-informed decisions.[3]

The Cycle of Competitive Intelligence

The CIA describes the intelligence cycle as "the process by which raw information is acquired, gathered, transmitted, evaluated, analyzed and made available as finished intelligence for policymakers to use in decision-making and action." There are five steps which constitute this cycle: [4]

- planning and direction
- collection and research

- processing and storage
- analysis and production
- dissemination and delivery

THE CHALLENGE

There was a requirement to have a centralized repository for keeping and tracking industry and company information. The various types of information includes company news, industry policies, financials of companies as well as industry, deals, Mergers and Acquisitions, trip reports, industry reports, company pipelines, latest technologies, compliance and regulatory information, address book and so on.

Some of the above information was scattered at various databases or they are unstructured. Also some information was supposed to be gathered as and when it gets published. We decided to come out with a solution in the form of a CI portal. The real challenge was to integrate and organize all the information into a single platform, with emphasis on easy accessibility. That includes full text searching and browsing by various parameters.

Another challenge was system should support accessing the content based on the user roles, as certain information is classified as confidential and protected.

THE SOLUTION

Planning and Decision Making

As information is scattered, software was needed to integrate them in a single platform. We looked for paid software and open source systems. The software readily available in the market was not fitting our requirements and the custom built software was too expensive. So we started scouting for open source system that may fit into our requirements. We evaluated several content management systems and rounded off Wordpress as a suitable solution. We have chosen Wordpress for simplicity, quicker adoption and availability of various modules fitting to our requirements.

About Wordpress

WordPress started as just a blogging system[5], but has evolved to be used as full content management system and so much more through the thousands of plug-ins, widgets, and themes. WordPress is Open Source software, which means we are free to use it for anything from our personal blogs to a Fortune 500 web site without paying anyone a license fee and a number of other important freedoms. Wordpress has great community in addition to online resources like the forums and mailing lists for resolving our queries.

Wordpress is based on the popular PHP, MySQL platform and can be easily installed on any server with minimum hardware and software configuration.

Collection, Analysis and Processing

As mentioned earlier there were several databases in isolation, also some information was available in internal newsletters, presentations, reports etc.

Type of Collection

- **News :** Industry News available in public domain.
- **Industry & Analyst Reports :** An external link with the abstract.
- **Pipeline :** Link to companies pipeline
- **Trip Report :** Internal reports circulated by scientists/ business executives
- **Address Book :** Contacts lists
- **Monthly CI :** A template to capture strategic information

Wordpress helps in organizing the content into pages and posts. Each page may contain posts of a particular document type. For Example, Pipelines page can have various posts having pipeline of different companies. We created pages for each type of collection like News, Trip repots, Pipelines etc.

Categorization

Major content of this portal was industry news available publicly which we are tracking on daily basis. We felt need for taxonomy to categorize the news items for the ease of accessibility. The news items were categorized broadly as per the type of the news. See the figure 1 for the snapshot of categories.

Tagging

Apart from categorizing the news items, we felt the need to describe the content of the news items for better retrieval of information, so we used the inbuilt functionality of Wordpress – Tagging. Tagging is an uncontrolled vocabulary where any number of terms can be associated with a particular news item.

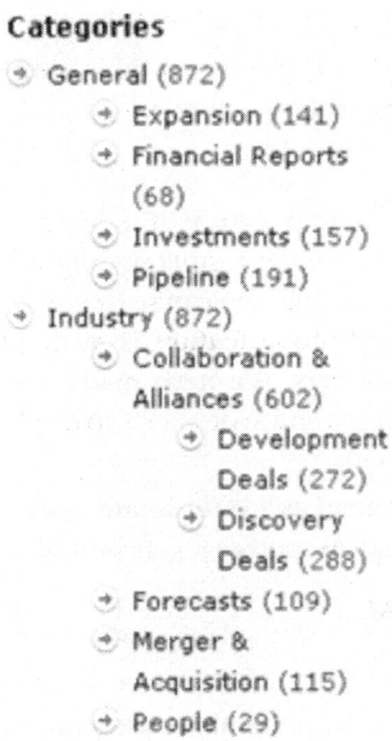

Fig. 1. Categories

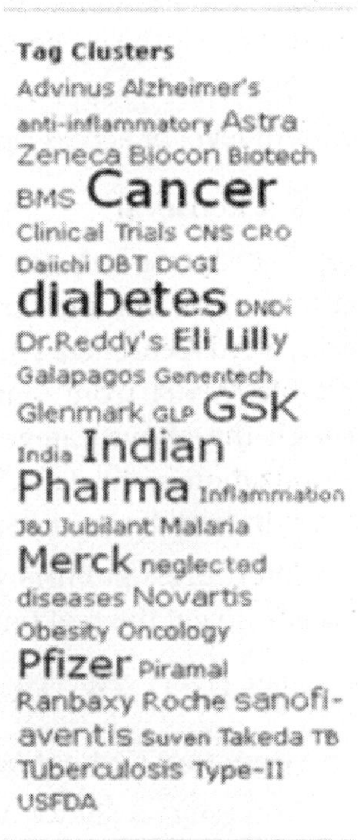

Fig. 2. Tag Clouds

Each news item is tagged with important key words of the

news. For example- In a news item with a Drug discovery deal between two companies, the company names, therapy area (cancer, diabetes etc) and drug targets are tagged. This feature of tagging also allows users to create their own tags, if not available in the list.

Tag clusters are created based on the tags. The size of the tag determines the number of items tagged. The bigger the tag, the higher the number of items associated with that tag. See the figure 2 for the Tag cluster.

Authentication and Access

In order to use single sign on system and to authenticate users, we installed **"Active directory authentication"** plug-in of Wordpress. This plug-in use windows authentication and allows the users to use the in-house email id for logging in to the system.

Users are grouped into different roles as per their profile. Different level of access rights assigned to each role.

Search & Retrieval

Wordpress has a very good search feature; it indexes full text of the content and displays the search results highlighting the keywords searched. Phrase search and Boolean search is also available. Apart from search, the browse feature is available through the above categories and tags. We have made some customization in the default templates and style sheets to display the results based on our requirements.

Wordpress publishes the content as RSS feeds and one can subscribe to get the real time update as soon as it gets published.

PLUG-INS USED FOR THE PORTAL:

Active directory authentication

This plug-in allows WordPress to authenticate users against an Active Directory domain.

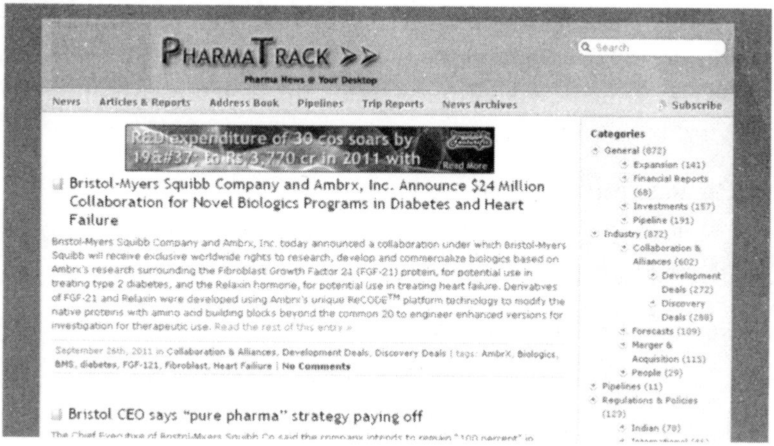

Fig. 3. Screenshot of Home page of the Competitive Intelligence Portal-PharmaTrack

Featurific Wordpress

An effortless interface to highlight the featured story slideshow. Installation is automatic and easy, while advanced users can customize every element of the Flash slideshow presentation.

Cforms

Cforms is a feature rich form plug-in for WordPress, offering convenient deployment of multiple Ajax driven contact forms.

Wassup

Analyze the visitor's traffic with real-time statistics. The aim of WassUp is the knowledge of what the visitors do when they surf the site. WassUp provides flexible, easy-to-read views into visitor's data that is customizable by time periods, visitor types, search keywords, and much more.

WP-Cumulus

WP-Cumulus allows one to display the site's tags, categories or both using a Flash movie that rotates them in 3D. The sources code for the Flash movie is available from wordpress.org.

Wordpress has a very big developer community and continuously developing new plug-ins/widgets and improving the features. Some new Wordpress plug-ins worth mentioning, but not used in our portal, are

WP Calais Auto Tagger

The plug-in uses the Open Calais API to perform semantic analysis of the post text and suggest tags.

TextWise Similarity Search

The plug-in automatically suggests related content

Rate This Page

Allow the visitors to rate the article posts and pages and show rating report system.

CONCLUSION

In our experience, Wordpress is a very useful tool for capturing, organizing and presenting the Competitive Intelligent information. This portal helps in accessing diverse information at one place and thereby saving time. The system can be used to do strategic analysis over the period of time, for example one can do merger & acquisition analysis over the years or analysis of deal making trends.

REFERENCES

1. Wordpress **http://wordpress.org** [15 September 2011]
2. Wordpress Extensions Home **http://wordpress.org/extend/** [15 September 2011]
3. Wikipedia : The free Encyclopaedia **http://en.wikipedia.org/wiki/Competitive_intelligence** [16 September 2011]
4. Aurora WDC.com Competitive Intelligence **http://www.aurorawdc.com/whatisci.htm** [16 September 2011]
5. Cipher : Research Consulting Services for Business Professionals **http://www.cipher-sys.com/what%20is%20competitive%20intelligence.html** [16 September 2011]

FOOTNOTES

1. http://en.wikipedia.org/wiki/Competitive_intelligence
2. Gilad, Ben. "The Future of Competitive Intelligence: Contest for the Profession's Soul", Competitive Intelligence Magazine, 2008, 11(5), 22
3. http://www.cipher-sys.com/what%20is%20competitive%20intelligence.html
4. Arik R. Johnson, http://www.aurorawdc.com/whatisci.htm
5. http://wordpress.org/about/

8

Developing a Cost Effective E-Library : *My Experience of Working from Home!*

Giridhar Kunkur

Librarian, Prin. Welingkar Institute of Management Development and Research, L Napoo Road, Matunga (CR), Mumbai 400 019

ABSTRACT

Technology offers many advantages than disadvantages. It has made our life easy, simple, comfortable and even luxurious. It has helped us a lot to connect with people and that is the reason we say - we are living in a global village. If situation demands, we need not necessarily work from office or a physical library environment all the time to deliver services.

In this case study, I am trying to explain how I managed to work effectively from home using simple technology available free of cost and as a team member, in developing an E-Library for a hospital in Bengaluru. No matter where we work and what technology we use, the challenge before us as librarians is the same - Teach /help people how to find reliable, accurate, pinpointed and relevant information when they need.

Keywords. E-Libraries, Cost effective digital libraries, Working from Home, Using Google Sites, RefWorks, Dropbox.

WORKING FROM HOME!

When I left the British Council Library particularly after serving as head of "the busiest among the British Council Libraries in the world" in Mumbai and joined a newly established QMed Knowledge Foundation, a not- for- profit organization with a broader objective of "Empowering the Medical Information User" as its Program Director, I was in a different work scenario altogether –a small but professionally enriching work place and my Sweet Home!

Because of the long distance that I had to travel in Mumbai to reach my office, I was given an option of working three days from home and three days from the office!

Now, "Working from Home" was a real big challenge for me!

I wanted to prove that I was sincere, honest, do not waste my office time with my family members and at the same time contribute significantly to the newly established organization to achieve its goals. The team at QMedKF was though small, but very effective, knowledgeable, tech savvy and absolutely committed

They said, "Girish, you will be working from home - using simple technologies such as Google Talk for official discussion/ communication, Google Docs for working on strategy papers and other documents which can be seen simultaneously by all those with whom there are shared, Google Calendar to look at who is doing what, where and when. Besides this, you will be using Outlook express for e-mail, Drop Box for sharing big and hefty files, Skype for Tele and Video conferencing, working on websites, databases like PubMed, software such as RefWorks etc".

All in all, I was expected to work using a very simple, but very effective technology. I must say that daily, sharp at 10 am, at home, with my Google Talk on, people in the office could see me that I was at work. Along with Good Morning messages, the colleagues were sending me the list of activities that I was expected to accomplish during the day! We had even agreed on my lunch and tea breaks! It was a great experience – I could never sit idle even for 5 minutes while I was working from home.

Most of my tasks were related to working on policy and strategy documents for the organization including marketing plans and promotional activities focusing on Medical and Health Information services and the scope was rather unlimited.

I would like to share with you my experience of working on an E-Library project – most of the time from home!

E-LIBRARY PROJECT

As part of my job, I was also responsible for working on the e- library projects for Medical Associations, Hospitals, and Research Institutions etc. One such project was to set up an E-Library for a reputed hospital in Bangaluru. It had a small special library too. However, one of the issues that the hospital was facing was the access to information which it had gathered over a period of time. Each Doctor/Consultant in the hospital had a lot of digital stuff in the form of articles, presentations, slides, research documents, case reports, videos, charts etc as their personal collection but scattered across the hospital stored on their respective PCs , Laptops, CDs, Pen drives etc and very little was available in the library. No one had any clue as to who had what and where. Many were having softcopies of articles downloaded from databases like PubMed, some were written by them and published in national and international journals.

We were expected to collect all this electronic information, organize and make it available as a central repository and retrievable using a library management software with all possible searches such as by author, title, subject, keywords, media, type, etc and provide online access to full-text so that they could get information quickly as well.

Another problem was that of budget. The hospital did not want to spend a lot of money on this project. They wanted it to be an affordable and at the same time, wanted the system to be reliable and efficient.

So, the objective for us was to provide them with a simple and cost effective solution. The main task before us was to co-ordinate the collection of scattered information in the hospital and work remotely with them from Mumbai to create their e-library.

INFORMATION COLLECTION AND SYNCHRONIZATION

For collecting the information, we decided to use the file synchronization/back-up service of the Dropbox (**www.dropbox.com**). This service is available free of cost for up to 2 GB space. When Dropbox client is installed say on two computers, the contents of the Dropbox folder would synchronize automatically between them and saved files are available from the Dropbox website. So, we installed Dropbox client in our office in Mumbai and one of the PCs at the hospital in Bengaluru. We taught the person in the hospital who was co-coordinating with us on how to use the Dropbox and she managed to collect all the digital stuff that was available with the consultants/doctors and put them in the Dropbox which was then shared with us in Mumbai.

WEB BASED DATABASE MANAGER

Since the number of documents given to us for creating the E-Library was just about 700 items, keeping in mind that the hospital did not have a qualified Librarian to manage their resources, we preferred to go in for an "easy to handle", user-friendly, reliable and low cost library management software. We selected RefWorks (http://www.refworks.com) - a web-based bibliography and database manager that helps build Library database by importing references from text files or online databases and other various sources such as PubMed, ABC- CLIO, CSA, EBSCOHost, NISC, BiblioLine, OCLC First Search, Ovid, ProQuest, etc. It also accepts all sorts of references like from a web page, newspaper article, section of a book, DVD and many other types as well. Thus, it is an online research management, writing and collaboration tool designed to help researchers easily gather, manage, store and share all types of information, as well as generate citations and bibliographies.

LINKS TO ARTICLES/DOCUMENTS

All bibliographic details of the items in the drop box were entered in the RefWorks. For providing the links to the full-text of articles and other items like PowerPoint presentations, slides, research documents etc, first we created a Google Site using our Gmail account and created a webpage in which we could upload the articles, presentations, slides etc that were moved from the Drop box and stored in computer hard disc. However this activity had a limitation as only 100 items could be uploaded on one Google Site. For adding more than 100 items, we needed to create the required number of Google Sites which was only a simple task.

We copied the links of uploaded items from the Google site and pasted in the Links field of the RefWorks for accessing the full-text documents. There is a feature called Term Assistant in the RefWorks. It appears while manually entering the author name, journal title or descriptor. The Term Assistant closely follows what is being typed and displays information already in the RefWorks database which one can choose to select to populate the appropriate field. Besides, when a new name, periodical title or descriptor is added to a reference that is not already in the database, RefWorks automatically adds it to the Term Assistant.

After importing all the references/items in the RefWorks, it has an option of organizing them in many ways – it could be by topic, type, folder name, class etc and searching and retrieving was easiest and fastest with both Quick and Advanced Search options.

Once the data was imported on the RefWorks and links were provided to access the full text articles, PowerPoint presentations, slides, documents, we made sure that every single link worked. We did a trial run of retrieving the documents online for about two weeks to get satisfied ourselves with the system and fix any teething problems.

COSTS

The costs involved were only the annual subscription to RefWorks database management system which was rather very economical. Other expenses were related to travel costs to Bengaluru, staff and overhead costs.

TRAINING

In order to ensure that this e-library was handled confidently by the people on their own once it was handed over to the hospital and make them build it further, we prepared a User Manual. It provided step by step instructions on how to use RefWorks and how to create Google sites and provide links for full-text articles.

We also conducted a training session in the hospital to teach people how to use, retrieve and further build this library. The hospital management which once had a great difficulty in accessing the valuable information they had was very happy and highly satisfied with this e-library which was delivered to them at an affordable cost.

It was a great fun working from Home making good use of simple technology and building effective E-libraries!

REFERENCES

1. RefWorks : A User Guide – QMed Knowledge Foundation
2. **www.refworks.com**
3. www.dropbox.com

9

Success v/s Best Practices in Academic Libraries

Keshava
Associate Professor, DLIS, Tumkur University, Tumkur,
Manjunath Lamani
Librarian, Govt. First Grade College, Dharwad,

INTRODUCTION

Library and Information Services of Higher Education institutions plays an important role in enhancing the quality of academic and research environment. Library is the place of support for the entire range of academic activities on an educational campus. In today's high-tech learning environment, the library as a learning resource is taking up increasingly more academic space and time in the life of a learner. Several factors are forcing academic libraries to change. The drivers of change include social and economical factors which affect higher education in general and libraries in particular. The main three factors behind the change are: 1. Changes in literate habits, 2. Changes in students and the curriculum, and 3. Changes in the technological infrastructure.

Globalization is playing major role in making today's

students more focused and demanding. At the same time it is introducing resource crunches and concept of value for money even in education sector. In this scenario, only those libraries can excel and satisfy its users which can develop best practices with the available resources.

MEANING & DEFINITION

According to http://en.wikipedia.org (Accessed on 28-07-2011) Best practices are commonly used where no specific formal methodology is in place or the existing methodology does not sufficiently address the issue. The idea is that with proper processes, checks and testing, a desired outcome can be delivered more effectively with fewer problems and unforeseen complications. In addition, a "best" practice can evolve to become better as improvements are discovered.

According to NAAC report -2006: A best practice may be innovative and be a philosophy, policy, strategy, program, process or practice that solves a problem or create new opportunities and positively impact the whole organization (NAAC, 2006). If one thinks with an open and creative mind, in almost every aspect of library a range of best practices can be evolved. Collection and library environment are indispensable assets of any library especially in an academic library. These aspects develops image of the library. Almost all the services and outputs of a library are associated with these two aspects. These can be strengthened further with the help of additional best practices. Best practices are nothing but developing tailor made services, reaching beyond with available resources and delighting the customers. Some best practices practiced in various libraries in India and across the globe are discussed below:

BEST PRACTICES BASED ON LIBRARY COLLECTION

Library Collection is an indispensable asset of any library especially in an academic library. To improve the existing condition of library collection, the libraries have to find out different modes of collection development, maintenance and promotion.

COLLECTION DEVELOPMENT

A systematically developed collection gives rise to a sound collection which can meet the needs of library clientele. A well written collection development policy, a systematic plan of collection evaluation and regular stock verification policy are mandatory to assure the uniform growth of collection. While collection building, the libraries should make special efforts to generate special collection in a selected area. This special collection not only adds value to the collection but also promotes the library and improves library's image and usage. Developing portals for a given subject or creating social bookmarks can act as value additional reference service. The issue of lack of sufficient number of copies can be dealt with the use of technology. Practices of many libraries revealed that offering online past question papers; access to e-books and e journals reduces the demands for the print versions. Use of hybrid collection, Cd- mirroring system, access to library collection via Wi-Fi also proves beneficial to library users. Users still carry the image of libraries as free information providers. Today's resource crunch may affect this image of the library. To retain the traditional image of free of charge information providers to some extent libraries can collect and make available free booklets on various topics published by Government bodies and NGOs.

COLLECTION MAINTENANCE

For better use of the existing library collection it should be in good condition and shelved properly and promptly in its respective place. Collection in good condition demands proper handling of collection by both library staff and users. Training them about how to handle the library material correctly can reduce wear and tear of collection. Appropriate shelving conditions and regular repairs can enhance the life of library collection. Lack of well trained manpower was a common problem in almost all college libraries, which caused delays in proper and prompt shelving. Techniques like RFID (Radio Frequency Identification) prove to be boon in this regard and are being widely used in worldwide libraries. A unique advantage of RFID systems is their ability to scan books on the shelves without tipping them out or removing them. A hand-held inventory reader can be moved rapidly across a shelf of books to read all of the unique identification information. Using wireless technology, it is possible not only to update the inventory, but also to identify items which are out of proper order. Another application of RFID technology is automated materials handling. This includes conveyor and sorting systems that can move library materials and sort them by category into separate bins or onto separate carts. This high-speed inventorying and automated materials handling improves the shelving condition and lack of handling leads to maintenance of condition of books (Lindquist, 2003).

RFID improves the efficiency of services and saves time of library staff and users to a great extent. On a long term basis the system is highly cost beneficial for libraries as it offers higher scale of security. However, given the high cost of the equipment, this application is not being used widely in college libraries. Currently studies are being held worldwide to develop cost effective and standard RFID systems (Scott & Cadoo, 2004).

There are many other techniques which can simplify and speed up the document retrieval process. Software like Book Finder Map, manual color coding systems, proper tags and nameplates are some of the modes to improve access to collection. Masses of dead collection or less used collection crowd the shelves which act as a barrier to users in locating the required document. Compact storage of less used collection as observed in St Joseph's College, Tiruchirapalli or London Business School Library saves the user's time in retrieving documents. Use of colour codes as observed in London Business School Library, indicating different subjects and different issue period also saves lots of user's time in collection retrieval and improve collection usage. All these efforts make library collection available to users in time.

COLLECTION PROMOTION

For improvising the use of collection one should popularize the same. Displays of newly acquired books and lists of additions were some of the common efforts. There are many ways to make the users aware about the library collection. Displaying list of top ten books, favourite books of celebrities raises the use of books. Theme based displays, book exhibitions, quizzes and treasure hunts are some of the interesting cost effective modes. Bookmarks explaining about various databases, brochures giving one liners about 4-5 interesting books were highly appreciated by library users of Valdosta State University, USA, City University, UK., etc. In UK, there is a practice to develop detailed source guides giving all types of information sources such as books, journals, electronic databases, dictionaries, encyclopedias, statistical databases, indexes, reports, bibliographies, glossaries, list of other libraries on that subject, etc; and how to access the same. This practice can be followed by any college library especially to assist the students and faculty for their project work. With the widespread use of internet one can also go for posting personalized advertisements about information sources, new arrivals of one's interest on the top/side/bottom banner 'ads' on the web. Many libraries such as Lean Resource Center Library of Ford Motor Company, Dallas Library of University of Texas, Iowa State University library experienced positive results from such web marketing (Swart, 2000; Giles & Crossno, 2000). Such personalized ads about library resources and services not only save the users' time but make them aware about the library's collection and facilities. These efforts improve the library use and reduce unused collection.

Outside India, library orientations are held on a regular basis. They are more than just a tour or introduction to library and its facilities. For example, Odum Library, West Georgia conducts orientations for library and its facilities, subject specific resources, searching online databases and searching/evaluating information on the web on a regular basis. This service is highly appreciated by library users, especially research students who respond to it positively. In majority of libraries in U.S. and U.K. separate library staff is assigned for library orientations. Madurai Kamaraj University, Madurai and University of Hyderabad experienced that hands on experience provided to library users during library orientations about using internet and various e-resources increased effective library usage. Lady Doak College, Madurai and Loyola College of Social Sciences, Kerala found resource utilization, bibliography compilation orientations inculcate reading habits and self study among the students especially undergraduate students (NAAC, 2006). Long back in 1986 in National seminar on "Role of libraries in new education policy" under the auspices of Indian Public Library Association and Rajasthan Library Association, held at Beawar it was concluded that to promote effective use of libraries, "Library use education" should be introduced in the pre-college schooling. The expert committee on college libraries, Trivandrum, 1994 under the directorship of V. P. Joy also suggested minimum of five hours in the first term of the first year for all students should be devoted to orientation lectures to be given by library professionals. These lectures should introduce the students to arrangement of information in various reference books (Nath, 2001). Kerala Agricultural University college of Horticulture adopted these guidelines and had taken a unique formal curriculum approach to give library orientations. It developed a course module on Library and Information Science using a blend of theory and practical sessions. Training in locating information using OPAC, different databases and resources and internet was included in the course material. This program received increased level of commitment as it was a compulsory part of the curriculum. Library had evidence about increased usage of resources and relevant quality information retrieval due to this course. Such efforts could make the library orientations more formal mode of imparting importance of library (NAAC, 2006). Various college events at different venues can be utilised to promote library and its services to users not visiting the library. Equipping the staff with required resources and skills can make the orientations more informative and attractive.

Displays are effective mode of promoting libraries. It was observed during the survey that almost all the libraries limit their displays to newly arrived books and/or book jackets. Users were not exposed to various kinds of displays. As a result users' expectations about displays were below average. Expanding the horizons of displays can interest more users and attract them towards the library. Displaying theme wise poems, pictures, newspaper clippings, resources, will no doubt make the libraries more happening places to visit. H R College, Mumbai experienced enhanced user appreciations and footfalls in library increased due to theme wise displays. One of the displays on train bomb blast of Mumbai just on the next day of bomb blast showing library compiled articles and books on how to deal with the disaster, blood bank directory, list of volunteers, NGOs, details about railway help desks and declared helps by various bodies was highly appreciated by the users. Such timely, informative displays connect the library with the users more strongly. Odum library, West Georgia also proved successful in attracting users towards libraries with the help of their innovative and interesting displays. Different monthly basis displays are held in the library on various topics such as professionals like poets, journalists, etc; subjects like advertising, genealogy, etc; ideas like how to convert unwanted or damaged books into useful items.

BEST PRACTICES BASED ON LIBRARY ENVIRONMENT

Library Environment has an in-depth effect on everyone who comes within its periphery and has a large impact on an organization's performance. Appropriate location, lighting, ventilation, arrangement of furniture is must to make the library user friendly. The lighting is basic requirement of any library. However it should vary as per the task area. Uniform lighting in different areas of a library such as stack area, open area reading rooms, reading carrels, computer area, audio-visual section and so on is not recommendable.

Maintaining sufficient ventilation and suitable temperature is other basic necessity of library. Studies showed that increased ventilation and controlled temperature increased performance of the occupants. A user friendly environment should make the users more confident and efficient library users without requiring help from the library staff. To create such environment libraries should improve access to library resources and services with the help of proper signage, maps and colour codes. While designing the library, one should keep in mind all types of users and their requirements. Care should be taken for easy access of differently-abled users with the help of ramps, special gates, sufficient aisles, special lift passes and special signage systems. As practiced in many college libraries abroad, audio tours of libraries, detailed maps and brochures serves as a great help for libraries. Introduction of virtual customer service representative like Cosmo, informative websites and dedicated telephone lines act as efficient help counters. Website performs the role of an effective help desk and promotional tool for libraries. Website offering facilities like "Ask a Librarian", provision of bibliographies, new additions, maps of collection and online catalogues solve lots of users' queries from their homes. Software like London Business School's "Article Finder" which checks all the subscribed databases as well as library catalogue and helps the users to locate the required online source.

Maintenance of silence and appropriate library timings are the basic expectations of library users. A number of factors such as location, building structure and interior design of the library and discipline of library staff and users play an important role in maintenance of silence. To develop soundproof, noise free library environment, one has to pay more attention towards both library's interior and student discipline. Offering carrels, library staff taking regular rounds is being practiced and producing favourable results in many libraries. For suitable timings, understanding user needs, being flexible and sensitive to their timely needs is must. Offering extra library hour, services and space during peak periods is essential. Offering 24 hour or extended hour reading rooms, converting available classrooms or other places into reading rooms during the exam periods online services are some of the measures taken by various libraries to deal with the user demands for extra seats. One can also try the remedies used by London School of Economics Library. During exam time they convert library meeting rooms into study rooms and temporarily switch off PCs provided in the library and convert those cubicles into reading carrels. The library allows users to do advance booking for reading space via library website. Reservation of study spaces by leaving one's belongings while taking breaks is not permitted. Security patrol staff issue yellow and red cards to defaulters. This procedure allows maximum utilization of limited seats.

Safety is a major issue of concern in developing a positive library environment. Libraries did make efforts at securing collection with the help of lock and key system, security staff, baggage counters, grilled windows, under observation gates and vigilant library staff. The belongings of the library users which have to be deposited are also kept secured by the library attendants. It was observed that the safety of library collection got more attention than safety of library users and staff. More structured efforts by provision of training and supervision; suitable equipment; safe systems of work improves the overall safety of the library. Keeping in mind the safety issue while designing each and every work area, equipment and service of the library, enhances safety of library. For example while dealing with collection one should give more attention towards shelf heights and packing densities; aisle width; removal of infrequently used volumes from open shelves, storage position of heavy materials, binding policies (volume size of bound periodicals, etc.) for offering maximum security to the users and staff. The appropriate light, air quality, equipments, furniture and fixtures of library as per standards are safe to use and enhance productivity. Appropriate employment practices (such as use of dedicated staff, etc.) and clear-language text including safety tips, charts, diagrams, checklists and illustrations simplify the processes and reduce risk factors. With internet new areas of dangers have entered the library. Training the users about the threats, declaring clear cut policies about use of equipments, site etc., using filters and firewalls improves the scenario.

College libraries have to create an image of being interesting and happening place to attract the young generation towards them. Many events can be organized to promote library activities. Various college events such as sports day, cultural day and special dates such as national day, environmental day should be effectively used to promote library resources and services. It advertises library collection and services on different subjects. Organising events like book talks, book displays, film reviews, etc. attract more users towards library. These create awareness about library products and services.

Displaying useful information to users such as importance of various days, vocational guidance, events happening in the local area or in a specific subject field, etc. interests many users and gives them a reason to visit libraries. It gives the library an image of information treasury useful even for its daily routine and helps to enhance user's knowledge and skills. Encouraging user participation in various library activities and user representation on various library activities and committees develops a feeling of participation. Ingram Library, West Georgia has a regular feature in their library bulletin explicating students experiences about "How library benefited me" to inspire others. Such articles, videos or talks of achievers and alumni about sharing their experiences at library and tips to use it effectively can attract users towards library.

CONCLUSION

To cope with the timely challenges, every library has to identify and develop its own tailor-made best practices to enhance the collection development process, services dissemination and use of the library as a whole. Appropriate planning, fore thinking, a detailed analysis of user base, objectives of the affiliating institution and its future strategies should be taken into account while planning any best practice. Many library stakeholders grumble that any best practice means involvement of a lot of resources especially in terms of money and equipments. In fact it requires active participation, willingness, creativity and problem solving attitude from the library stakeholders. Developing best practices, analyzing and revising them at a regular interval will lead to continuous improvement in overall performance of the library and the whole institution.

REFERENCE

1. Lindquist, M. (2003, August, 1-9). RFID in libraries: Introduction to the issues. Proceedings of World Library and Information Congress: 69th IFLA General Conference and Council on Access Point Library: Media - Information - Culture, Berlin, Germany. Retrieved February 21, 2007, from http://www.ifla.org/IV/ ifla69/papers/161e-Lindquist.pdf
2. Nath, M. (2001). Handbook of library services. Jaipur: Pointer Publishers.
3. National Assessment and Accreditation Council (NAAC). (2006). Library and information services: Case presentations. Bangalore: NAAC.
4. Scott & Cadoo, L. (2004). RFID use within Libraries: An Australian context. Retrieved May 18, 2007, http://conferences.alia.org.au/ newlibrarian2004/zobjects/ presympppapers/ doowebsitepaperfinal.pdf
5. Swart, S. (2000, Oct. - Nov.) Marketing my corporate library on the web. Marketing Library Services, 20(2). Retrieved May 7, 2007, from http:// www.infotoday.com/ mls/oct00/swart.htm

10

The Digital Divide: Bridging the widening Gap

Manjula N Kadadallimath
Librarian, Army Institute of Fashion & Design, Doorvani Nagar, Bangalore – 560 016

Vani Hiremath
Officer, Information Resource Centre, Tata Consultancy Services, Bangalore – 560 066

ABSTRACT

The digital divide refers to the gap between individuals, households, businesses and geographic areas at different socio-economic levels with regard to their opportunities to access information and communications technologies (ICT's) and to their use of the Internet for a wide variety of activities. It includes the imbalance in physical access to technology and the resources and skills needed to effectively participate as a digital citizen. In this article, an effort has put into discuss the impact of digital divide in education, across geographies and role of Libraries in bridging the gap. In the late 1990's the term ICT gained popularity among scholars, policy makers, and advocacy groups. There are various initiatives such as Consortiums and Library networks across India are also discussed in this article.

Keywords : Digital Divide, Information haves and have not's, ICT Impact. Bridging the digital divide gap and global digital divide.

INTRODUCTION

Society is divided on many basis like Socio-Cultural, Technological, Educational and Political etc. For our topic we can divide the world in to two groups on the basis of access to the Information Technology gadgets can be as

1. People who have access to modern information technology devices.
2. People who have don't have access or the skill to use modern information technology devices modern technological gadgets.

Such as, the telephone (both landline and mobile phones), TV, Internet and many. The term 'digital divide' became more popular among relevant players, such as scholars, policy makers, and advocacy groups, in the late 1990s. The more concerned area in this aspect is the education system and many more sociological aspects. For instance, the digital divide exists between the educated and the uneducated, between economic classes, and, globally, between the more and less industrially developed nations" [1].

The digital divide refers to the gap between person to person, business and geographical areas at different social and economic levels. The opportunity to access information and using information and communications technologies (ICT), and the use of the Internet for a wide variety of activities in performing day-to-day activities. It includes the differences both in physical access to technology and the resources and skills needed to effectively participate as a digital savvy. This very access/ skill set divide reflects the access of various social groupings to information and knowledge, typically gender, income, race, and geography. The term global digital divide refers to differences in access between countries in regards to the internet and its means of information flow [2].

DEFINITION

According to World English Dictionary, Digital Divide is the gap between those people who have internet access and those who do not.

According to Cultural Dictionary, Digital Divide is a term that describes the division of the world into two camps, those who have access to the Internet and other advanced information technologies and those who don't. The term highlights the issue that those who do not have access to such technology are potentially destined to futures where they will be at an economic disadvantage

The other web definitions of the term Digital Divide are:

- The divide between those who can read well and take full advantage of the treasures of information that will be so widely available, and those who are not fully literate and cannot take advantage of easily accessible information resources.
- "Refers to the gap between individuals, households, businesses and geographic areas at different socio-economic levels with regard to both their opportunities to access information and communication technologies (ICTs) and to their use of the Internet for a wide variety of activities.

WHAT IS DIGITAL DIVIDE?

According to an estimate today, there are 429 million people online globally at any point in time; this represents only 6% of the world's entire population. "Even among highly developed nations, there exists a vast difference in the availability of household Internet access. Among all the nations worldwide, Sweden ranks the highest percentage of home Internet connections at 61%; following up with the Spain, which trails the list with only 20% of its homes connected." [3]

In this article, there is an effort to know how Digital divide affects in Geographies, Education, Library and Information Science and its services and so on.

GEOGRAPHIES

The geographical digital divide is a term used to describe the great disparity in the opportunity to access the Internet and the information and educational/business opportunities tied to this access between developed and developing countries. The global digital divide involves "geographical, economic, educational, and social aspects" which influence the levels of information communication technology (ICT) development in each country across the geographies. A 2002 World Economic Forum report on the global digital divide found that, 88% of all Internet users are from industrialized countries that comprise only 15% of the world's population.

As the internet progressed from 2000s onwards it became more sophisticated, leading to widening of the digital divide; which is resulting in the lag of those to whom the internet is least available .Countries with a wide availability of Internet access such as United States of America, United Kingdom and most parts of Europe can advance their economics of those countries on a local and global scale. In these western societies, commerce, and social interaction is almost entirely Internet based to a larger extent. Andy Grove, the former Chairman of Intel, predicted that "by the mid-2000s all companies will be Internet companies, or they won't be companies at all". Those countries like India where the Internet and other Information and Communication technologies (ICTs) are not accessible to the large; illiterate communities/masses and societies thus not benefiting fully from the information age and cannot be competitive in the global economy. [4]

EDUCATION

Education is one area where the digital divide is most prominent and prevails today in much geography even today in this ICT/ Internet era. In the context of schools and the digital divide, present day approach focus more on how students use computers, than simply looking for whether there are computers or Internet connections in the education institutions and so on. Public libraries and afterschool programs have also been shown to be important access and training locations for disadvantaged/ drop-out youth [5].

The E-Rate program (officially the Schools and Libraries Program of the Universal Service Fund) in the United States, authorized in 1996 and implemented in 1997 by the federal government, directly addressed the technology gap between rich and poor schools by allocating money from telecom taxes to poor schools without ICT/technology resources [6].

OVERCOMING THE DIGITAL DIVIDE

Overcoming the digital divide depends on what aspect of the digital divide is being investigated and subsequently countered, which depends on the expected impact of the deployed ICT. The first step, which includes may be providing access, itself meets significant challenges from income restrictions. For example, providing ICT access to the poorest of the society would require a great reduction in access prices on part of services provider.

Many Multinational Corporates as part of their corporate citizenship program, help to lessen the divide, often doing so through education systems which draw on information technology. This technology often includes low-cost laptops/ notebooks, handhelds (e.g. Simputer, E-slate etc.), tablet PCs, Mini-

ITX PCs and low-cost WiFi-extending technology such as antennas and WokFis. Technology material for the classroom can also be made available by lowering the costs, including projectors [7].

One of the main challenges in overcoming the digital divide is to widen the influence of the respective policies from those carried out by the particular authorities, to the entire public sector. One way in this direction may be, mostly national Internet programs are led by national telecom authorities, who can work it out to reduce the costs in access and devises to enable reduce the gap of Digital divide [8]. Much thought needs to put in this direction to reduce the gap.

Some cities across the countries have started programs to bridge the divide for their people includes; residents, school children, students, parents and the elderly. One such initiative sponsored by the city of Boston, founded in 1996, was called as the Boston Digital Bridge Foundation. It especially concentrated on school children and their parents, helping them to make both equally and similarly knowledgeable about computers, using computer application programs, and navigating the Internet. In 2010, the same City received a major grant from the federal government to provide internet access and training to underserved populations such as parents, children, youth, and the elderly [9].

LIBRARIES ROLE IN BRIDGING THE GAP

The idea is that some information and communication technologies are vital to quality civil lives are not new anymore. Popular opinion is that the Internet and other ICTs have transformed/ transforming the society, improving understanding between individuals, systems and cultures, eliminating power differentials, realizing a truly free and democratic society globally, and other benefits.

As the systems get more sophisticated and the desire to overhaul and remake those systems gets more intense, libraries need librarians who are technology savvy and back office staff who are pure ICT complaint. There's no doubt that today's reference librarians need a strong ICT skill set than ever in meeting the challenges posed by both technology and ever demanding user requirements, thus reducing the gap.

Libraries are the only places where individuals enjoy the freedom of access to information for lifelong learning. And they are playing a vital role in bridging the digital divide where all services are provided to the society (regardless of age, race or language). Indian libraries have been changing their role from traditional storehouses of information to providing access to information from any part of the world, just like those in other developed world countries. Today the professional librarians are being recognized as information disseminators or communicators rather than custodians of books as in the earlier age. Although digitisation has been a slow process in the country of India, many encouraging steps and several projects are taken-up by the government to bridge the digital divide such as the National Science Digital Library (NSDL), Vidya-Vahini Project, and Digital Mobile Library.

As the usage of Library increase the Demands of users also getting increased and Individual libraries does not have enough capabilities/ facilities to provide better services and they are trying to form a larger communities such as consortium to give better services, quantitatively and qualitatively, as a result of that a large number of library resource sharing networks, such as the INDEST Consortium, CALIBNET (Calcutta), DELNET (Delhi), BONET (Bombay), PUNENET (Pune), MALIBNET (Madras), MYLIBNET (Mysore), HYLIBNET (Hyderabad), ADNET (Ahmedabad), ERNET (Educational and Research Institutions), SIRNET (CSIR Laboratories), INFLIBNET (Universities and Research Institutions) and DESINET (Defense Laboratories) etc are working to fill the gap of digital divide.

The nonprofit organisation such as Knight Foundation announced in Oct 2009 that it is working with communities across the U.S. to make libraries more relevant in the information age. Lady Bird Johnson once said that the only entry requirement to a library is interest. The foundation is working at local libraries to make them the centers of excellence for the digital and media training by funding the project at the local level .The foundation has installed and also financed computer labs in underserved areas, recruited multi-lingual tech tutors, installed wireless Internet in some libraries, and set up job centers for online employment searches and career research.

Some of the popular Initiatives in Bridging the Digital Divide Gap worldwide are;

- Wikipedia Foundation
- International Development Research Center
- Blackboard
- Web Accessibility Initiative (WAI)
- WebAIM
- World Economic Forum
- Equal Access to Software and Information – EASI
- @lis online Initiative
- Close the Gap Initiative
- Social, Economical and Political Change

CONCLUSION

The digital divide not only affects access to resources and services, but also affects their opportunities to use technology. In addition, people from low-income families may not be able to enter the competitive world with sufficient technology know-how and use background.

Closing the gap between those with access to computers and the Internet, and the skills to use those tools to best advantage is important for promoting economic opportunity: as more and more jobs rely on computer skills, the computer illiterate are closed out of more and more economic opportunities. As more information and services are transmitted online, computer illiteracy will push those on the downside of the digital divide further to the margins of society. For example, the use of the Internet would lead to a more democratic society as public participation in election and decision making processes increases. If already under-represented people continue to be unable to participate in such forums, the digital divide will reinforce a socio-economic and socio-political divide. Such factors translate to the lesson that closing the digital divide will have huge advantages for both the current digital disadvantaged, as well as for society at large.

The digital divide is not indeed a clear single gap which divides a society into two groups. Researchers report that disadvantage can take such forms as lower-performance computers, lower-quality or high price connections (i.e. narrowband or dialup connection), difficulty of obtaining technical assistance, and lower access to subscription-based contents.

REFERENCES

1. American Library Association. What is the digital divide?. Accessed on September 10, 2011 at http://www.ala.org/
2. Patricia, J.P. (2003) 'E-government, E-Asean Task force, UNDP-APDIP'. From: http://www.apdip.net/publications/iespprimers/eprimer-egov.pdf
3. Digital Divide Network. Accessed July 30, 2002 at http://www.digitaldividenetwork.org/content/sections/index.cfm?key=2
4. Burks, Michael R. (2001). "Economic Factors Involved with Universal Internet Access and People with Special Needs hi- A Working Paper", Internet Fiesta, March 1–2, Sofia, Bulgaria
5. Sullivan, J. Et al (2009). Work and Play in the Information Age: Technology Usage in Boys & Girls Clubs. University of Washington: Seattle.
6. "New Report Shows How E-Rate is Connecting Communities and Schools to 21st Century Academic and Employment Opportunities", National Coalition for Technology in Education and Training, Washington, DC, February 28, 2007
7. Geekcorps using Mini-ITX PCs. Accessed on 10th Sep 2011 from http://www.iesc.org/geekcorps
8. Martin Hilbert (2011). "The end justifies the definition: The manifold outlooks on the digital divide and their practical usefulness for policy-making", Telecommunications Policy, 35(8), 715–736

9. "City of Boston Receives $4.3 Million Grant That Will Give Training, Computers and Opportunity to Underserved Communities", City of Boston press office, September 14, 2010

10. Digital Divide. Accessed 12th September 2011 from http://en.wikipedia.org/wiki/Digital_divide

11. Neena Singh (2007). "Bridging the Digital Divide in India: Some Challenges and Opportunities" Vol. 17, NUMBER 1Spring 2007.

http://www.worlib.org/vol17no1/singh_v17n1.shtml

11

Infrastructure Development : A Case study of Government College for Men, Kurnool

S.Jahan Ara
Lecturer in LIS, Government College for Men, Kurnool-518002
Dr. D.Chandran
Professor, Dept. Of Library & Information Science, School of Arts, Sri Venkateswara University, Tirupati -517502

ABSTRACT

Library and information has gained absolute importance in the knowledge society. For human development information is as essential as the oxygen to individual survival. Lack of access to information resources is a death knell to social development and international peace. Access to information avoids ignorance, fundamentalism, wars and obstinacy hence provision of libraries and channels to information access is essential for the survival of democracy.

Information and communication technology (ICT) have made a profound impact on the life and work of people. In the context of library landscape, the impact of ICTs is seen in the areas of library automation, library and knowledge networking, information storage and retrieval. LIS education and practice have been profoundly influenced by the electronic resources and the internet based services. But, the library information professionals (LIPs) are faced with a diametrically opposite situation with declining library budgets on one side and growing user expectations on the other. The information and knowledge seekers are overwhelmed with the growing information deluge in the digital age. So, it is inevitable for LIPs to develop information literacy skills among the end users and bring order to the web based chaos.

INTRODUCTION

Information needs knowledge management, knowledge networking, institutional networking, Institutional repositories and library consortia, digital age and computer anxiety, digital preservation, personal and professional competencies, user orientation, user education, user satisfaction and change management according to the users perspective pave a challenging path to LIPs. So, LIPs have become multifaceted personality to handle all types of work in the Information Resource Centre (IRC).

Use of modern technology in library has great relevance in the context of fourth law of library science. "Save the time of the Reader \ User," in which the internal efficiency of the Library develops. IT facilitates collection, storage, and organization, processing analysis, Presentation, Communication and Dissemination of data. The main reason for adoption of ICT are information explosion availability of information in machine readable form and multi use of machine readable records by many users for any number of times and users can access information irrespective of time and location of the information source.

NEED FOR THE STUDY

The turbulent change of the society from Guten Berg to Charles Babbage effects transition of the LIS education. The Librarian is now called as the ebrarian\ Knowledge Manager \ Information Scientist.

The change from the book store of houses to the Virtual Library has come out with the effort of the ICT. IT applied to the field of LIS.

The article is about a case study of the Government College for Men, which was established in the year 1971 with 1200 books only and how it has changed its landscape to the present situation of 20000 books, CD/DVDs section and an internet based device to know the information which is a "click," away.

OBJECTIVE OF THE STUDY

The main objective is to know and have a clear picture of changing infra structure changes the environment of services from the good old book reading to the latest developed one – Virtual reading environment. The infra structure changes that have taken place in the Government College for Men (GCM) from 2005 onwards reflect in the content management and services available in the Information Resource Centre. How the changes taken are in the fallowing way:

Implementation plan for modern technologies in GCM, Kurnool: The changing role of a traditional functions and services of the LIPs:

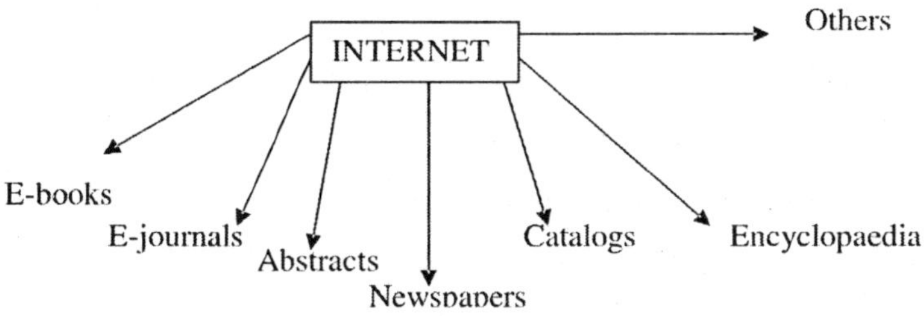

PHASE-1

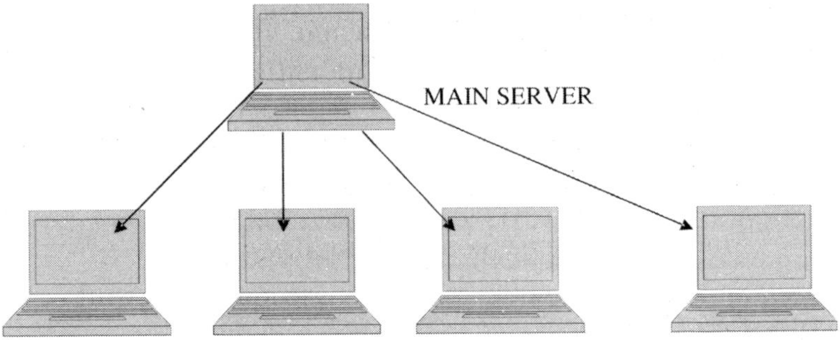

PHASE-2

Main Services available now in the Library due to change in the infrastructure:

1. Free Online Journals: eg; http:// www. jodi.ecs.soton.ac.uk/

   http://www.information.net

   http:// www.springerlink .com

   It provides students and researchers with electronic access to more than 45000 e-books, 2000 peer reviewed Springer journals as well as 23000 protocols for laboratories.

2. Free online books: http://www.free ebooks.net

   http://www.etext.libvirginia.edu/ books.

3. Free Encyclopedia: http://www.britannica.com.

4. Free News Papers: e.g.: http://www.dinamalar.com

   http://www.hinduonnet.com

5. Free Online Dictionaries e.g.: http://pdictionary.com

   http://www.wesu.edu/library/odlis.htm

6. Free abstract service: http://www,wkap.nl/kaphtml.htm/ to CSEARCH

7. Free Online Catalogue Service: http://www.catalog.loc.gov/

   http://www.pindia.com

   In GCM to save the time of the Reader / User the important

websites which are useful for them are written on a board where they can search for freely available online e-journals, e-books other information sources like news clippings which are useful for research work.

Examination Cell Service

In GCM when the Examinations are going to start, the Librarian has to keep ready all the previous and expected question papers for the stakeholders. The model papers for competitive examinations are also taken care for the final year students.

Helpline Centre

From 2008 onwards Library is also acting as the Helpline centre for the students. According to Sri. S.R. Ranganathan Reference service is "Personal service to each reader in helping him to find the documents answering his interest at the movement pin-pointedly, exhaustively and expeditiously."

Telephone or Cell Phone Service

If the user asks any question or any query to the Librarian through phone or mobile, he /she should give the proper answer and guide the user in a right way to the information.

Online Enquiry Service

If the user want any information regarding his research or seminar or any topic for competition through online then it should be answered.

E-mail Service

E-mail service has the advantage of providing more complete answers than what could be possible be given at a busy reference desk. When answering a question though e- mail, the Librarian usually has more time to think about the question, the users information needs and if necessary consults with other colleagues who have more related expertise or knowledge.

Chat Based Service

Sometimes any announcements of the tests and internal competitions and other things are sent through the instant messaging.

Virtual reference: real-time reference line on the web is the latest trend in Libraries.

E.g.: http://www.libraryspot.com/spotlight/cdrs.htm

http://www.cpi.org

Inter Library Loan Service

GCM is having loan facilities and vice versa with other colleges in Kurnool. Staff and students from other colleges approach our Library for the Model Question Papers, reference Material and for their research work in different fields.

CHANGES IN COMPULSORY FOR LIPS

The above are the advantages of the implementation of new technologies in the Library, GCM, and Kurnool. LIPs should not fear that the new emerging technologies will replace the traditional services completely. Though the staff and students go through the news everyday on their Pcs and Laptops they prefer to go through the Newspapers with a cup of coffee or tea in their hand.

WHAT IS NECESSARY?

LIPs should have fallowing qualitative change:

- Software skilled / trained
- They should use internet base e- courses which are plenty
- To adopt e-publishing this is being increasingly accepted by the users.
- To face the challenges of ICT and utilizing it in LIS environment.

Major challenges experienced by the LIP staff at GCM, Kurnool while undergoing the changes in infra structure:

LACK OF FINANCE

In Government sector, the budget released for the Library purchase of books and journals will be very less. For infra structure and for equipment the funds given by the Government are very meager and it will not meet the demands of the users. The Knowledge Commission has recommended to strengthen the Libraries and its infra structure but in practical the situation is very pitiable.

Inadequate Infrastructure

Web accessibility is the most important point and it has great impact on virtual learning. The supply of computers and other supportive equipment is highly impossible in a Government College where as the US schools are having 24x7 online technical help and programme participants need not visit the school (1993 Syracuse university started the virtual learning)

Lack of knowledge and training

Though LIPs have interest to learn more and do the Best due to lack of knowledge and training, they are helpless and they will a fear to touch and operate the system.

Insufficient Contact Classes

In my GCM , the students are from the rural areas. They did not have enough knowledge to work in the digital environment. So, they should be given some exercises to operate the system. Information literacy classes are taken for them so as to enable them to learn the other things on their own and get acquainted. If the systems are less and the numbers of students are more –it is insufficient for them to learn and operate.

Lack of High Quality Teaching Staff

At sometimes, the elderly staff does not pay much interest towards the virtual learning and are reluctant to guide the students. At the age of 18 to 21, if the students are guided properly then their future will be bright and at same time they will show interest to learn and achieve something.

Lack of Evaluation

As there is no committee or body which evaluates the productivity of the college, it reflects on the result of working condition of the staff and students. If it is regularly evaluated, the LIPs will improve in their quality of service. On the other, the evaluating body should announce some bonus /increments to LIPs for their best workmanship. **The infrastructure of the Library should also be increased at a regular basis to cope up with the demand of the users.**

Lack of Supporting Policy at National Level

As there is no common National Policy in India the States have different type of syllabi and curriculum in different courses. The courses have different syllabi even in a single State. If all are brought under one Umbrella and adopt a common policy then it will be easy to compete on National Level. The methods and standards will be the same. NODLINET, INFLIBNET, UGC-edusat are trying but they did not reach the nook and corner of India. Common Network of Higher Education in all over India is needed for the all round development of the students whether he studies in a city/taluq/ village.

SUGGESTIONS FROM THE INSTITUTIONAL POINT OF VIEW

Patronization of UGC

UGC should appoint an Advisory Committee with faculty representation from all leading LIS institutions to be involved in all major decisions relating to the supply of software, e- learning equipment, conducting training programmes, evaluating the performance and standards of the Institution and updating it periodically both in quality and quantity.

Accreditation

It is very essential to establish some professional agency at the National Level which can undertake the work of accreditation in LIPs , Curriculum , Nomenclature, standards, salaries etc. etc.

Policy Formulation

The policy should emphasize the need for practical training and necessary infrastructure requirement. It should be taken from the point of common user from Kashmir to Kanyakumari.

SUGGESTIONS FROM THE STUDENT'S POINT OF VIEW

1. The common student studying in a Government College should get all those facilities / services accessible to that one in a corporate college.
2. The Government of India should take interest in providing all the information of all facilities, courses available to the student category.
3. The scholarships in various categories, mode of applying, the sty fund, fee structure, hostel facilities etc. etc. through a common network of Higher Education.
4. Every citizen of India and student should feel free to take part in all types of competitions and National Level Examinations. They should be aware of the information and material for preparation through the Common net.
5. The infra structure should be given priority in the Government sector as the rural people and the poor will come into these college for study. So, it is the most important to be care of for the development of the country and the youth.

ONE THING TO THINK:

Though we adopt all the modern technologies as infra structure and say that we are developed, it has its own consequences when the trouble arises in the system and every one feel that the new modern infra structure gives a new problems to face and solve.

Think of when you lost your entire term paper because your hard drive crashed. That is the part of danger of our digital world.

We do not know how to store things for safe keeping hundred of years into the future. Without stable HARDCOPIES, everything that has been "born digital" is at risk.

While e- books are great replacing paper books. The most recent calculations estimate that people need to read at least 100 books a year on their e- readers to break even with books on environmental impact. But it is a lot more difficult to recycle an e- reader than a paper book.

Source: http://www.treehugger.com/

REFERENCE

1. Anandan. C, Gangataran .M : Digital Libraries From Technology to Culture
2. Jain. A. K. et. al: Marketing information products and services: A Primer for Librarians and information professionals
3. Bushing, M. C.(1995), Library's Product and Excellence, Library trends, Vol 43 No. 3,pp.384-400
4. Shiva sukula Electronic Research Management what, why and how.

12

Information Needs and Information Seeking Behaviour of PG Dental Students in South Kanara and Udupi Districts: A Case Study

Pooja R
Senior Librarian, Kasturba Medical College, Mangalore-575001

INTRODUCTION

Health practitioners need information management skills to cope with the growing volume of medical knowledge. The ability to quickly access, track, coordinate, critique, and store information is essential for daily decision making related to patient care, education, and research. In addition, changes in the health care systems of industrialized countries have placed new demands on health care services. Delivery of care has become interwoven with adoption of and adoption to computer and information technologies.

Dental hygienists function in a constantly changing information environment and need to keep up to date in the practice of their profession. Not only does information facilitate their ability to make valid decisions and statements about dental hygiene, but information also enables hygienists to provide quality care to their patients. Information is a crucial resource in the operation and management of organizations. Timely availability of relevant information is vital for effective performance of managerial functions such as planning, organizing, leading and controlling. A well established and well designed information system to facilitate users of library is essential to the success of any institute.

User studies are starting to be recognized as an important part of the information package. Information providers like the library need to be aware of their users' information requirements as well as their information seeking and information retrieving methods in order that they might be able to provide better services. A lot of research has been done to find out the information needs and information seeking behavior of various categories of users of information systems.[3]

BACKGROUND TO THE STUDY

From our experience of the everyday world, we see that people are in consistent, if not constant interaction with texts of a variety of types, for a variety of purposes. We read newspapers, we watch television, we go to picture galleries, we use libraries, we engage with advisory services; in order to know about our world, to be entertained, to understand, to learn, to become informed, to do our work, to help us solve our problems. [11] An essential feature of all of these activities is precisely our interaction with these texts. By interaction, we mean that, in such activities, people are not just passive recipients of messages, but rather active seekers of texts, and active constructors of meaning from these texts. They look for texts of potential interest; they make judgments about the usefulness or interest of texts by engaging with them, they interpret texts in order to understand them. Thus, our engagement with texts and our interpretations of them are central to our being able to use them for our goals, whatever they may be.

In the situations which lead to information-seeking behaviors, our interactions with texts often take place within the context of systems, social and technical, which are constructed to support us in accomplishing the goals of the behaviors. Such systems include, for instance, libraries, information centers, advisory services, and information retrieval (IR) systems. The study is therefore explicitly concerned with the issue of how to identify PG dentists' information needs and the information sources they use to meet their needs in clinical settings.

CURRENT STATUS OF THE STUDY

Electronic publications are rapidly replacing printed materials in personal, professional, and educational collections. Libraries have substituted many, if not most, titles in their journal collections with electronic subscriptions, and many books are now available in digital format. With laptops a required tool for many students, electronic books in various formats often replace some or most textbooks required by instructors. For numerous reasons, including environmental preservation, cost savings, convenience, and flexibility, schools are selecting digital textbooks over printed books.

Considering the rapid changes in information provision in the 21st Century with computerized access, digitized information formats, and the overload of resources on the Internet, the access and retrieval capabilities of users who are traditionally accustomed to manual information library systems is questionable. Atkinson (1997) enumerates these as the circumstances under which it was worthwhile to reexamine issues of user behavior in academic settings. Hence this study seeks to investigate the process Postgraduate student's library use while seeking information.

NEED AND SIGNIFICANCE OF THE STUDY:

The advent of personal computers and the internet followed by the introduction of online electronic journals and databases at the beginning of the 1990s led to the development of online academic resources and the transformation of the practice of scholarly communication. The ease of access and ease of use provided by electronic resources made it easier for researchers to access and share scientific knowledge. Today, the use of online electronic resources has become widespread in almost all fields of scientific research. Health sciences librarians have been advocating the use of indexes and abstracts for as long as these products have been available.

The study of Information Needs and Information Seeking Behavior of university students especially in developing countries has been a significant and eventful issue from the last few decades. The current domain of information atmosphere is rich, characterized by an explosion of information sources and providers, a multiplicity of methods for accessing information, and a redundancy of content from multiple sources.

PURPOSE OF THE STUDY

Dentists, like any other health care providers, need to continuously update their knowledge base to stay competent in their profession and provide high-quality health care for patients. Identification of student's behavior towards seeking knowledge and their needs regarding information is a difficult task. Considering the importance of education and information for quick learning, objective of study is formulated which is to understand the information needs and seeking behavior of PG Dental students in South Kanara and Udupi Districts. The librarians need to manage the important resources and make them accessible to attain cost effectiveness in the university library services and promote the use of library information resources. Hence the purpose of this study is to identify general dentists' information needs and the information sources they use to meet those needs in clinical settings so as to inform the design of dental information systems and their awareness about resources.

OBJECTIVES OF THE STUDY

This study sought to establish ways of improving the information–seeking behavior of Post graduate students and to attain their goal, the study stipulated the following objectives:

1. To determine the information needs of PG Dental students.
2. To determine whether the library serving the dental colleges is able to meet those information needs of PG Dental students.
3. To determine the usage of the dental college libraries by PG dental students.
4. To determine the information seeking behavior
5. To establish the problems that PG students encounter in information seeking.
6. To suggest strategies of improving their information seeking behavior.
7. Population of the study:

   The Dental colleges under study are

1. College of Dental Surgery- Manipal.
2. Manipal College of Dental Sciences- Mangalore,
3. K.V.G. Dental College & Hospital, Sullia,
4. Yenepoya Dental College & Research Institute , Mangalore.
5. A. B. Shetty Memorial Institute of Dental Sciences, Deralakatte ,
6. J. Institute Of Dental Sciences, Mangalore.

8. Distribution of Questionnaires:

The distribution of questionnaires among different colleges is shown in Table 1

Table 1. College wise distribution of responses

Name of the college	Questionnaires distributed	Responses received	Percentage
AB Shetty Institute of Dental Sciences (ABSIDS)	90	59	65.55
Yenepoya Dental College (YDC)	85	73	85.88
AJ Institute of Dental Sciences (AJIDS)	55	55	100
KVG Dental College (KVGDC)	36	36	100
Manipal College of Dental Sciences (MCODS), Mangalore	80	73	91.25
Manipal College of Dental Sciences, (MCODS) Manipal	85	79	92.94
TOTAL	**431**	**375**	**91.2**

DATA ANALYSIS

After the survey the collected data were analyzed by using the software packages like SPSS and MS EXCEL.

1. The preference towards channels of information seeking:

Table 1. The preferred channels/modes of information seeking

S.N	Channels/Modes of information seeking	Respondents	Percentage	Ranking
1	Search the internet	292	77.9	1
2	Browse the library	253	67.5	2
3	Consult teachers/friends	179	47.8	3
4	Attending conferences	144	38.4	4
5	Consult the librarian	43	11.5	5
6	Others (TV, Mobile phone)	4	1.2	6
	Total	**375**	**100**	

From the Table 1 it is established that since this is the era of Information Technology 77.9% of respondents prefer internet as their main channel for information seeking since by this method users can get advanced, updated information related to their field of interest very speedily. Still the traditional method of seeking information through library is not lagging behind since 253 respondents (67.5%) prefer their mode of information seeking through library. The other important channels are consult the colleagues (47.8%), attending conferences (38.4%), consult the librarian (11.5%), and very few respondents (1.2%) use some other modes such as TV and mobile phones as their channels for seeking information. It is established that information seeking through librarian is less (11.5%).

Purpose of Library use

Table 2. Purpose of Library use

S.N	Purpose of Library use	Respondents	Percentage	Ranking
1	To read books	292	77.9	1
2	To read Journals	258	68.8	2
3	To issue & return Library materials	137	36.5	3
4	To photocopy materials	135	36	4
5	To use computer	107	28.5	5
6	To read your own documents	54	14.4	6
7	To read news papers	51	13.6	7

From the Table 2 it was established that

- Majority of the respondents visit the library to read books (77.9%) and journals (68.8%) since this is the most important source of current information.
- Others use the library to issue and return library materials (36.5%), to photocopy library materials (36%), to use the computer (28.5%), to read their own documents (14.4%), to read news papers (13.6%), to request inter library loans (1.6%) and others (5.1%) come to library to meet their colleagues and friends.
- It is observed from the Table 4.6 that respondents who visit the library to use the computer are less (28.5%). This may be because as it is observed in most of the libraries under study there is no good number of computers with internet

facility. Due to this reason students are unable to use the computer in the library.

- Since in most of the colleges under study personal books are not allowed inside the library, number of respondents who come to the library to read their personal books are also less in number (14.4%).

Frequency of Library Use

Table 3. Frequency of library use

S.N.	Frequency of Library Use	Respondents	Percentage
1	Everyday	104	27.7
2	Once in two-three days	155	41.3
3	Once a week	73	19.5
4	Occasionally	43	11.5
	Total	**375**	**100**

The Table 3 reveals that maximum number of respondents (41.3%) uses the library once in two-three days, 104 (27.7%) use daily, 73 (19.5%) use once a week and 43 respondents (11.5%) use the library occasionally.

Reasons for not visiting library regularly

The main reasons are- library location which is not convenient (13.9%), lack of time(9.1%) and lack of computers with internet facility (8.3%) The other reasons include –using information sources from the internet (4.8%) inconvenient library hours (4%), lack of awareness about library resources and services (3.7%), lack of relevant library resources (3.7%), availability of information and information sources from other colleges (2.7%), and from friends and teachers (1.1%).

Table 4. Reasons for not visiting the library

S.N.	Reasons	Respondents	Percentage	Ranking
1	Location not convenient	52	13.9	1
2	No time to do so	34	9.1	2
3	No convenient access to computer with internet access	31	8.3	3
4	Use information sources available on the internet	18	4.8	4
5	Library hours not convenient	15	4	5
6	Do not know full range of library services available	14	3.7	6
7	Library resources not relevant to work related information need	14	3.7	7
8	Use information sources available from another organization	10	2.7	8
9	Use information sources available from friends/teachers	4	1.1	9
	Total	**192**	**51.3**	

Purpose of Information seeking

Table 5. Purpose of Information seeking

S.N	Purpose	Respondents	Percentage	Ranking
1	For updating knowledge	284	75.7	1
2	For preparing exams	210	56	2
3	For doing research work	172	45.9	3
4	For writing paper & presenting paper	154	41.1	4
	Total	**375**	**100**	

Table 5 reveals that

- Majority of respondents' (75.7%) purpose is to update their knowledge and for preparing exams (56%).
- The other purposes for seeking information are for research work (45.9%) and for writing and presenting paper (41.1%).

Information Media

Table 6. Information media

S.N	Information Media	Respondents	Percentage
1	Print Books / Journals	164	43.7
2	Online Books/ Journals	184	49.1
3	Both	27	7.2
	Total	**375**	**100**

The Table 4.11 signifies that most of the respondents (49.1%) would prefer to use online books/journals. Still 164 users (43.7%) prefer print books/journals and 27 (7.2%) would like to use both medias for their reference works.

Type of Resources Used in the Library

Table 7. Important library resources

S.N	Library resources	Responses	Percentage
1	Print resources available in the library	251	66.9
2	E Resources available from the library's website and internet	160	42.7
3	Resources (print and online) referred by librarian	17	4.5
	Total	**375**	**100**

The Table 7 shows that

- A good number of respondents (66.9%) prefer to use print resources from library, than e-resources (42.7%) available from the library's website
- Very few respondents (4.5%) get librarian's help to locate their information sources which may be either print or online sources.
- This shows that although it has been revealed that they prefer online resources over print resources (Table 4.11) since in most libraries under study, print resources are available in upper limit number when compared to e

resources respondents have to prefer print resources only without any option.

It also shows that only few respondents (4.5%) get librarian's help to locate their information sources.

Computer & Internet Knowledge

Table 8. Computer & Internet knowledge

S.N.	Conversant	Respondents	Percentage
1	Yes	298	79.5
2	No	77	20.5
	Total	**375**	**100**

From the Table 8 it is clear that 79.5% respondents are familiar with the use of computer and internet. Still 20.5% respondents are not acquainted.

Use of Internet

Table 9. Use of Internet

S.N.	Internet Use	Respondents	Percent
1	Yes	347	92.5
2	No	28	7.5
	Total	**375**	**100**

According to Table 9 vast majority of respondents use the internet (92.5%) and few respondents (7.5%) don't use the internet.

Purpose of Internet Use

Table 10. Purpose

S.N.	Purpose	Respondents (n-375)	Percentage	Ranking
1	Communication	333	88.8	1
2	Education	306	81.6	2
3	Entertainment	199	57.3	3
4	Research	187	53.9	4
5	News	134	38.6	5
6	Sports	52	15	6

This table 10 reveals that

- The majority of the respondents (88.8%) use the internet for communicational purpose and for educational purpose (81.6%).
- 57.3% of respondents use the internet for entertainment,
- 53.9% of respondents use for research purpose ,
- 38.6% of respondents use the internet for news,
- Only 15% of the respondents use internet to get information about sports.

Search Engines used

Table 11. Search Engines used

S.N.	Search Engines	Respondents (n-375)	Percentage	Ranking
1	Google	329	94.8	1
2	Pubmed	129	37.2	2
3	Yahoo	39	11.2	3
4	Alta Vista	4	1.2	4
5	Lycos	1	0.3	5
6	Others	-	-	-

As shown in Table 11 majority of respondents opined that they use Google (94.8%) as their main search engine. The respondents also would like to use Pub med (37.2%) , Yahoo (11.2%), Alta Vista (1.2%) and Lycos(0.3%) for their information needs.

Search Online Data Bases

Table 12. Search online data bases

S.N.	Search	Respondents	Percentage
1	Yes	265	70.7
2	No	110	29.3
	Total	**375**	**100**

The Table 12 reveals that utmost respondents (70.7%) use online data bases for their information needs.

Use of e mail for communication

Table 13. Use of e mail

S.N.	Use of e mail	Respondents	Percentage
1	Yes	333	88.8
2	No	42	11.2

The Table 13 reveals that majority of (88.8%) respondents use e mail for communication

Criteria for Evaluating Information

Table 14. Criteria for evaluating information

S.N.	Criteria	Respondents	Percentage	Ranking
1	Accuracy of Information	295	78.7	1
2	Ease of use and access	289	77.1	2
3	Relevance and Comprehensiveness	130	34.7	3
4	Reputation of source	115	30.7	4
5	Timeliness	80	21.4	5
6	Price	46	12.3	6
	Total	**375**	**100%**	

It was revealed from Table 14 that

- While evaluating information respondents give more importance to accuracy (78.7%) and easy accessibility (77.1%).

The other factors are timeliness (21.4%), relevance and comprehensiveness (34.7%), reputation of source (30.7%) and price (12.3%) for the evaluation of information.

Problems faced while seeking information in the library

Table 15. Problems faced while seeking information in the library

S.N.	Criteria	Respondents	Percentage	Ranking
1	Material is not available	158	42.1	1
2	Incomplete information materials	119	31.7	2
3	Lack of time	57	15.2	3
4	Information scattered in too many sources	52	13.9	4
5	Lack of awareness in using library resources	48	12.8	5
6	No convenient access to computer with internet access	31	8.3	6
7	Library staff are unwilling to service	25	6.7	7
8	Information available is outdated	20	5.3	8
9	Information is too vast	13	3.5	9
10	Information sources are far away located	9	2.4	10
11	Do not know how to use the catalogue	7	1.9	11
	Total	375	100%	

From the Table 15 it was revealed the major problems that the respondents come across are – information material of their choice is not available (42.1%) and also the material that they get contains incomplete information (31.7%). They also complained that lack of time (15.2%) is also a dominant barrier in accessing information. The other problems that they encounter are – non cooperation from library staff, far away located information sources, lack of knowledge about the use of library catalogue, lack of awareness in using library resources, scattering of information in too many sources, vast quantity of information and also non availability of current information.

User education/orientation programme

Table 16. User education/orientation programme

User education	Respondents	Percentage
Yes	116	31
No	259	69
Total	**375**	**100**

The Table 16 reveals that majority of respondents (69%) have not received any user education programme and 31% of them have trained in using the library and its resources.

Necessity of user education

Table 17. Necessity

Needed	Respondents	Percentage
Yes	250	96.5
No	9	3.5
Total	**259**	**100**

From the Table 17 it is found that a vast majority (96.5%) of the respondents opined that user education is important and very few (3.5%) of the respondents opined that user education is not needed.

FINDINGS

- The study collected the data from 375 PG Dental students of which 182 were male students and 193 were female students and is from nine different specialties of Dentistry.
- It has been found that majority of respondents prefer Internet as their main channel of information.
- It is significant that their main reason to use the library is to read books and then the journals.
- It is revealed that respondents visit the library once in 2-3 days and they spend 2-3 hours/day in library.

- The main hurdles for not visiting the library are lack of time, lack of computers with Internet facility in the library and the location of library which has no convenient access.
- It is remarkable to note that students seek information for updating their knowledge in addition for their exam purpose.
- It is found that most of the respondents would prefer to use online books/journals. Other users prefer print books/ journals and few of them would like to use both medias for their reference works. It is important that even in this electronic era students get information through print resources also in the library.
- It is significant that latest trends and events in the field of dentistry are the main continuing education needs.
- It is acclaimed that maximum number of respondents from all the departments are computer literates, majority of them use the internet and they use the internet for communication and education .They get access to internet primarily from their home and hostel. Google is the main search engine that the respondents prefer to use.
- Majority of respondents make use of online databases and they search for these databases independently and very few respondents get help from others.
- Majority of respondents uses e mail frequently for communication.
- It has been identified that while evaluating information respondents give more importance to accuracy and easy accessibility.
- It was found that all the libraries under study are average in providing books and journals in both print and online media and in providing services like current awareness service, Inter Library Loan Service etc and certified that their library staffs are helpful in providing these facilities.

- It is apparent that the two main problems they faced while seeking information materials are – non availability of materials and incomplete information in the materials they selected.
- It was found that more than 60% of respondents not received any user education or orientation programme in using their library resources and facilities and they suggested for user education so as to be aware of library resources and its services.

CONCLUSION

The results of this survey suggest there are differences in information-seeking and computer application practices among Dentists. Information seeking is motivated by a wide variety of needs, including personal, professional, entertainment, etc. In summary, practicing dentists feel strongly the need to keep up with new techniques for patient care; they seek other types of information less frequently. Innovation is an important factor. These needs seem to be met best by professional colleagues, personal book and journal collections. PG Dental students use the library mainly to read books and journals due to lack of availability of sufficient e resources in their libraries. Lack of sufficient number of computer with internet is one of the main barriers for them to use the library regularly.

It is apparent that the Internet has firmly established a place in the lives of many dental professionals. The respondents in this survey reported that majority of dental students are computer literates and they use a variety of Internet services such as email and online databases for their information. The results of this study emphasize the belief that the internet is becoming a valuable asset to the dental profession. Through internet they access online resources which are the preferred media of information for dental students. In addition to this it is important to note that even in this electronic era many students get information through print resources also in the library. The Internet provides a wealth of information. The students are using the Internet significantly and it occupies an important place among various information sources. It is widely used by the students for their research purposes and it plays an active role in searching of information.

Students still depend on print media. Electronic media has not replaced print media. The students need to get skills for searching on the Internet. The information searching practice needs a methodical training to gain the quality in information searching. Of course, "three elements are essential to users in the evaluation of online information retrieval systems: interface design, system performance and collection coverage" (Xie, 2004). The observation of these elements and training the users will enable users to get useful and relevant information.

REFERENCES

1. Atkinson, J.D. & Figueroa. (1997). Information seeking behavior of business students: a research study. *Reference Librarian*, 58, 59–73.
2. Kuhlthau, C. C. (1993). A principle of uncertainty for information seeking. *Journal of Documentation*, 49, 339-355.
3. Singh K.P. (2007). Information seeking behavior of agricultural scientists with particular reference to their information seeking strategies. *Annals of Library and Information studies*, 54(4), 213-220.
4. Shelstad, Kristen R. (1996). Information retrieval patterns and needs among practicing general surgeons: A state wide experience. *Bulletin of Medical Library Association*, 84(4), 490-497.
5. Udupi District. Retrieved on 16-8-2011 at http://en.wikipedia.org/wiki/Udupi_district.
6. Dental colleges in Karnataka. Retrieved on 10-8-2011at http://www.karnataka.com/education/medical/dental-colleges.html
7. Schleyer Titus, K.L. (1998). A Profile of current internet users in dentistry. *JADA*, 129(12), 1748-1753.
8. Satish Kumar, H T. (2011). Approaches to information seeking by life scientists of Defense Research and Development Organization, India. *Annals of Library and Information Studies*, 58(1), 17-23.
9. Nwezeh, Chinwe M. T., & Shabi, Olabode Muftau., (2011). Information-Seeking Behavior of Doctors at the Obafemi Awolowo University Teaching Hospitals Complex, Ile Ife, Osun State, Nigeria. Journal of Hospital Librarianship, 11 (2), 126-139.

•

10. Lasserre, Kaye E., & Foxlee, Nicola. (2011). Health Sciences Librarians' Research on Medical Students' Use of Information for Their Studies at The Medical School, University of Queensland, Australia. Medical Reference Services Quarterly, 30(2), 141-157.

11. Khan Shakeel.A. (2011). Information Needs and Information-Seeking Behavior: A Survey of College Faculty at Bahawalpur. Library Philosophy and Practice (e-journal), 95, 484-489.

12. Umeshareddy, Kacherki & Thombare Mahesh J.,(2010).Print vs. e-Journal and Information Seeking Patterns of Users: A Case Study of SPJIMR .*DESIDOC Journal of Library and Information Technology*, 30(1), 22-25.

13. Gowda?Vasappa. (2010). Information seeking patterns of researchers in the University Libraries in Karnataka state. *Journal of Information management*, 47(1), 23-28.

14. American Dental Association. Dentistry definitions. Retrieved on 21-1-20 from http://www.ada.org/prof/ed/specialties/definitions.asp.

15. Schleyer Titus K.L. (1999), Is the Internet useful for clinical practice? *JADA*, 130 (10), 1501-1511.

13

Library and Information Services @ TATA Consulting Engineers Limited (TCE) : A Case Study

M N Divya
Librarian, Tata Consulting Engineers Limited, Bangalore

Dr. Syed Shahameer
Chief Manager – Administration,
Tata Consulting Engineers Limited, Bangalore.

ABSTRACT

Engineering consultants are the most information hungry community as they need to keep abreast with the developments in engineering design and other fields. Library services are the best possible medium for catering to this information hungry community. An estimate suggests that most of the decisions are taken with paltry 30% of information availability, 30% on ones experience and the rest of 40% on Gut-feel basis. Well equipped Library and Information centers and skilled professionals make this equation changed by improving on % of information availability and thus enhancing the engineers/ technologists experience levels to arrive at accurate decisions which is the need of the hour. This article provides the insight of an engineering consultants library and information centre at Tata Consulting Engineers.

Keywords. Tata Consulting Engineers Limited, TCE Library and Web based Information Services.

INTRODUCTION

Tata Consulting Engineers Limited (TCE) is one of India's leading engineering consulting organization. Established as Tata-Ebasco Consulting Engineering Services in 1962, the company is now a wholly-owned subsidiary of Tata Sons Limited. TCE is an ISO 9001 - 2008 certified by Lloyd's Register Quality Assurance.

TCE offers a wide range of multi-disciplinary services in project engineering across several sectors. The firm has completed more than 6,500 assignments, including the engineering of several power plants with total installed capacity of over 50,000MW, several large urban water supply and waste water projects (including those for smaller towns), facilities inside battery limits and offsite facilities for several chemical and industrial plants. TCE has always endeavored to provide state-of-the-art technology and cost-effective solutions to its clients. This in turn has helped TCE to earn an international reputation and awards for engineering excellence.

TCE has over 3200 highly qualified and experienced professionals on its rolls. Design offices are located in several cities in India - Mumbai, Bangalore, New Delhi, Chennai, Kolkata, Pune and Jamshedpur and a subsidiary in Qatar.

TCE has successfully carried out several assignments overseas — in South East Asia, the Middle East, Africa, Europe, Asia Pacific, Australia and America. TCE has done projects funded by:

- World Bank
- Asian Development Bank
- United Nations Development Programme

- Japan Bank for International Cooperation
- United Nations Industrial Development Organization
- World Health Organization
- United States Agency for International Development

TCE'S INDUSTRY FIRSTS

- India's first 800 MW rating supercritical thermal power unit at Coastal Gujarat Power Limited, Mundra.
- India's first under creek tunnel of 3.6 m diameter at Kasheli for water transmission system of Brihanmumbai Municipal Corporation, apart from four tunnels of 3 m diameter using tunnel boring machine in Mumbai.
- Detailed engineering of India's single largest water supply and sewerage project in Bangalore for Bangalore Water Supply and Sewerage Board.
- 150 MW pumped storage unit 1 at Bhira for Tata Power Company Limited
- World's largest steerable radio telescope (GMRT) 30 dishes each 45m diameter at Narayangaon for Tata Institute of Fundamental Research
- Asia's biggest optical telescope (2.3 m dia) for Indian Institute of Astrophysics
- Dismantling and transportation of 60,000 TPA DMT plant from USA and redesign & reerection at Patalganga for Bombay Dyeing.
- Asia's biggest clear water pumping station at Bhandup (1900Mld) for Brihanmumbai Municipal Corporation
- The first submarine cooling water tunnel (468 m) at Kalpakkam for Nuclear Power Corporation
- Continuous polymerisation and direct melt spinning polyester staple fibre plant for Swadeshi Polytex.
- The first 160 MW Trombay Unit-IV thermal power unit in India for Tata Power Company Limited

LIBRARY AND INFORMATION SERVICES

TCE Library brings a set of unique skills and strengths to projects, thus enabling the company to achieve excellence and customer satisfaction in a wide range of industries and business sectors. To achieve this TCE Library is completely aligned to the organization's Vision, Mission and Values.

The aim of the Library and Information Centre is to establish, develop, manage, continuously review and update a comprehensive information system utilizing the information centers like British library, Indian Institute of Science Library and other TCE Libraries. Through this data network information is provided to the staff and senior management to assist in preparation, execution, follow-up, evaluation and development of plans, programs and policies in various business units. Ultimately, the information helps in raising the standards of Engineering, Organizational, Scientific efficiency and productivity in the organization.

LIBRARY COLLECTIONS

TCE Library always strives hard to create a bench mark and sustain it by helping the organization's focus areas of today and future/new technologies. The Library provides all the required material and information services to Power, Infrastructure, Architecture and town planning, Chemical, Industrial, Mining, minerals and metallurgical, Nuclear and Construction Business Units.

Over the last 40 years, TCE Bangalore library has developed from a small referral Library to a size which has the following collections,

- Books - (4300)
- Standards - National and International (4500)
- Reports - In-house project reports, conference/ workshop/ seminar reports etc. (830)
- Periodicals/Journals Subscribed (60)

- CD's / DVD's (130)
- Maps

TCE Library has pioneered in delivering all the regular services listed below.

Information search services to the engineering community

Library and Information services centre does cater to a wide variety of information search requests using the available in-house sources. We also use the domain experts located in different offices through our IT network in sourcing the required information. We use their expertise to answer a particular query or we help them in establishing a link with the expert to proceed further.

Document Delivery Service

- We use our own TCE libraries across the country and borrow required materials on ILL.
- TCE Library also has memberships with many industrial and academic research libraries, sourcing the required articles and clearing the required copyrights is a continuous process.

Standards Reference Services

TCE being a consulting company, focus on the deliverables is mainly dependant on National and International Codes and Standards. Library plays a major role in maintaining quality, accuracy of the projects. Earlier type of hardcopies is now replaced by electronic format. All standards bought are LAN network version and made available to all the TCE employees across locations and at sites.

Newspaper Clipping Services:

Articles and Information related to company, business is collated from publications, newspapers, scanned and stored for future reference. The information which is required to be shared is sent by a creative mailer.

Content highlights from journals

Whenever a new hardcopy of the journal/ magazine issue is received, Library sends out the contents page of the particular journal/ magazine to all the staff. The decision makers may not have time to reach out to the library, but library reaches out to their desks providing information services. This service is one of the highly applauded products of TCE library. Contents of the journals which speak about the new work or any innovations, articles which is related to our projects, new technology are scanned and a creative mailer along with the link to scanned document is sent to all the employees.

Circulation of books and standards

TCE uses SLIM software and barcode scanner assisted library transactions for efficient tracking and circulation.

Interlibrary loan

Within TCE libraries of different locations tradition of borrowing books is widely practiced. This is made possible by online access of all the libraries by the employees at all locations.

Role of Librarian in today's Business Scenario (TCE in specific)

Apart from conventional library function TCE library aligns itself to the business requirements of the company. A sample of our activities are :

Power news: Research Views

Day to day happenings in the area of power sector (thermal, nuclear, hydro, wind, solar,) are collected and mailed to all. Help engineers to source relevant and current information.

Day to day news headlines: "Good Morning TCE"

A crisp news headlines from Daily news papers are sent to the employees in the morning as an information tablet to their desktop. Link is provided to each topic which leads to the relevant news details. This also includes – health tips, a quiz per day, did you know?, gold and silver rates, temperature, steel rates, cement rates, sensex etc.

Business news bits

New business opportunities within the country and outside the country are collected (Information such as tenders, bids etc) and forward to commercial department or to the concerned staff.

Innovations in the business sectors are snaffled, circulated and stored for records.

Newsletter of new additions

This news contains info on what are the new additions to library in that particular month. It contains news bits which speaks about the information such as new and revised standards, new memberships, any special activity done at library, etc.. Then what are the materials added, journals added.

Book Exhibition

Every year we conduct book exhibition inviting the different suppliers and all employees are given chance to read, choose and recommend books for the library.

Documentary Shows

A documentary movie is played every Friday on Engineering Disasters and Extreme Engineering. The audience are encouraged to discuss/debate relevant incidents in our projects and learning's are shared. Our senior advisors /consultants are also invited for these screenings to share their views with our junior engineers.

Book Bank

Academic books – A book bank of used books starting from class X onwards including engineering/other professional books collected from the employees are made available for use by our employee's children. Employee's children are encouraged to borrow from the library make use of it for their academic purpose and return it back to the library.

Technical Publications

TCE Library also helps the engineers/non technical staff in developing Technical Papers and presenting them in various forums which enhances their knowledge and also helps in brand building of TCE.

SUBSCRIPTION

To keep abreast of the latest information and to have access to the old/past information we have membership of some of the well known libraries and organizations.

OTHER LIBRARIES MEMBERSHIP

- British council library
- Indian Institute of Science Library
- Central Power Research Institute library

OTHER ORGANISATIONAL MEMBERSHIP

- Indian Green Building Council
- Confederation of Indian Industries
- Indian Desalination Association
- CICIND
- ISA Bangalore Section
- FKCCI
- Greater Bangalore Industries Association

TCE Library operates with a team of Library committee members drawn from different disciplines and is headed by a Chairman, (General Manager). Members conduct brain storming activities to motivate the users.

CONCLUSION

The need of the hour is to make libraries to be part of the business process so that the top management starts looking at them as not just knowledge repositories but as one of the more vibrant business process which can add value to the company's top &

bottom line. TCE Libraries have succeeded to a large extent in convincing the management by aligning itself to the today's business needs and contributing to the growth of the Company. TCE Bangalore Library has been taking a lead role and we have plans to introduce mobile library concept so that the relevant data can be accessed 24X7 in any corner of the Globe.

ACKNOWLEDGEMENT

Authors thank the management of TCE for the encouragement and guidance in publishing this paper.

REFERENCES

1. Tata Consulting Engineers (TCE) website http://www.tce.co.in/ accessed on 12th September 2011
2. Jamie McKenzie (1993). Libraries of the Future. Accessed from http://www.fno.org/libraries.html on 12th September 2011
3. Sohail Inayatullah. Which Future for Libraries? Accessed from http://www.metafuture.org/Articles/which-future-for-libraries.htm on 20th September 2011

14

Analysis of Usage of Intranet Services at Central Library, Alliance University, Bangalore

Pradeep.P.Kavi

Asst. Librarian, Central Library, Alliance University, Chikkahagade Cross, Chandapur-Anekal Road, Anekal 562106, Bangalore

ABSTRACT

The article traces the development of Intranet website at Central Library, Services provided and usage. Usage statistics have been obtained from Webserver log files. The analysis of the statistics reveals how the users have increased over the time and what are the main services they use on the website.

INTRODUCTION

Alliance University was set up under the aegis of Alliance Business School by an Act of the State Government in August 2010. At present, it offers BBM, MBA, EMBA, EPGP, M.Com and Ph.D degree programmes.

CENTRAL LIBRARY COLLECTION

The library which was started during 2005 at City campus at BTM Layout was shifted to Central Campus at Anekal in September 2008. It is housed in an impressive dome shaped building with pillared architecture spread over four floors covering a total carpet area of 55,000 sq ft and has seating capacity for about 1000 plus users.

The Library has rich collection of books in all streams of Management. The collection includes 30,167 books, 2500 plus e-journals, 110 print periodicals, 2468 Project Reports, 612 CD/DVD's and 286 Case Studies.

CENTRAL LIBRARY WEBSITE

The library house keeping operations have been completely automated using Easylib Library automation software. Initially, only the Web OPAC was available on the Intranet for accessing the library collection. However, as the number of e-resources like databases, e-Journals, e-Books increased, there was demand for an integrated website which would provide a single point access to all e-resources and also on services like Current Awareness, New Arrivals, Circulars & Notices, Subject Gateways, Weblinks etc.

Keeping these in mind, Library Intranet website was developed in the year 2009 using MS FrontPage and hosted on Apache webserver server running on MS Windows 2000 Server Operating system.

The website offers the following Information Services

- General Information about the Library and collection
- Access to Databases - brief information on the database, coverage and links
- Access to e-Journals – Title, link and User name/password
- Access to e-Books subscribed by the library and also links to free e-Books sites of interest to the University
- Web OPAC

- Digital Library (Institutional Repository using DSpace)
- Circulars with archives
- Library e-Newsletter
- Subject Gateways
- Weblinks (Links to websites referred by Faculty for their courses)
- Services (ILL, Institutional membership etc)
- User Guidelines
- FAQ
- Library Staff contact
- Publisher Contact
- Download section (Book indent, Membership form etc)
- Flash news

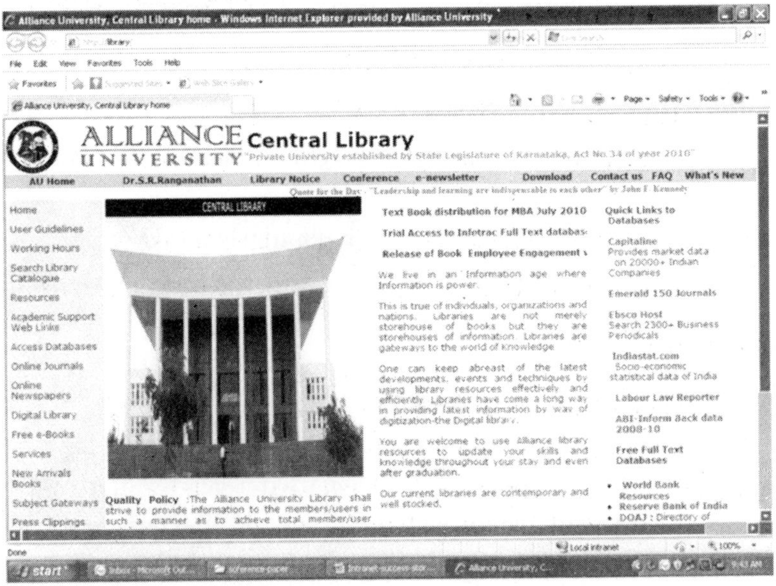

Picture 1. Screen shot of Homepage of Central Library

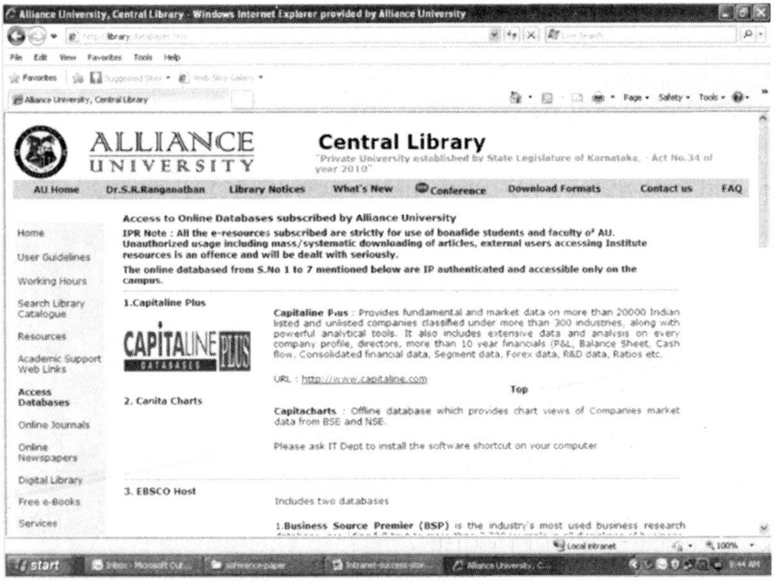

Picture 2 Screen shot of Databases access page

OBJECTIVES OF THE STUDY

1. To find out the frequency of usage i.e how often users visited the website
2. What are the services that are popularly used?
3. Problems faced by users in accessing the Intranet website

METHODOLOGY

ANALYSIS OF USAGE OF LIBRARY INTRANET WEBSITE

The study was conducted based on analyzing the log files generated by the webserver. We have used 'Deep log analyzer' a free software available for web server log file analysis.

Table 1. Hits to Library Website

S.No	Year	Hits	Average number of hits Per day
1	2009	32854	90
2	2010	70265	193
3	2011	53995	225

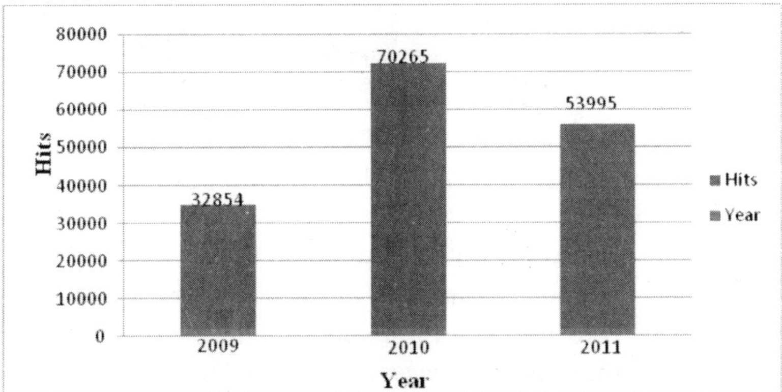

Graph 1. Hits to Library Website

Table 1 shows year wise hits to Library website. A hit is recorded every time a web browser (such as Internet Explorer or Firefox) requests a file from the web server. The file that is requested might be a page of text, an image, a banner advert, a piece of JavaScript, or any other file. A cursory glance at Table No1 shows that the hits have gone up from 32854 in 2009 to 70265 in 2010. That is, the number of hits has more than doubled. It shows the increase in users to the Library website. The figure for the year 2011 is also high at 53995 being the hits recorded till August 9, 2011.

Table 2. Visits to Library Website

S.No	Year	Visits	Average number of visits Per day	No of unique visitors
1	2009	3280	9	390
2	2010	9274	25	1167
3	2011	10803	45	1105

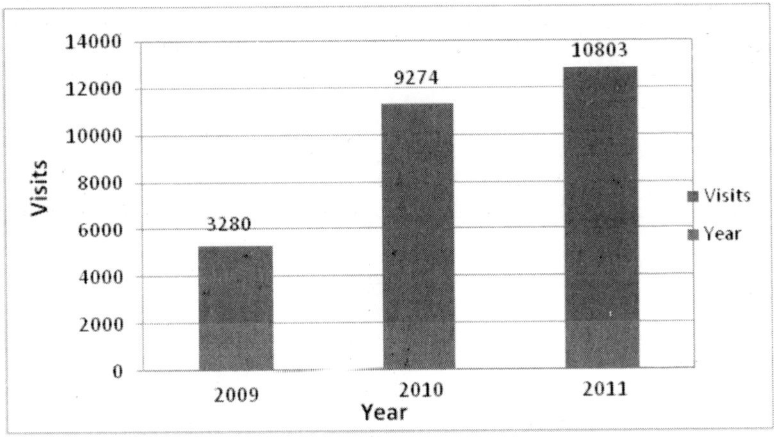

Graph 2. Visits to Library Website

Table 2 shows the number of visits to Library website. A visit will be recorded when a user visits the site one time and regardless of the number of pages the user views. A cursory glance at the table 2 shows that the user visits also has gone up from 3280 in the year 2009 to 9274 in the year 2010. The visits have almost trebled. The number of visits for the year 2011 is 10803 which is the recorded visits till August 9, 2011. This is also encouraging as it has crossed the last year figure.

Table 3. Services popularly used (Top 20 Pages)

S.No	FileName	Description	Page Views
1	index.htm	Library Home Page	33,919
2	databases.htm	Databases access page	6,127
3	opac.htm	Web OPAC	4,413
4	online_journals.htm	Online Journals access page	4,365
5	resources.htm	Library Resources (Collection details)	2,553
6	digital_library.htm	Digital Library - Institutional repository	2,387
7	new_arrivals.htm	New Arrivals Books	1,535
8	library_notice.htm	Circulars with archives	1,757
9	services.htm	Services (Institutional Memberships, ILL etc)	1,185

10	drupal	News Paper Clippings service	1,108
11	working_hours.htm	Working Hours	943
12	subject_gateway.htm	Subject gateways	936
13	academic_weblinks.htm	Web links (Links to websites referred by Faculty for their courses)	832
14	rules.htm	User Guidelines (Rules, member privileges etc)	829
15	e-books-free.htm	Free e-Books	818
16	what_is_new.htm	What is New	683
17	staff.htm	Staff information	640
18	conference.htm	Conference alert	713
19	download.htm	Forms download (Book indent, membership form etc)	591
20	contact.htm	Contact information	486

Table 3 shows the number of page views for top 20 pages (for the years 2009-11) arranged in descending order. The maximum numbers of views were for Library Home Page; a snapshot of which is shown in Picture 1. It so happens that as we have given links to databases subscribed from this page itself, users need not visit the database access page once again. The next important service used is the Databases access page. This page gives details of databases subscribed, brief information on the coverage and links. The third important page that users have used is the Web OPAC page for searching Library Catalogue. The next two services popularly used are the e-Journals access page and Resources page respectively. It means that Databases, Web OPAC and e-journals are the three most sought after services from the users.

PROBLEMS FACED BY USERS IN ACCESSING INTRANET WEBSITE

During September 2010, we conducted an online user survey which included questions on problems faced by users in accessing the Intranet website. The sample consisted of 72 users.

We can see from Table No 4 that majority of the users (91%) are aware of Library Intranet website and just 9% are not aware.

Table 4. Questionnaire on Problems faced by users and their response

Problems faced	No of responses	Percentage
Not aware of Library Intranet	7	9
Did you face any problems in accessing website	15	20
Did not get the required information	3	4

To address the issue, students were made aware of Intranet website during Orientation itself and this information has also been included in Student handbook. This apart, we invariably include link to Library Intranet website in all our e-mail communications, notices etc. Twenty percent of users have reported that they faced some problem in accessing Intranet website. On further enquiry, it was found that most of cases related to access from users laptop computers which needed a onetime setting. These problems were rectified by IT Dept. Four percent of users have reported that they did not get what they want. On further enquiry, it was found that either they were not able to get the full text of the article through the databases subscribed or faced some problem with Easylib Web OPAC.

CONCLUSION

As discussed in the preceding sessions, we have tried to analyze the users' behavior on what services on the Website that are popularly used, how often they use and the problems faced by them in accessing the website. The figures obtained after analyzing the log files are encouraging as the user base has increased manifolds over the years. It gives us enthusiasm to provide more Intranet based services. The analysis presented in the preceding pages shows only a partial view of usage. Many Hits and Visits are not recorded because users may have saved the web pages on their computers and access the page offline. Also, caching is another reason due to which Webserver does not get hits. The Browser simply pulls the page from its cache, thereby not recording a hit.

15

Managing and Sharing Knowledge through Portal: Mysore University Library Experiences: A Case Study

Mallinath Kumbar
Professor and Chairman, Dept. Library and Information Science, Manasagangothri, University of Mysore, Mysore -570005

Tejashwini B
UGC-Junior Research Fellow, Dept. Library and Information Science, Manasagangothri, University of Mysore, Mysore -570005

G. Kiran Kumar
Research Scholar, Dept. Library and Information Science, Manasagangothri, University of Mysore, Mysore -570005

ABSTRACT

Knowledge sharing in an organization is always a difficult task, but in academic institutions knowledge sharing is most essential process. University of Mysore is almost a century old academic body which is India s most efficient and popular education institute along with the vast amount ongoing researches. The modern technology as pros and corns of its own kind it brings loads of information to people's doorstep, desktop and in more advanced form on everyone's finger tips. Everyone is moving from publishing to e-publishing due its easiness, dissemination of information worldwide. People now wake up in morning write in blog, face book and twitter no more diaries are used as before. Today information is produced in terabyte speed. This information and knowledge has to be shared for its better application and usage, but there barriers like language, political security, closed access etc. in India especially UGC pays crores of money to E-resources access and the INFONET constria is made to share knowledge among all the universities to make utilization of this large amount of information and knowledge. Mysore University library Information portal is playing a key role in bridging information resources, peoples and intellectual properties in knowledge sharing environment. This paper describes the experiences of Mysore University Library Information Portal an effective feature for knowledge sharing in academic organization.

INTRODUCTION

An academic institute like University of Mysore is a knowledge organization. The knowledge in higher education is always shared in high rate percentage than in any other organizations. Before going in to knowledge sharing platform of University of Mysore we have to understand what exactly knowledge is? Oxford online Dictionary defines "Knowledge" as "facts, information, and skills acquired through experience or education; the theoretical or practical understanding of a subject" and Collins online dictionary defines "Knowledge" as" the facts or experiences known by a person or group of people". Thus we can understand that knowledge is prolonged skills obtained through information, experience and through education also. As public programs and services grow more complex and interdependent, knowledge and information sharing across the boundaries of government agencies, levels of government, and public, non-profit, and private sector are essential elements for developing electronic applications.

These applications are typically based on information and knowledge beyond the jurisdiction of one agency or one level of organization. Sharing knowledge and information through information technology (IT) enablers provides strategic advantages for persons to improve decision-making and enhance the quality of services and programs. Such sharing is the foundation for development of integrative applications, resources sharing, effective adaptation to new environments, and the enhancement of organizational learning.

Despite the importance of knowledge as an asset, few organizations truly understand how to manage knowledge to achieve their goals. To actualize knowledge management, firms frequently turn to technology-based information systems such as knowledge repositories and expert databases. These information systems, developed to support and enhance organizational knowledge processes, are referred to as knowledge management systems (KMSs). Much of the literature on KMSs has focused on the process of capturing and disseminating knowledge. However to gain a competitive advantage from knowledge, firms must accomplish more than the redistribution of existing knowledge, they must generate new knowledge.

BACKGROUND

All organizations also operate within their external environment, i.e. society. An analysis of types of society may be helpful as it allows us to consider the aspect of sharing information and the management of knowledge from quite different perspectives. For example, Van DerRijta's (2007)work was concerned with the two concepts of societies which display characteristics associated with individualism and collectism. These types of societies are important and a means of charting differences in the concept of sharing (Chen et al., 1998; Hofstede and Hofstede, 2005). All the relatively new "free" Eastern European societies have in common a sense of uncertainty about the future and this aspect has important consequences regarding the need to share and trust information. Uncertainty can be viewed from two areas, that of "relational uncertainty" (according to Berger, 1975) where it is difficult for employees to predict the beliefs and behaviour of colleagues and the that of "informational uncertainty" where the accuracy of the actual information is called into question – as addressed in the information seeking literature (Burke, 2003, 2006, 2007; Choo, 2001; Kulthau, 1993; Davenport and Prusak, 2000).

Both these areas are concerned with three issues. The first is the fear and trepidation experienced by organizational members about levels of accuracy and quantity of information; the second issue is about both trusting the source of the information and a willingness to trust co workers enough to share information whilst the third issue is about having sufficient relevant knowledge to make quality decisions. The project builds on these premises and investigates the barriers to one of these major KM processes – that of sharing information. Sharing generally happens within the context of an information system or a KM system and in order to discuss KM sensibly, we must start with a clear definition. KM can be defined as being about the management of all information in organizations in such a way as to enhance the progress of the organizations aims and objectives. More formally, KM can be defined as "the generation, representation, storage, transfer, transformation, application, embedding and protecting of organizational knowledge"(Schultze and Leidner, 2002).

BARRIERS OF KNOWLEDGE SHARING:

Everyone is aware of importance of knowledge sharing in an organization but still the knowledge sharing is not happening to great extent due to barriers of knowledge. According to Andreas Riege there are around three-dozen barriers for knowledge sharing in an organization which flows from

- Individual barriers like not trust on others, less motivation etc.

- Communication barriers like language, verbal representations etc.
- Cultural barriers like scared, unwillingness to learn/share with other cultural peoples.
- Political barriers like security issues, confidentiality.
- Along this we have one more major barrier of knowledge sharing in E- environment i.e. "Digital divide". The term refers to gaps in broadband network access. The term means not only unequal access to computer hardware, but also inequalities between groups of people in ability to use information technology fully. Bharat Mehra defines "digital divide" In context as simply the troubling gap between those who use computers and the internet and those who do not".

We may try to ignore these barriers in academic organization to some extent, but there lies one more major barrier of ICT for knowledge sharing i.e. "Closed access". A large amount of knowledge will be shared only with person who can buy/ subscribe it. If a person is subscribed to journal of Mathematics than he will be able to access only journals of mathematics. It may look simple but it's not if the same person likes to read or to acquire knowledge from interdisciplinary subjects of mathematics like physics astronomy etc. A single individual will not be able to afford the journals of his interests. This same case can be implied to an academic institution, in a developing country like India there is not much investments for higher education. Thus UGC came up with the constria idea. Where resources can be shared throughout universities of India without any limitations to particular area or particular organization and every university library plays a vital role to fulfill the objectives of UGC.

KNOWLEDGE PORTAL

A portal simply in Oxford online dictionary means"a door or entrance to..." . According to the free online dictionary of computing, portal can be defined as "a website that aims to be an entry point to the Worldwide Web, typically offering a search engine and/or link to useful pages, and possibly news or other services". A portal more than simply an archive to information , portals facilitate a dynamic exchange of Knowledge, data, information by compiling content from multiple sources, they limit redundancy and effectively increase the dissemination of information. A library portal serves as integrated interface to a wide variety of digital resources and web based library services. Web portals are also important tools for users to access and utilize library.

A library portal serves as an integrated interface to a wide variety of digital resources and web-based library services. Web portals are also important tools for users to access and utilize library and information services over a network. An informative home page provides the users helpful information about the library, its collection, and services. In addition, library portals also host links to important internet resources useful for the parent organization. The dynamic linking capability of the web has provided users unrestricted access to information, and to librarians an effective method to organize the contents. It has thus become mandatory for libraries to develop their portals to provide users access to their resources.

UNIVERSITY OF MYSORE LIBRARY WEB PORTAL EXPERIENCES

University of Mysore was established by the Maharaja of Mysore Dynasty, His Highness Sri Krishnaraja Wodeyar IV and his Dewan, the renowned engineer - statesman, Sir M.Visvesvaraya, on July 27, 1916. The main campus of the University, created in 1960, lies in a picturesque area of 739 acres at the western end of the Kukkarahalli Lake. The University now encompasses 122 affiliated colleges and 5 Constituent Colleges (with an aggregate of 53,000 students). In addition, the University has 37 post graduate departments, 8 specialized research & training centers and 2 post graduate centers that together offer about 55 regular academic programmes to 3,500 students. It also runs a number of employment-oriented diploma courses and certificate programmes. The post graduate departments are reputed for excellence in advanced studies and research, and have attracted projects and grants worth crores of rupees from many national and international institutions. The University has developed excellent infrastructure for curricular and co-curricular activities. The Mysore University Library offers a collection of over 8 lakh books, 2,400 journal titles and 1 lakh volumes of journals. The main campus features an amphitheatre, an auditorium, a swimming pool, and hostels for women and men with modern amenities and comforts.

Mysore University library is one of the oldest and largest University Library in the country and Mother of other University Libraries in Karnataka. The Library started functioning in the year 1918. It has a glorious record of 91 years of worthy service with resource collection 6 Lakhs volumes in its systems today. The inception collection of the library was around 2311 books which was housed in Jubilee building and later moved to Maharaja's college campus and finally the library shifted to new building at Manasagangotri Campus in 1965.

Table 1. Mysore University Library collections

Format of Resources	Total in No.
Books	4,35,000
Periodicals	1,26,000
Archrivals materials	75,000
Thesis and dissertations	4,000
CD-ROMs	250
Microform	255
Microfiche	10
Audio cassettes	26
Video cassettes	250
Total	**6, 40, 800+**

Access to this collection has been provided to patrons of library within campus. The users of library can access to this resources whenever they needed. They can barrow the resources with membership to library or can read within library.

Table 2. Users Category with Numbers

Category of users	Total in No.
Post-graduate students	3,500
Research scholars	350
Teaching staff	150
Non-teaching staff	250
Others (including Visitors)	100
Total	**4,350**

Library with this no of patrons and this huge amount of collections it's difficult easy task to provide access to all users at time. This is about physical collection but Mysore University Library contains a huge amount of E- Resources which include e-journals, databases etc. The following table tries to give a picture of libraries E-collection.

Table 3. E-resources Collection of Mysore University Library

Format of E-Resources	Total in No.
Access to full text journals	7064+
Bibliographic databases	12+
Search engines	4+
Open access journal Directories	4+
Open access E-books sites	11+
Thesis and dissertation directories	6+
Open access data sites	20+
Blogs with special scientific information	20+
Institutional Repositories (Indian)	27+
Institutional repositories(other countries)	5+
Open access Institutional Repositories	2 +
Total	**7195+**

In table there plus sign for every column because each

database, directories contains n number of journals and n number of articles. Thus it becomes an essential step to develop portal through which data, information and Knowledge can be shared.

In the year 2008 UGC sanctioned 100 crores of Money to University of Mysore to enhance infrastructure facilities for students. Mysore University Library started a new Project to upgrade the services of Library. The library is automation Project is on going with Koha software. Mean while a temporary portal as been created for access of E-resources. A portal is not complete yet but we can't make users wait until the portal with all features developed, so a temporary portal with some basic features has been in use at present. Following are the objectives and plan for developing portal of Mysore University Library.

- A configurable and integrated interface to multiple resources
- A unify searching across different metadata schemes like MARC, Dublin core etc.
- Unify searching across multiple systems , including multiple sources of library systems.
- To provide full and integrated management information and usage statistics
- To provide dynamic reference and citation linking.

Along with these objectives the portal is going to contain all the web 2.0 applications and features like weather update, academic calendar , online document delivery services , and web profile server, My search, RSS feeds, TOC alerts, My interest, ask my librarian, profile customization, personalization, virtual tour of library floor plan, SDI, virtual reference services etc.

At present the portal is performing basic function like providing access to all the E- Resources, within library and within campus services. In May 17 , 2010 a completely upgrade centre of information with more than 300 computers providing access to E- Resources of Library within library and campus Wi-Fi. The user is given a unique user id and password so he can access through online from home also. A screen shot of Mysore University Library shows the features provided by library to access the available E-resources.

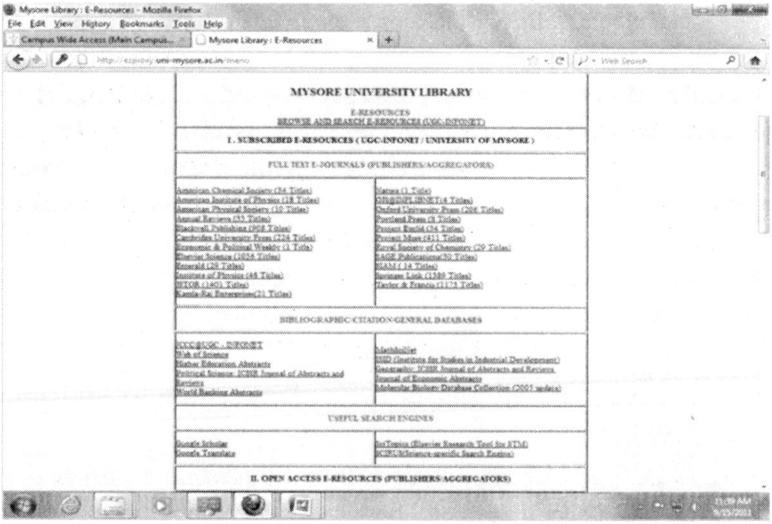

Fig. 1. Shows the list of E-resources of Mysore University library.

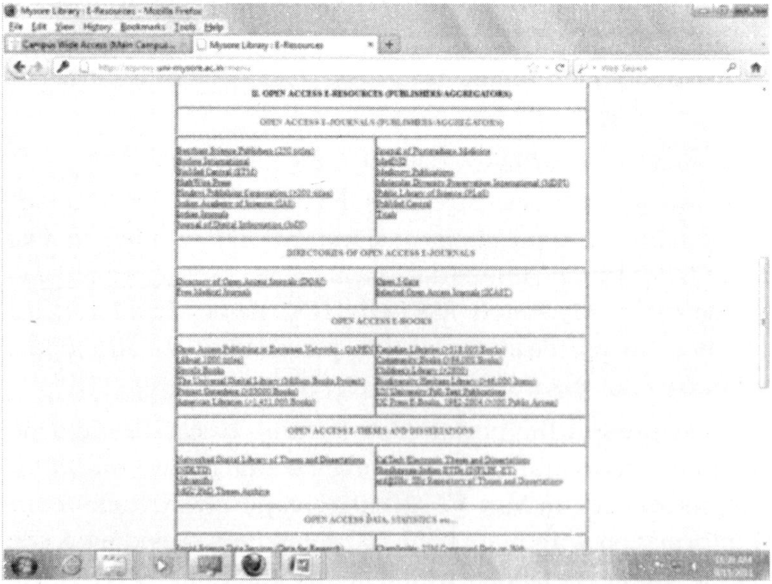

Fig. 2. Shows the continued list of E-resources of Mysore University Library.

Because the portal is a growing collection of knowledge and experience, ongoing development continues through periodic reviews and additions to the Website.

It's important to note that although the project timeline was sectioned into four distinct phases, new content and iterations of the site's design were migrated weekly. At present the with the library and Information centre (computer room/DIRC) statistics of users visit to library we can proudly say that this has brought a positive change and drastic increase of users to library from day to day.

CONCLUSION

The amount of increase in library user's visit to library shows that portal of library is playing a key role in dissemination of information and sharing of knowledge among University of Mysore library patrons. Once the automation project gets completed we are expecting more no of library users to library and a maximum utilization of available resources in library. The knowledge management and sharing of resources is done effective through this portal. In the Knowledge Management (KM) arena, portal systems are assuming a more prominent role for organizations to collect, manage and disseminate resources in an automated, specific and relevant way. Universities use portal to provide a uniformed user interface and to integrate disparate information systems important to their academic missions and operations. One important sub-system of enterprise portal, the library information portal (LIP), has been playing a key role in bridging information resources, people, and intellectual properties in the knowledge management and sharing environment

REFERENCES

1. Mysore University Library website from: **http://www.uni-mysore.ac.in/university-library/** (accessed on 15/09/2011)
2. Alavi, M. and Leidner, D.E. (2001), "Review: Knowledge management and knowledge management systems: conceptual foundations and research issues", *MIS Quarterly*, 25 (1), 107-32.

3. Argote, L. and Ingram, P. (2000), "Knowledge transfer: a basis for competitive advantage in firms", *Organizational Behavior and Human Decision Processes*, 82 (1), 150-69.

4. Argote, L., Beckman, S.L. and Epple, D. (1990), ' 'the persistence and transfer of learning in industrial settings", *Management Science*, 36(2), 140-54.

5. Baron, R.A. and Markman, G.D. (2000), "Beyond social capital: how social skills can enhanceentrepreneurs", *The Academy of Management Executive*, 14 (1), 44-56.

16
Unique Collections @ Raman Research Institute Library : A Case Study

Vrinda J. Benegal
*Raman Research Institute, C.V. Raman Avenue,
Sadashivanagar, Bangalore -560080*

ABSTRACT

A research library collection is a key asset of the parent institution. Raman Research Institute Library is a Repository of its scholarly Information and strong special collections. Our main criteria being collecting and exposing of any materials in all formats like rare books, archives and manuscripts, audio, and video, and digital, etc. A considerable amount of old and valuable material in these formats faces risks of being permanently lost and hence a beginning is made to identify, collect, preserve and at the same time to expose more of these materials to boost their use in learning and research.

CHANGING SCENARIO OF SCHOLARLY INFORMATION

ARL (Association of Research Libraries), [1] defines "Special Collections" broadly to include distinctive material in all media and attendant library services. The special collection plays a unique role in Transforming Research Libraries.

ABOUT THE INSTITUTE

Sir C.V. Raman is one of the most renowned scientists produced by India. Sir C.V. Raman won the Nobel Prize for Physics in 1930, for his pioneering work on scattering of light.

The Raman Research Institute was founded by Prof. C.V. Raman in the late forties. Since 1948 he was Director of the Raman Research Institute at Bangalore, established and endowed by himself. After his demise in 1970, it was reorganized as a national institute for research, which is an autonomous institute engaged in research in basic sciences. The main fields of research at the Institute are Astronomy & Astrophysics, Light & Matter Physics, Soft Condensed Matter and Theoretical Physics. The research activities include work in Chemistry, Liquid Crystals, Physics in Biology, and Signal Processing, Imaging & Instrumentation. [3]

The Raman Research Institute Library was founded by Sir C V Raman and ever since has served as a constant source of both highly specialized and general knowledge for the institute members. Throughout the years, the library has continuously expanded trying to provide adequate literature for the growing research activities at RRI.

The principal goal of RRI library is to preserve the record of knowledge from the past and present, through its large collection and to carry out this responsibility into posterity.

Special collections of RRI library is holdings of all kind of **materials** made accessible to the Research scholars and its scientific community, while to collect and keep the items and information for its maximum use.

RRI Library has the most notable collections of these materials:

- Charts and Atlases, Sky Survey Maps
- Slides of famous Astronomers and physicists, Observatories, and about Astronomy.

Astronomers of the past. (A set of 50 slides), Other slides like Neptune Kit (A set of 12 slides), The radio Universe. (A set of 40 slides), Telescopes of the world. (A set of 50 slides), The Hubble space telescope. (A set of 25 slides) etc.,

- Collection of photographs of famous Scientists
- Newspaper Clippings both in print and digital forms
- Library has housed several CD's, Video Cassettes & DVD's

Book Collections

- **Scientific Biographies** : are a collection of Biography of renowned scientists
- Selected **Popular Science** book collection is popular among general readers
- RRI Theses
- Project work of visiting students
- Hindi books
- **Collected Papers & Historic Works** :
- The collected papers of Albert Einstein, Selected papers of S. Chandrasekhar, and Mathematical Papers of Isaac Newton and others
- Collected works of Mohandas Karamchand Gandhi (70 Volumes)

3. C.V. Raman – A Pictorial Biography

This is a pictorial biography of the Nobel Laureate Sir C.V. Raman. Here the author has nicely depicted Raman's early life and his work , has illustrated it with rare photographs and letters which is narrative and readable . This biography is one of a special publications of its kind and is a brief biography of C.V. Raman which unfolds his life and work through the medium of photographs.

C.V. RAMAN A PICTORIAL BIOGRAPHY, NOBEL SCIENTIST

You have reached your maximum guest watch list limit of 10 items.

Please remove some items from your watch list in xMy eBay if you want to add more.

This item has been added to your guest watch list in My eBay.

Raman's Collection of Books

The present library has been developed around the library started by Prof. C.V. Raman with his personal collection of about 3000 books. Among these, there are few old and classic books in which Raman's signature can be found. These books are kept separately and it is named as " Raman's collection" .

Memoirs of RRI

The Golden Jubilee of the Raman Research Institute was celebrated in the year 1998. As a part of this library was asked to compile all the publications of RRI of the past 50 years dating from 1949-1998. As a result of this the library brought out collection of publication namely the Memoirs of RRI in 50 volumes. The compilation of these volumes was done using DBase and its now being updated regularly. It is now a part of our special collections which is made available both in print and digital form.

Miscellaneous Collections

These are collection of books, papers, etc., of eminent persons deceased and received as gifts and have been taken into library collection for the use of students and faculty.

We have a good number of books of the following scientists:

1. Prof. Ramaseshan's Collection
2. Prof. Satish Dhawan's Collection
3. Prof. V. Radhakrishnan's Collection

Indian Academy of Science

The Academy was founded in 1934 by Professor C. V. Raman (Nobel Laureate) and was registered as a Society under the Societies Registration Act, on 24 April 1934 Prof. C.V. Raman was its President from 1934-1970. Current Science, founded in 1932 is published by the Current Science Association in collaboration with the Indian Academy of Science. Raman was responsible for scientific publishing in India and it was under his direction Current science journal become most popular. We have good collection of both publications and special issues of these in the library.

The publications activity of the Academy in recent times has grown up tremendously and the number of Periodicals published now is eleven. It covers all major disciplines in science and technology. Now the Indian Academy Of Science is considered as one of the single largest scientific publishers in the country and its scientific journals has occupied a most important place in India.

The most important publication being

- RAMAN(C V) / Scientific papers of C.V. Raman. Vol.1:

Scattering of light

- RAMAN(C V) / Scientific papers of C V Raman Vol.2: Acoustics
- RAMAN (C V) Scientific papers of C V Raman. Vol.3: Optics
- RAMAN(C V) / Scientific papers of C V Raman Vol.4: Optics of minerals and diamond
- RAMAN(C V) / Scientific papers of C V Raman. Vol.5: Physics of crystals

- RAMAN(C V) / Scientific papers of C V Raman Vol.6: Floral colours and visual per caption

Special Publications of Academy

Indian Academy of Science brings out some titles, including conference proceedings Published as special issues of journals and made available separately. A public lecture of Indian Academy of Sciences, held at the Raman Research Institute, December 18th, 1989, Bangalore.

DIGITAL COLLECTIONS: THE RRI DIGITAL REPOSITORY

The RRI Institutional library is a storehouse of digitized information of documents of its scientific community. The emphasis given is more largely on the collection of its founder Sir C.V.Raman, which has a large collection of newspaper clippings about Raman dating back to the 1930s.

Unique Feature [2] of our repository are:

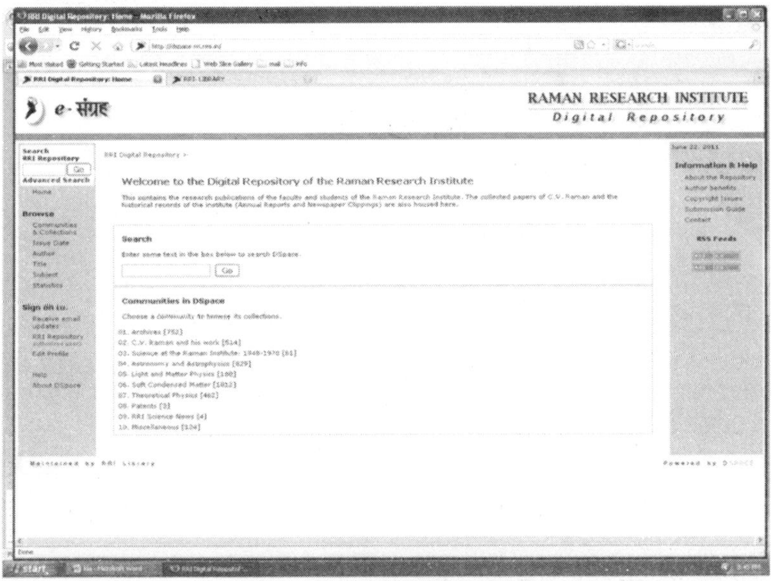

Fig. 1. RRI Digital Repository

- Newspaper Clippings from Raman Archives.
- Lectures and miscellaneous writings of Raman
- Collected papers of C.V.Raman
- Articles and biographical materials on Raman
- Huge source of information on C.V.Raman and his work

IMPRINT COLLECTIONS

This is a festschrift and a volume of learned article collection of an individual presented as a token of appreciation to the scholar at the time of his/her retirement. The research papers of all the scientists are put together in the form collected works. This collection of all scholarly papers is made available on a single Platform which we call it as "Imprints Collection". It gives more information about the authors. This in itself is a significant Special collection of the library which denotes their contribution to scientific literature in particular and to its scholarly community in general.

Fig. 2. RRI Imprints Collections

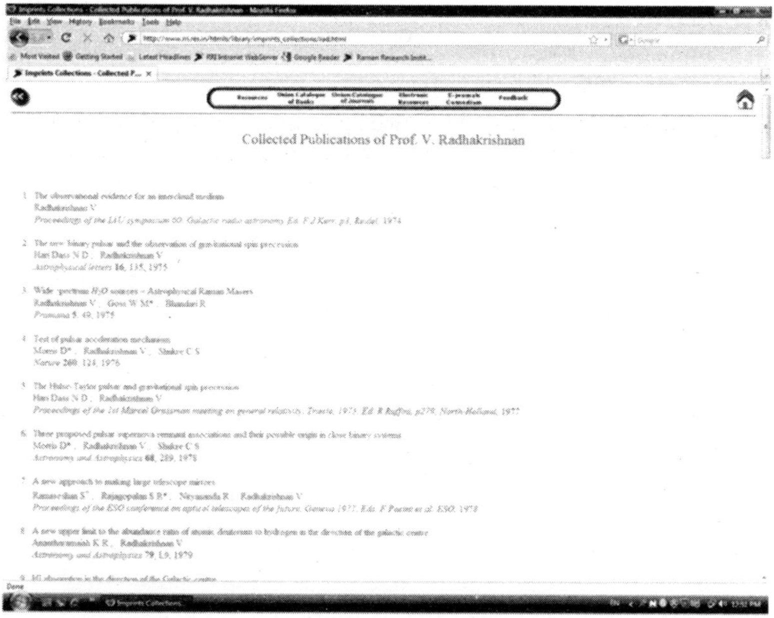

Fig. 2. Raman Research Institute Imprints collections – Screen Shot

CONCLUSION

The Digital Repository of the Raman Research Institute is rich in its collection of information on C.V. Raman and his work. It serves as a Resource sharing tool simply because many of Raman's papers are on open access. Thus our library acts as an incredible historical source of information. Be it a transformation from traditional library to digital library or name it as a facilitator of information, the library will ever remains as a valuable repository of its institution and always remain as the custodian of the collections in both its paper/print and digital formats, there after catering the knowledge to its scientific community. Finally, it is kind of a mission of connecting to scientific fraternity of the world through our special collections by means of digital repository.

REFERENCES

1. http://www.arl.org/rtl/speccoll/transforming research libraries> the Unique Role of Special collections.
2. Isaksson (E) et al. Eds: Library and Information services in astronomy VI: 21st Century Astronomy Librarianship, From New Ideas to Action. (ASP Conference Series, 2010, Vol.433, p215)
3. Annual Reports of RRI

17

Standardization of Activities and Services in MS Ramaiah Institute of Technology (Autonomous) Library in the ICT Era

SF Kattimani
Dy. Librarian, MS Ramaiah Institute of Technology, MSR Nagar, MSRIT Post, Bangalore - 560054

M Manogar
Librarian & Head, MS Ramaiah Institute of Technology, MSR Nagar, MSRIT Post, Bangalore - 560054

Ramesh R Naik
Associate Professor, Dept. of Studies of Library & Information Science, Karnatak University, Pavate Nagar, Dharwad

Shankar Nadoor
Asst. Librarian, MS Ramaiah Institute of Technology, MSR Nagar, MSRIT Post, Bangalore - 560054

ABSTRACT

The present era is popularly known as 'information era', where there is prominence and importance for information. The new technological applications especially Information and Communication (ICT) have accelerated the Research and Development and led information explosion. The combinations of different technological disciplines such as Computer Technology, Information Technology, Telecommunication Technology, Satellite Technology, Digital Technology and Electronics have contributed to the emergence of Information and Communication Technology. The Information and Communication Technology applications transformed the libraries into Electronic libraries, Digital libraries, Learning Resourcc Centres, Virtual Learning Resource Centres and Virtual libraries. In the changing scenario of information environment the professionals have to be more interactive, collaborative and dynamic so that information can be made available to all those who seek it regardless of physical boundaries, formats and time constraints. The emerging trends in digital technologies and their applicability to information handling activities added new challenges to library professionals. The paper presents the standardization of activities at MSRIT library services such as Resources development, reference/referral services; ICT enables service, user education, E-learning services, skills, and automated services to the user community.

Keywords. ICT, standardization, MSRIT, library services, user education, skills, e-learning, automated library services. NPTEL, E-Vidya.

INTRODUCTION

The library plays in important role in an educational institution, by providing necessary reading materials and information for higher education and research. A college library occupies a premier position by providing ample scope and encouragement so that individual's needs and requirements are fulfilled. The process of learning, which takes place within the four walls of a classroom or laboratory, should be augmented by a variety of resources in the library. One of the key qualities of an ideal college library lies in its capacity to enable the students to use their leisure time with meaning and purpose. This should enhance the chance of spotting the inherent talents in them and to launch into instructive and absorbing hobbies thereby laying a strong foundation for a good, responsive and responsible life. Furthermore, the library by virtue of its position in the hierarchy of higher education takes an individual to the world of recorded ideas and apprises him/her of the lively issues of life and challenges. Standardization of activities and services of the libraries, are the best ways to perform an activity that leads to a superior performance. These pertain to the processes, standardizations, and systems identified in private organizations that perform exceptionally well and are widely recognized as improving organizations performance and efficiency. Successfully identifying and applying best practices can reduce costs and improve quality.

Need for Standardization in Library Activities and Services

As per the Operational Practices of National Board of Accreditation (NBA) for Library, the adequate provision of library resources and information services, appropriate to the academic level and scope of an institution's programs, is essential to teaching and learning. The level of library resources needed in relation to their programs and to provide a range of support to meet these needs. The size of collections and the budget allowed for library resources and services do not ensure adequacy. The quality, relevance, accessibility, availability, and provision of support services ultimately will determine the adequacy of an institution's efforts. In assessing library resources and services, **Accrediting Council for Independent Colleges and Schools (ACICS)** requires that an institution, at a minimum, shall:

- Develop an adequate base of library resources
- Ensure means to access these resources
- Develop a continuous assessment strategy for library resources & information services
- Provide adequate staff to support library development, collection organization and accessibility

- Ensure that library services are provided to all learners, including those at non main campuses and
- Provide training and encouragement for students and faculty to utilize library resources as an integral part of the learning process. [1]

STANDARDIZATION IN MSRIT LIBRARY

Standardization of library activities and services helps to function the library effectively and efficiently. Standardization of library activities and services are already propounded by Dr. S.R. Ranaganath, but this standardization is limited to print collection only. Due to the invention of ICT and its applications to the libraries, the function and services of the libraries are also transformed. As such the present study is an attempt to reveal the standardized activities and services of the MSRIT Library. It covered both print and non-print materials, especially ICT based learning resources.

About MSRIT

Industrious and enterprising, an Engineering Contractor of all India repute, a person with a lavish common sense, Dr.M.S.Ramaiah, an illustrious son of Karnataka founded "Gokula Education Foudation" in the year 1962 as one of his bold ventures to perform service to society through a private educational system, without looking for any form of assistance from other agencies. Under the aegis of this foundation was born "M.S.Ramaiah Institute of Technology" in the same year. Another landmark was thus created in the history of technical education of India to impact much needed engineering education and an access was provided to all those who had been denied such an opportunity till then, in all parts of country and outside.

The M.S.Ramaiah Institute of Technology now boasts of offering Bachelors programmes in disciplines 1)Civil Engineering 2) Mechanical Engineering 3) Electrical and Electronics Engineering 4) Electronics and Communication Engineering 5)

Chemical Engineering 6) Computer science & Engineering 7) Industrial engineering and Management 8) Instrumentation technology 9) Information sc and engineering 10) Telecommunication engineering 11) Medical Electronics 12) Biotechnology and 13) Five year Bachelor of Architecture. And Masters programmes (M.Tech) in 1) Structural Engineering 2) Manufacturing Science & Engineering 3) Computer science & engineering 4) Digital Electronics & Communication 5) Software Engineering 6) computer Application in Industrial Drives 7) Digital Communication 8) Computer Integrated Manufacturing. 9) Master Business Administration (MBA) 10) Master of Computer Application (MCA).

MSRIT Library

The Library began its existence in 1962. With its modern collection, knowledge resources and innovative information services fills an essential role for Students, faculty and the surrounding community in their intellectual pursuits. It is Centralized Air Conditioned hybrid library with the state of the art technological applications with a carpet area of 3748 sq. mtrs. It holds knowledge resources predominantly related to Engineering, Technology, Management and allied subjects.

MSRIT Libraries

As per Fourth Law of Library Science "SAVE THE TIME OF READER" on this base MSRIT libraries are divided into Six libraries apart from the Departmental libraries and all the libraries are controlled & maintained by the Main Library (Library and Information Centre-1).

Note: 1st Year Library is exclusively for 1st year students of all branches (Except MCA, MBA) can avail the books and journals. All the libraries are looking after all the Library professionals except the Departmental libraries maintained (except procurement of library resources) by their dept faculty members.

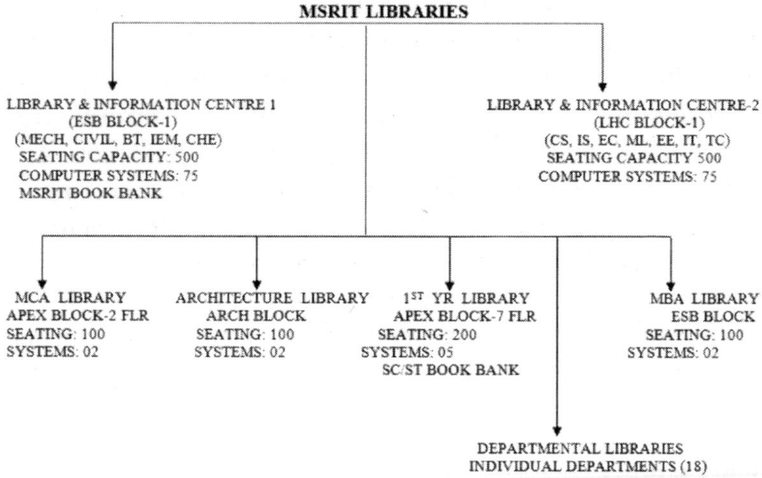

Fig. 1. Libraries

Library Mission:

"THE LIBRARY'S MISSION IS TO PROVIDE COMPREHENSIVE RESOURCES AND SERVICES IN SUPPORT OF THE RESEARCH, TEACHING NEEDS OF THE COLLEGE COMMUNITY"

Objectives of Library

- Understand the research, teaching and learning needs of its users
- Build collections and create tools to support research, teaching, and learning.
- Provide access to and promote the discovery and use of local and external information resources
- Ensure the preservation a long-lasting availability of library collections and resources.

ACTIVITIES AND SERVICES

The Library process is an extremely important primary support service provided by MSRIT. The library and the associated library facilities are indispensable services in support of imparting and acquiring competent and up-to-date professional knowledge. These necessities helped to develop a well equipped modern library to provide up to date library services by using modern technological applications.

Resource Development

The library resources development is major task of the library and the these resources to make availability to the user community

- Print Materials (Books)
- Print Materials (Hard copy Journals)
- Bound Volumes
- Code Books
- Standards
- Non Print Materials (offline databases)
- e-resources accessible through web

As on 1st September 2011 the library resources collection are as under:

Table 1. Library Resources

Sl.No	Name of the Resources	As On 1st Sep 2011
1	BOOKS	73790
2	JOURNALS (National & International)	284
3	MAGAZINES (General & Technical)	42
3	JOURNALS BOUND VOLUMES	4500
4	CODE BOOKS	1195
5	STANDARDS & SPECIFICATIONS	1421
6	PROJECT REPORTS	4000
7	MSRIT BOOK BANK SCHEME	4300
8	SC/ST BOOK BANK SCHEME	2970

Book/Periodical Selection

The Heads of departments take stock of the available books, analyze the requirements for new books and other materials based on the curriculum, changing technologies and request from staff and students and accordingly prepare lists of the required books etc in prescribed indent form which is available (**http://www.msrit.edu/system/files/indent.pdf**) and they send such lists to the Principal for further processing. The library also organizes the books exhibition every year to facilitate the faculty, students to browse, select, and buy books for their personal use or to recommend to the library. The principal, after perusal and consultations with the library committee and the Heads if required, approves the lists with any modifications if deemed necessary and then forwards these lists to the Librarian for further processing. When an Indent is received, Acquisition Section assigns it a unique indent registration number and then sends an acknowledgement within three working days to the indenting department quoting the indent registration number. This will enable the indenting department to follow up its indent when required. MSRIT BOOK BANK SCHEME In this scheme students will give their required books in the beginning of the every semester (individual can give 2 books requirements), such list of books consolidated and finalized and it will be sent to the principal approval, once get approved from principal the process will start. SC/ST BOOK BANK all faculty, students and library staff will select the books and directly sent to the government approved vendors.

Procurement of Books /Periodicals

Librarian will send these indents to three Approved vendors to get quotation, once get sealed quotations the quotations will open in the library committee meeting will make comparative statement and finally the librarian obtains a budgetary estimate for all the materials requested and submits the same to the Principal after review by the Library Committee. Based on these estimates, the Principal consultation with the Library Committee and Heads of departments and the Librarian may revise the indent lists. Librarian sends this final list for approved by the Principal to the Purchase department for further processing. In accordance with the purchase process, purchase order is placed for the required books and the other library items. The librarian follows up the purchases with the vendors. On receipt of the library items indented for, Acquisition department has them inspected, verified and validated to ensure that they meet the purchase order requirements, are free from any kind of damages either in content matter or material conditions. Deviations if any are notified the Purchase department for further action.

Storage, Handling, Preservation & Presentation

Books/Journals indented for lending, reading and reference are openly stored for easy identification and easy retrieval and are free from physical handling issues. Books are arranged in APUPA patterns, using Dewey Decimal Classification (DDC 22[md] Ed). The books are arranged Department-wise in a helpful sequence. Regular inspections are made to check the books for damages either by users or environmental factors (water, moisture, dust and pests). In case of damages, remedial measures like rebinding will be taken up. As a preventive measure against damages by environmental factors, termite treatment is done periodically as appropriate. As a value added practice, information regarding new arrivals is made available to all regularly through notices.

Budget

The library budget will allocated by the management every financial years to purchase the books, journals, periodicals, computer peripherals, magazines etc., every year budget will increase 15 % to 20 % . (During the financial year 2011-2012 the budget was Rs. 1, 10, 00000.00) is allotted.

Upkeep and Stock Verification

Books and other library items are stored and displayed neatly, cleanly and in order, Stock Verification of the books etc. is done once a year on a test checking basis and once in three years comprehensively by using Bar code scanner. During this exercise, all the departments are involved. In this process, books and other items are checked for damages, mutilations and relevance also and accordingly librarian, under the guidance of the library committee and under the approval of the Principal initiates repair, replacement, and discarding actions.

Surveillance System

In the Academic Libraries, Security of the Library materials is a challenging Job. For this purpose, the library has installed 20 CCTV Cameras at every corner of the library along with the four security persons. The library has planned to install RFID Technology in future.

Library Committee

Principal constitutes a Library Committee of 11 people, consisting of the Librarian, 7 Staff members and 3 Students members. One of the staff members is designated as the Chairman of the committee and the Librarian acts as the convener. This committee normally meets once in a month. However, the Chairman, with the permission of the principal, may convene a meeting on any day with prior notice to the members. The chairman, with approval of the Principal, will take decisions regarding all operational aspects of the committee. Proceedings are being circulated to the Principal, and all Departments Heads.

LIBRARY SERVICES

Reference Services

Bonafide student and staff members are allowed to use the library for reference; Students deposit their Identity cards with a Library official before drawing the books for reference. Such cards will be returned after the reference books are returned. Staff members affix their signature in a register meant for the purpose to use the reference materials. Reference books are not allowed to use outside the reference section and cannot be issued. In case of request for one hour will be allowed on genuine cases only.

MSRIT Book Bank Scheme

Students can recommend two books of their choice in the beginning of the every semester for procurement. Such books borrowed can be retained for a semester. While returning they have to pay 20 % of the cost of the books after discount.

For e.g.: If Books cost Rs. 100. After 25% of vendor discount cost became Rs. 75

The library will collect 20% of the Rs. 75 it means Rs. 15. The main motto of this scheme is to increase the reading habits of student's, non commercial scheme.

SC/ST Book Bank Scheme

Scheduled Tribe and Scheduled Caste students can avail this scheme, in this scheme library will issue two books, issued books can be retain whole semester.

Library Working Hours

The library remains open all working days except government holidays, the working of library is observed as follows:

- 9 AM TO 9 PM –Monday to Friday
- 9 AM TO 4:30 PM – Saturday & Sundays
- 9 AM TO 12 Midnight – During Examination
- 9 AM TO 9 PM- Saturday & Sundays During Examination

Membership

All the students, faculty members, and staff MSRIT and Research scholars of VTU (Visveswaraiah Technological University, Belgaum), who are engaged in Research under the faculty of MSRIT. Constituent colleges of GEF (GOKULA EDUCATION FOUNDATION), a member of MSR Groups are eligible to become members of MSRIT library. The Borrower Cards will be issued as per the following description. Each card can be issued one book only.

Table 2. Membership Descriptions

Sl No	Category	No's of Cards
1	Students (Under Graduate)	02
2	Students (Under Graduate) Book Bank Scheme	02
3	Students (Post Graduate)	04
4	Students (Post Graduate) Book Bank Scheme	02
5	Students (UG & PG) SC/ST Books	02
6	Research Scholars	02
7	Regular Faculty Members (All Departments)	10
8	Probationary Faculty Members (All Departments)	05
9	Visiting Professors	02
10	Emeritus Professors	02
11	GEF (MSR) Group Colleges	10
12	Staff of MSRIT (Non Teaching)	02

Charging and Discharging

The Circulation System of MSRIT Library is one of major tasks of the library professionals. Every day on an average 2000 transaction are carried out. The charging and discharging of Materials are Complete Automated by using Libsys Library Software. All Materials and Borrowers cards are Bar-coded, the entire issue, return and renewal of materials requires 6 Bar-code Scanners. For Scanning it will 4 to 5 seconds for each material. The Circulation of MSRIT Library timing is observed as follows.

9 AM TO 6 PM on all working days.

9 AM TO 4:30 PM on Saturday.

Books will be issued as per Table 3 Durations.

The Books may not be renewed, in case of any reservation for students. MSRIT BOOK BANK SCHEME Books once issued cannot be renewed. Faculty and Staff of MSRIT can return, get issued and get renewal of books at any time. SC/ST Books can be return, issue and renew any time during the circulation hours. Librarian may recall any book from any member at any time. A fine of 50 Ps per day for 10 days and Rs. 1 per day for subsequent days will be levied as optional for Students. Book Bank Scheme books and SC/ST Books there is no any fine will be levied. In case of any books lost, damaged, defaced borrower has to replace new copy with latest edition or has to pay triple of the present book cost. CD/DVD's and Periodicals will be issued for overnight on demand.

Table 3: Statistics of Books Circulation

SL. No	Members	Description	Duration of loan of Books
1	Students (UG&PG) All Semester	2 Books	15 days' with 2 Renewals
2	Students (UG&PG) All semester	MSRIT Book Bank Scheme	During the Beginning of the Semester for One semester
3	Students (UG&PG) All semester	SC/ST Books	6 Months
4	Research Scholars	2 Books	One month with 2 Renewals
5	All Faculty and Staff of MSRIT		One Semester
6	GEF (MSR)	10 Books	One year (every year membership can be renewed)

Institutional Membership

The Library has subscribed to British Council Library, Bangalore (BCLB), Indian Institute of Management, Bangalore (IIMB) , Central Manufacturing Technology Institute, Bangalore (CMTIB), and DELNET , Books can be borrowed and online access to their Communication skills, and e-resources. It is extending the facility of Books etc to our faculty and students.

Competitive Examination Books

Popular series of Aptitude Books, GMAT, GATE, TOEFL, GRE Verbal Communication Books etc have been kept in the library for the benefit of users. On demand these books will be issued for fortnight.

Reprography and Printing Facilities

Library provides photo-copying and printing facilities. Important material from the books drawn for reference can be photo-copies and related references material downloaded from the internet can be printed. The librarian, in consultation with the Principal, prescribes the fee for such services from time to time.

Standards:

The library is having 1421 national/international standards.

- National/International standards are also controlled as in the case of books/journals etc. with respect to procurement and maintenance.
- Librarian obtains information from each teaching department regarding any National/International standards being used in the department and consolidates this information to have a master list of all the required national/ international standards.
- Librarian keeps track of updates of all the relevant standards. This maybe done by registering with the publishers concerned to be on their regular mailing lists, scanning regularly the relevant trade journals and also by soliciting such update information from the departments concerned through specific requests once a semester.
- Upon the receipt of information about update of any national/international standards, librarian communicates the same to the Heads of the departments concerned and also to the Principal. The Heads in turn assess their requirements and indent for the updates if required. Principal also may instruct the librarian to procure the updates in the general interest of the institute. The process of procurement, maintenance etc is similar to that of books.
- Updating the national/international standards available in the library is never done automatically by the librarian as

it any interfere adversely with the planned implementation of the teaching process. It is always based on specific indents from the Heads or Principal.

Examination Code Books

Library is having Design Data Books, Code books, which are required for Examination are added and updated according to student strength and requirement. These books will be supplied to the examination room on examination dates, room invigilators are the accountability of these books after the examination over on the day, and they have to submit to the library immediately.

ICT ENABLED LIBRARY SERVICES

Library Automation

Library Automation process started in the year 2001-02 with the installation of the Library Management Software **"Libsuite"**. It was fox pro based multi user software. The data entry of all the resources was done and put to use for some years till we switched on to more advanced LMS package **Libsys**. Libsys 7 cloud computing based modular integrated ,full pledged client based Management system software the java based user friendly online catalogue called Libsys Web-Opac, was purchased, and all the data is converted in to the new database. This enables us to handle complex operations like Circulation, Serial Control, Acquisition, Web OPAC etc using multiple features. A dedicated server has been kept for this purpose. All the Library materials are bar-coded and issued by using bar code scanners.

Digital Library

Digital Libraries that are setup in both Library and Information Centre-1 (ESB BLOCK-1) and Library Information Centre-2 (LHC BLOCK-1) Libraries are well facilitated with 150 High-end configured TFT Monitor Computer Systems are connected 20 mbps leased line of karturi broadband systems. It is connected to the backbone through one of the routing switches.

The library has 3 high end configured servers. 8 Systems for OPAC, and remaining are to access online journals, e-resources, e-books, and other databases. The complete LHC block is WI-Fi enabled.

Library Website: http://www.msrit.edu/node/36

The Library website is a mirror of MSRIT Library, what are the resources available and services provided in the library are provided, Portal is comprises of profile of the library and details of services, resources available in the library.

Fig. 1. Library Website

Books and Journals

The library web site revealed the books and journal collection department-wise, added to the library from time to time.

Web OPAC

The Bibliographic databases can be accessed with printed indexes. The system includes a word based search using Boolean operators that can narrow down a search to meet very specific needs. Further, features of these systems are periodic list of recent additions to the library. The members can find the materials checked out to them and reserve materials. The various searching options under LSWIN OPAC are

- SEACH (Simple, Additional, Advanced)
- BROWSE
- NEW ARRIVALS
- JOURNALS
- PATRONS

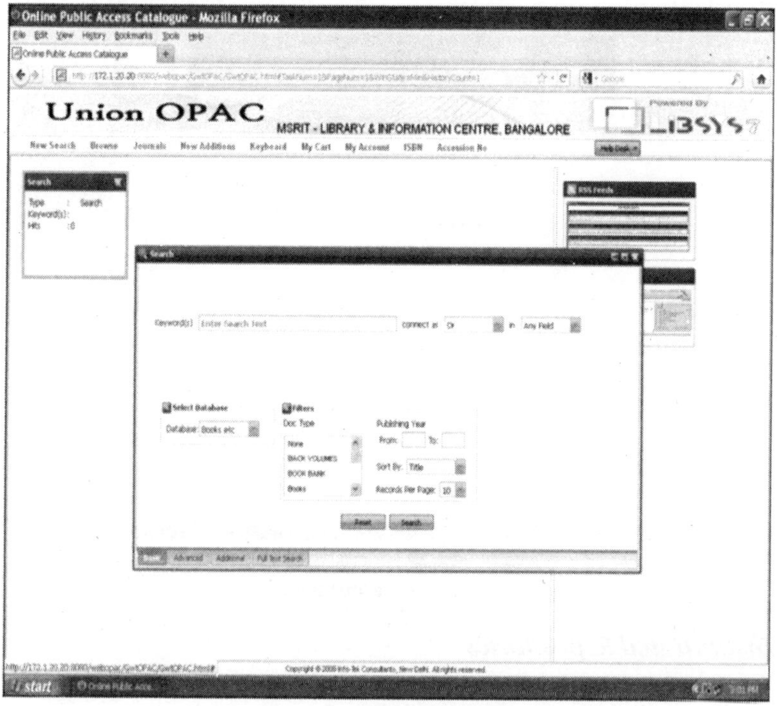

Fig. 2. Lirary Web OPAC

E-Resources

This link will indicate the complete web address and links of the online journals which are subscribing the library. Library has been subscribing nearly 991 major full text national and international e-resources in the field of Engineering and management through INDEST-AICTE Consortium, New Delhi and others, such as " IEL ONLINE, ACM Digital Library,ASCE and ASME Digital library, MathSciNet, Springer Link, Canadian Journal of Chemical Engineering, N-Digital Online E-resources can be accessed. Users are given full support in accessing the e-journals or searching the articles. On request the articles will be downloaded and forwarded to their e-mails.

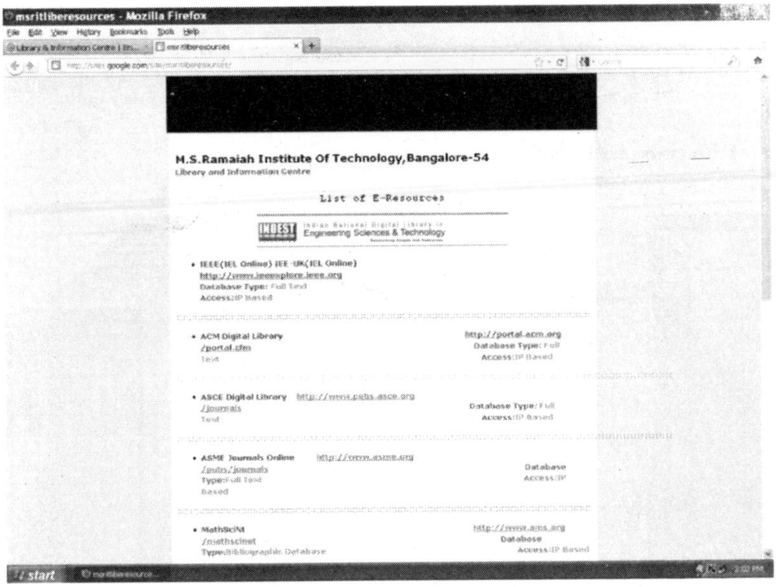

Fig. 3. E-resources

Institutional Repositories

Institutional Repository is an organized collection of e-resources or publications of Faculty and Students of MSRIT and MSRIT related news and activities. The faculty publications, Project reports, Question papers, Seminar papers, and Theses are being uploaded on to the Digital Library Server using DSPACE and are accessible with the Campus. And outside the campus for members only by using their personal user name and password. Digitization process using HP 7800 Scanner is being carried out.

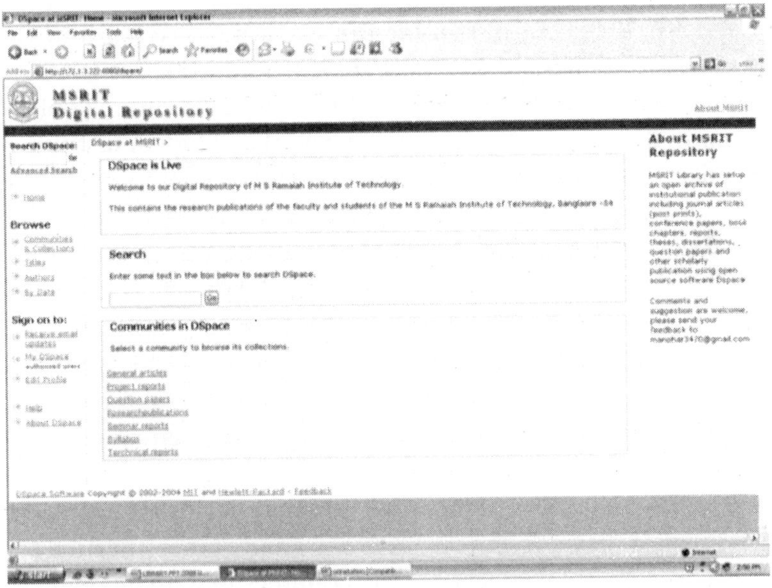

Fig. 4. Old Version of Dspace

Fig. 5. New Version of Dspace

E-Vidya & NPTEL

NPTEL is an acronym for National Programme on Technology Enhanced Learning which is an initiative by seven Indian Institutes of Technology (IIT Bombay, Delhi, Gawhati, Kanpur, Kharagpur, Madras and Roorkee) and Indian Institute of Science (IISc) for creating course contents in engineering and science.NPTEL as a project originated from many deliberations between IITs, Indian Institutes of Management (IIMs) and Carnegie Mellon University (CMU) during the years 1999-2003. A proposal was jointly put forward by five IITs (Bombay, Delhi, Kanpur, Kharagpur and Madras) and IISc for creating contents for 100 courses as web based supplements and 100 complete video courses, for forty hours of duration per course. Web supplements were expected to cover materials that could be delivered in approximately forty hours. Five engineering branches (Civil, Computer Science, Electrical, Electronics and Communication and Mechanical) and core science programmes that all engineering students are required to take in their undergraduate engineering programme in India were chosen initially. Contents for the above courses were based on the model curriculum suggested by All India Council for Technical Education (AICTE) and the syllabi of major affiliating Universities in India.[2]

The e-learning package provided by VTU (Visvesvaraya Technological University) is extensively explored over the last several months various options for deploying NPTEL. VTU and other contents at VTU affiliated college campuses. Terra Incognitus Systems Research Alliance (TISRA) of Bangalore in association with VTU e-Learning Centre with hardware platform support from Sun Microsystems, have evolved an advanced E-learning deployment solution called E-Vidya. E-Vidya is a custom designed using proved open source technologies to support the following:

- NPTEL media content (129 courses)
- VTU media content (50 courses)
- Advanced Web 2.0 content management and community management

- Moodles –LMS
- Education content in Java Solaris, etc of Sun Micro System[3]

NPTEL, e-vidya Video streaming facility has been launched at MSRIT Library since December 2009; it is a facility for e-learning through Campus Network. Faculty and students can access the Video of their choice any time in the Digital library or across the Campus. By using common username and password. E-Vidya Server has been installed at the Digital Library of Main Library; the facility is a value addition to our Library service.

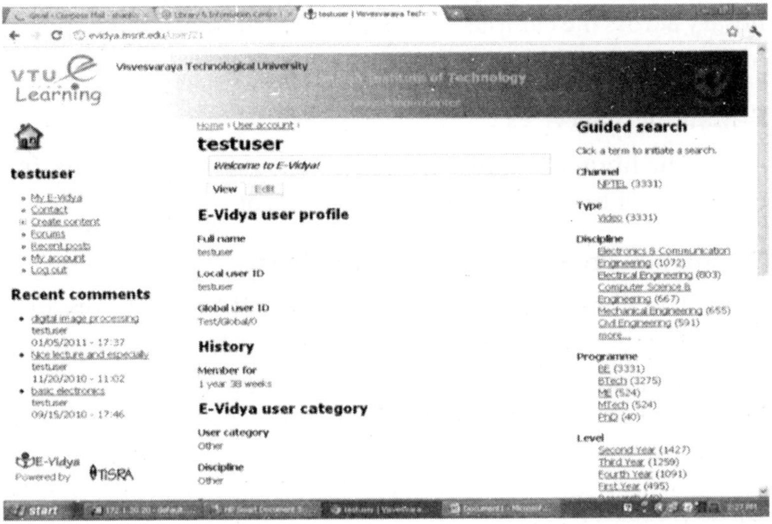

Fig. 6. VTU E-vidya E-learning

INFORMATION LITERACY PROGRAMMES

User Orientation Programme

The library will conduct user orientation every year for New Comers (First Year Admitted Students) on the day of first year inauguration ceremony. Further, at the beginning of every semester the library will conduct two week orientation programme to students and faculty members of different departments, to inform about the resources available in the library, various services provided by the library and how to access e-resources, digital library facilities etc.

Library Visit

All the Heads of various departments will bring the first year students and their parents to visit the library and the library personnel explain the services and facilities available in the library in brief.

Library Bulletin Boards

The library displayed various functions and activities of the library across the campus, which discloses the day today activities of the library including latest news, new arrivals list, etc.

E-Mail Alert Services

The library will provide e-mail alerts of new arrivals, free e-books, e-journals, and current contents of journals etc.

Orientation Programmes From Publishers

The library co-operate and helps publishers to organize presentations about their new products, new technology, etc and the leading publishers include Springer link, Cambridge press, Elsevier, Taylor and Francis, IEEE explore tips for effective searching programmes.

Library Brochure

The library distributes brochures to visitors, new students, faculty members and all the departments with updated information about the library regularly.

OTHER INITIATIONS

Internship Training Programme

The library provide one month Internship Training programme for final year M.L.I.Sc, students from various universities of Karnataka state. On completion of internship training the successful students will be given Certificates.

Conferences, Seminars and Workshops for Library Professionals

The Library organizes regularly workshops and conference to the library professionals to enhance new technologies in the library field and to interact with the experts in the concerned field.

Workshop

The library had organized "THREE DAYS NATIONAL LEVEL WORKSHOP ON DEVELOPING DIGITAL LIBRARY USING DSPACE" from 27th to 29 August 2008 for the benefit of professionals, About 60 participants from all over the country had participated.

Conference

The Library has organized "ONE DAY NATIONAL LEVEL CONFERENCE ON OPEN CONTENT MANAGEMENT AND ORGANISATION FOR TECHNICAL INFORMATION SERVICES" on 4th February 2011, Nearly 300 participants were attended all over India.

Forthcoming Activities

On the occasion of "GOLDEN JUBILEE CELEBRATION" 2011-2012, the library planned to organize Three days National Level Seminar in the Month of March 2012 and One Week Technical Books Exhibition in the Month of January 2012.

Student Satisfaction Survey

The library will conduct every year satisfaction survey of the selected students from various departments of all Semesters.

Suggestions and Complaints

A suggestion box is provided in the all libraries at a prominent place and a communication is displayed to all students/ users of the library to drop their suggestions, complaints, grievances, etc. regarding the library services into the suggestion box to facilitate implementation of corrections and corrective actions. The Librarian, in the presence of the library committee or Vice-principal, opens the suggestion box once a month and records the contents. The library committee analyzes such suggestions/complaints and formulates the corrections and corrective plans that are implemented after approval/further modifications by the principal.

LIBRARY HUMAN RESOURCES DEVELOPMENT:

Library Staff Development Programme

All the Library staff members are encourages attending the seminars, workshop and other professional activities to development their personal and professional careers.

Staff Structure

The Library staffs members are divided into two categories i.e., Professionals and Non professionals and all the staffs are assigned individual responsibilities into the six libraries.

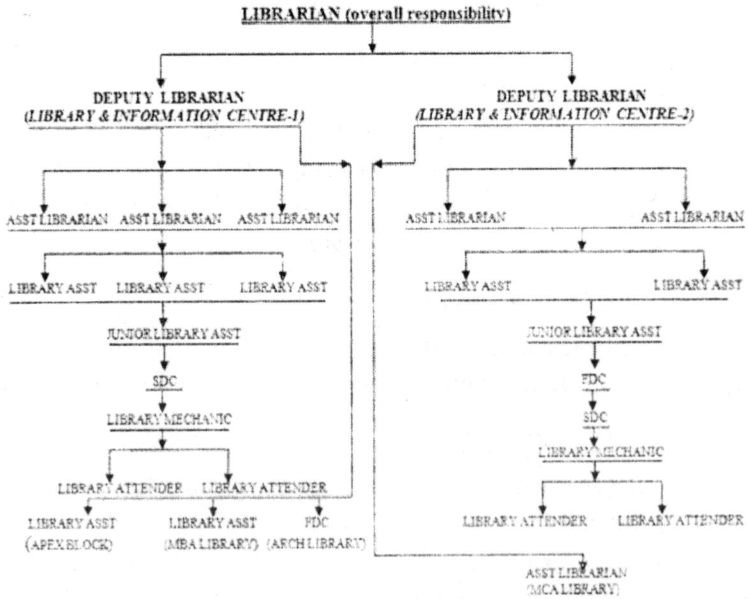

Fig. 2. Staff Structures

All the Asst Librarians and below cadre staff members will be assigned to work in the rotation shift duties.

Shift duties:

9 am to 4:30 pm - general duties

1:30 pm to 9 pm (male staff) &

4:30 pm to 12 midnight (male staff).

LIBRARY LINKAGES TO OTHER PROCESSES:

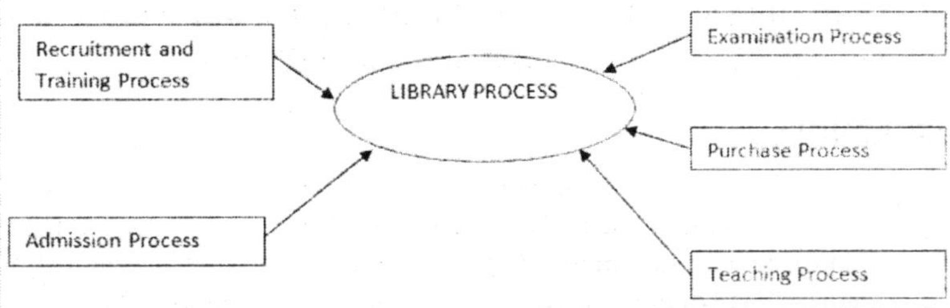

Fig. 3. Library Process

Library Process is the main supportive process for the teaching process and has links to many other processes.

- Purchase of all library resources are carried out in accordance with the purchase process.
- Issue of Borrower cards for students is dependent on Examination process for higher semesters and on Admission process for 1st semester.
- Issue of borrower tickets for staff members is dependent on recruitment process.
- Purchasing of library resources dependent on library requirement, which is in turn dependent on teaching process.

CONCLUDING REMARKS

As discussed above, the library is promoting reading and intellectual activities in the fields of science and technology. Further, it is noted that all the conventional services of the libraries such as circulation services, are already being automated, so as to save the time of the users. The functions and services of the library are interactive, as each of the function and activity of the library is related to another, so as to provide better services. It is emphasized that the orientation programmes organized by the library are have excellent feedback from the students and faculty members. The library is providing remote service facilities for the users located in the campus through Wi-Fi technology. Hence, it can be rightly agreed that both the concepts, that are "Standards of Modern Library (as stated by Dr. S.R.Ranganathan)" and 'library without walls' has been realized in the MSRIT library.

REFERENCES

1. An Informative Handbook of Norms, Standards & Procedure Prescribed by NBA (National Board of Accreditation) & Technical Education Quality Improvement Programme(TEQIP) of Ministry of HRD, Government of India, Chief Editor G.Pathan and Edited by Bhavana Sharma. Vol -1, pp 244-245.
2. Human Resource Development, India, 2010. NPTEL Brochure. A joint initiative of Indian Institutes of Technology and Indian Institute of science. e-Learning. Department of Higher Education, Ministry of HRD. New Delhi.
3. E-Vidya VTU Brochures.Vishswerayya Technological University, Govt of Karnataka, Belgaum.2010.

18

Development Plan of Libraries in Engineering Colleges at Solapur University, Solapur: A Study

Vijayakumar N Mulimani
Librarian, Sangameshwar College,
Saat Rasta, Solapur - 413 001 Maharashtra, India

ABSTRACT

This Paper Belongs to the actual Survey done during the year 2007-2008 and the thesis is submitted to the M.Phil Degree from Annamalai University. The article mainly gives the information of faculty members in Engineering and Technological institutes affiliated to Solapur University, Maharashtra state it highlights the importance of Engineering Library resources especially the reading materials provided by the engineering library and its effective use by the faculty. Library automation system and status of the present and future plan for 20 years. This article gives the future plan of the libraries existing in Solapur City and availability of huge information, resources and services. The digitized access is used by academicians of various faculties of i.e. civil, Mechanical, Electronics, Electrical and other such facilities. To do the positive and optimum utilisations of library digitization and networking is the requirement of time.

Keywords. Faculty members, Engineering, Technology, User survey, library automation and applications of technology.

INTRODUCTION

Library automation systems are designed and crafted computer applications that require considerable programming skills together with an extensive knowledge of the function needs of libraries and the exacting standards that are applied in such systems. Library automation systems are used to create and maintain large bibliographic databases some of the world's largest databases are bibliographic. For instance the world cat database of the online Computer Library center (OCLC) has more than 50 million records. Primarily textual in nature, records can be very large, having many variable length field. Some of which could be repeatable within a logical records. Field within records could be present in some records and not in others the records themselves could vary both in length and format.

Library automation systems provide the support needed to ensure consistency and accuracy in the content of these databases. To achieve this, the automation systems access several as external databases called authority files.

Library automation systems are expected to provide support so as to enable records to satisfy exacting international standards for bibliographic description and data exchange between different databases.

Library automation systems require sophisticated algorithms to index, serial and display information from the database created. Software technologies used in library automation systems include database management systems, client server architectures, search engine technology and software used in web based applications.

OBJECTIVES

The objectives of this research is how the teacher and

students get their information through the Internet researcher.

1) Does the Technical Institute provides update information for student & teachers.
2) To form standard libraries.
3) To provide e resources to maximum users of the library
4) To store update information.
5) To trace out use of e-mail services and search techniques used for information search.
6) To explore quality of the automation and computerization

The Technical Institutes for study are as follows:

1) Walchand Institute of Technology, Solapur
2) Bharat-Ratna Indira Gandhi College of Engineering, Solapur
3) Brahmdeo Mane Institute of technology
4) Vitthal College of Engineering, Pandharpur

METHODS USED FOR DATA GATHERING

The questionnaire as a tool for data gathering is used. In addition to a comprehensive questionnaire there is an observation and interview method to support data is also used.

To reach the perfection in process of data collection I have used a mixed comprehensive questionnaire which has given an opportunity to some open ended questions. The questionnaire consists of close ended questions too and some options are along with multiple choice questions also.

The data collected from the respondents is without prejudice. The collection of data is limited to only four Engineering colleges of Solapur University. They are 1) Walchand Institute of Technology 2) Bharat-Ratna Indira Gandhi College of Engineering 3) Bhramadev Mane Institute of Technology 4) Vitthal College of Engineering, Pandharpur.

Content Analysis of the Present data

The Present study is an effort to exploration the "Digitization

& Networking development plan of Technical Institute affiliated to Solapur University, Solapur.

Analysis and Interpretation

There are 4 Technical Instituted affiliated so Solapur University, Walchand Technical Instituted, Bharat-Ratna Indira Gandhi College of Engg. , Brahmadev Mane Technical Instituted, Vitthal Technical Institute, Pandhapru. This research is limited to these four Technical Colleges.

Table-1. Stream of four Technical Institutions Affiliated to Solapur University.

Sr. No.	Name of the Technical Institution	Streams
I	Walchand College of Institute	1. Computer Science & Engineering. 2. Information Technology 3. Electronics & Telecommunication Engg. 4. Civil Engg. 5. Mechanical Engg.
II	Bharat-Ratna Indira Gandhi College of Engineering	1. Computer Science & Engg. 2. Information Technology 3. Mechanical Engg. 4. Electronics & Tele.Comm. Engg. 5. Civil Engg
III	Brahmdev Mane Institute of Technology.	1. Computer Science & Engg 2. Information Technology 3. Mechanical Engg.4. Electrical.
IV	Pandharpur College of Technical Institute.	1. Computer Science & Engg. 2. Information Technology 3. Mechanical Engg. 4. Electronics & Tele.Comm. Engg. 5. Civil Engineering

There are 5 H.O.Ds. in Walchand Institute, 5 in Bharat-Ratna Indira Gandhi College of Engineering, 4 in Brahmadev Mane Institute, 5 in Pandharpur technical Instituted, Pandharpur. The Universe of study of the present research is expressed in the following table.

It is clear from table – 1 that there are 5 streams named Computer Science & Engineering, Information Technology, Mechanical Engineering, Civil Engineering, Electronics & Telecommunication Engineering in Walchand College, 5 Streams in Bhara-Ratna Indira Gandhi College of Engineering, 4 stream in Brahmdev Mane Institute of Technology and also 5 streams in Padharpur College of Technology.

Table 2. Table showing number of male & female H.O.D. members at various Technical Institutions.

Sr. No.	Name of the Technical Institution	Male H.O.D. Members	Female H.O.D. Members
I	Walchand College of Institute	04	01
II	Bharat-Ratna Indira Gandhi College of Engineering	05	00
III	Brahmdev Mane Institute of Technology.	04	00
IV	Pandharpur College of Technical Institute.	04	01

It is clear from table – 2 that there are total 17 H.O.D. members in the four technical institution where in male H.O.D. strength i.e 89.47% and 2 female H.O.Ds. strength i.e. 10.53%.

Pie Chart showing Percentage of Male and Female H.O.D.

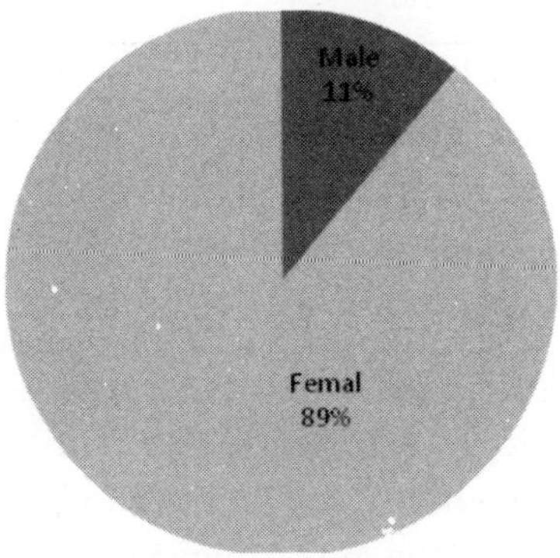

Fig. 1. Number of Male and Female H.O.D. members of various Technical Institute.

It is clear from Pie – Chart that percentage of Male H.O.D. is 89.47 and female teacher's is 10.53.

Table 3. Table showing number of books and Periodicals available at various Technical Institutions.

Sr. No.	Name of the Technical Institution	Total Books	Total Journals
I	Walchand College of Institute	25,275	95
II	Bharat-Ratna Indira Gandhi College of Engineering	11,000	72
III	Bramhadeo Mane Institute of Technology	12,250	65
IV	Pandharpur College of Technical Institute	20,000	85

It is clear from table 3 that there are 25,275 books, 95 Journals available in Walchand College of Technology, 11,000 books, 72 Journals available in Bhara-Ratna Indira Gandhi College of Engineering, 12,250 books, 65 Journals available in Bramhadeo Mane Institute of Technology and also 20,000 books, 85 Journals available in Pandharpur College of Technical Institute.

Table showing how many PC's are in the library and software connected at various technical Institutions.

Table 4. No. of PC's used in the library and software connected at various technical Institutions

Sr. No.	Name of the Technical Institution and software used in the library		No. of Computers
I	Walchand College of Institute	SOUL	06
II	Bharat-Ratna Indira Gandhi College of Engineering	OTHER	04
III	Brahmdev Mane Institute of Technology.	SOUL	04
IV	Pandharpur College of Technical Institute.	DELNET	08

It is clear from table 4 that there are 06 P.Cs.are available in Walchand College of Institute, 04 in Bharat-Ratna Indira Gandhi College of Engineering, 04 in Bramhadeo Mane Institute of Technology, 08 Pandharpur College of Technical Institute

Use of Internet as a Research Tool

All the 19 H.O.D. members have stated that they use internet. All respondents have stated that they use internet as a research tool. There is no negative response. Therefore it is clear that 100% respondent agree that they use internet as a research tool.

Table 5. Frequency distribution of Internet users.

Once in a day	Once in a Week	Once in a fortnight
12	04	03

It is clear from above frequency table that 12 respondents use internet once in a day, 04 respondents use internet once in a week, 03 respondents use internet once in a fort-night.

Search Engine Preference by the Faculty Members

Table 6. Search Engine Preference

Search Engine	No. of Preferences
Google	8
Yahoo	4
Altavista	2
Rediff	5

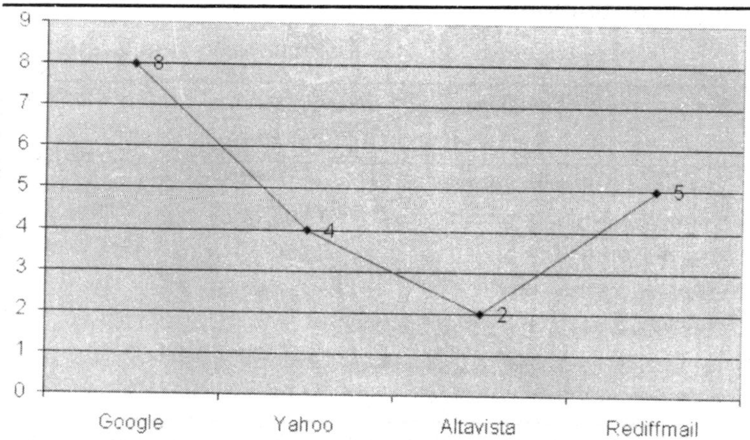

Fig. 2. Line graph showing Preference order of use of search Engine.

It is clear from above line graph that 8 respondents prefer google search engine, 4 respondents prefer yahoo, 02 Prefer AltaVista and 05 respondents Prefer Reddifmail Search engine for information Search on the internet.

Major Purpose of using internet by faculty members

The survey conducted to 20 faculty members:

Table 7. Purpose of using internet

To Search latest relevant Subject material	E-mail	Chatting	Others
11	04	02	03

It is clear from above frequency table that 11 respondents use internet for to search latest relevant subject material for their research purpose, 04 respondents use it for e-mail, 02 respondents use it for chatting and 03 respondents use it for other purpose.

Use of e-Journals

All the respondents have stated that they use e - Journals as a research tool. There is no negative response. Therefore it is clear that 100% respondents agree that they use e – Journals for their research work or as a research tool.

Table showing number of faculty wise e-Journals at Various Technical Institution.

Table 8. faculty wise e-Journals at Various:

Sr. No.	Name of the Technical Institution	Civil Engg.	Mech. Engg.	I.T.	C.S.E.	E.T.C.
I	Walchand College of Institute	12	25	10	15	20
II	Bharat-Ratna Indira Gandhi College of Engineering	-	15	15	18	10
III	Bramhadeo Mane Institute of Technology	-	08	05	10	12
IV	Pandharpur College of Technical Institute	-	40	10	20	20

It is clear from Table – 4 that there are 82 e-Journals

available in Walchand College of Institute, 58 e-Journals available in Bharat-Ratna Indira Gandhi College of Engineering, 35 e-Journals in Bramhadeo Mane Institute of Technology, and there are 10 e-Journals available in Pandharpur College of Technical Institute.

I) Pie-Chart Showing department wise Percentage of E-Journals.

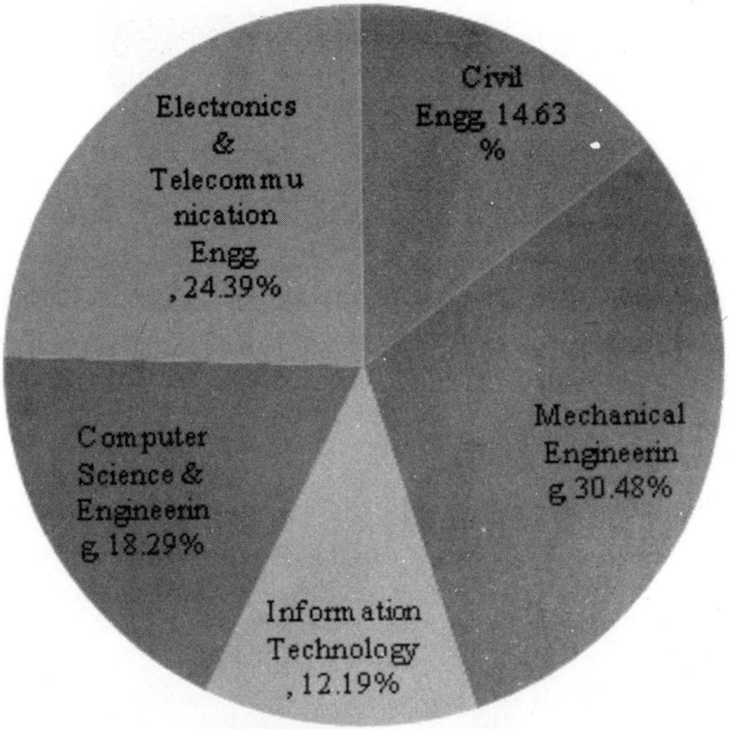

Fig. 3. Walchand College of Technology, Solapur

It is clear from Pie-Chart that Percentage of Civil Engg is 14.63% Percentage of Mechanical Engg. E-Journals is 30.48%, 12.19% of Information Technology e-Journals, 18.29% of Computer Science and 24.39% of Electronics & Telecommunication e-Journals available.

II) Bharat-Ratna Indira Gandhi College of Engineering Kegaon, Solapur

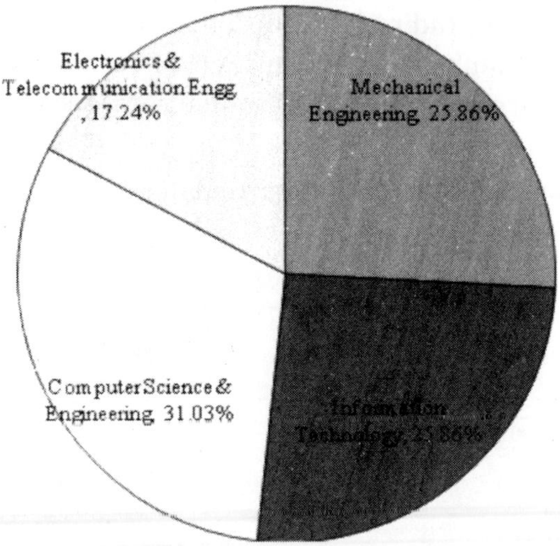

Fig. 4. Pie-Chart Showing department wise Percentage of e-Journals.

It is clear from Pie-Chart that Percentage of Mechnaical Engg. E-Journals is 25.86%, Informaion Technology is 25.86%, Computer Science is 31.03% and Electronics & Telecommunication is 17.24%.

III) Bramhadeo Mane Institute of Technology.

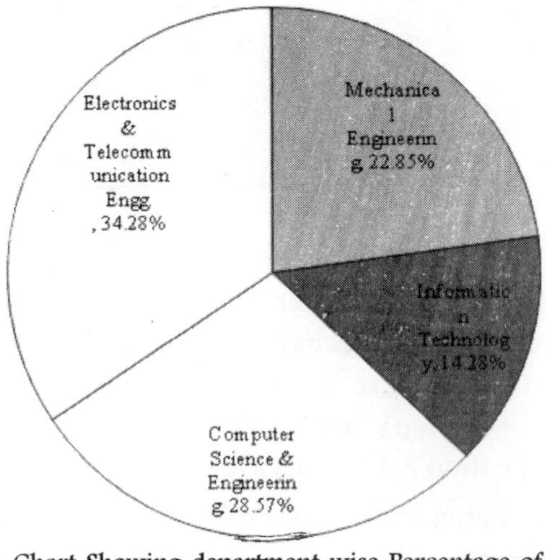

Fig. 5. Pie-Chart Showing department wise Percentage of E-Journals.

It is clear from Pie-Chart that Percentage of Mechanical Engg. e-Journals is 22.85%, Information Technology is 14.28%, Computer Science & Engg. Is 28.57% and Electronics & Telecommunication is 34.28%.

IV) Pandharpur College of Technical Institute.

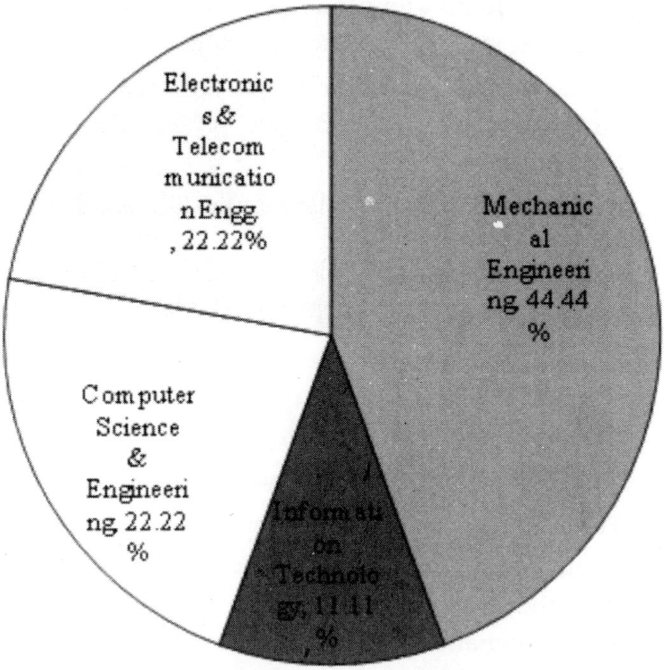

Fig. 6. Pie-Chart Showing department wise Percentage of E-Journals.

It is clear from Pie-Chart that Percentage of Mechanical Engg. e-Journals is 44.44%, Information Technology is 11.11%, Computer Science & Engg. Is 22.22% and Electronics & Telecommunication is 22.22%.

FINDINGS

1. All the respondents at various technical institutes have Computer knowledge the Percentage is 100%.

2. All the respondents of various technical institution use internet resources once in a day or other time.
3. All the technical institutions provide department wise e-journals on minimum rate for the teachers and Students.
4. It is found that 55.00% respondents use the internet resources and service for to search latest relevant subject material, 20.00% for e-mail purposes, 10.00% for chatting purposes, and 15.00% use it for some other purpose.
5. It is found that the libraries are well digitized with SOUL and other library software package and internet racecourses.
6. Development plan projection for next 20 years i.e. by 2027.

Present Staff Patterns

The staff in the library department is selected as per AICTE standard pattern.

i) One Librarian
ii) One Asst. Librarian
iii) One Library Asst, Per thousand students.
iv) Three Library Attendants per one thousand students.
v) Additional Lib Asst. subject to crossing limit of 1000 students i.e. in the first page college get one Lib Asst., three attendants and further attendant is admissible per 250 students. Thus, if the strength of students exceeds 2000 there will be one Librarian, one Asst Librarian, Two Lib. Asst. and Six Library Attendants.
vi) Today all the technical college libraries are having four qualified librarians, one Asst. Librarians, Eight Library Asst and fourteen library attendants. Some of them are looking after security and with and work duties.
vii) Future Plan Projection:-There is an average increase of 1.5% students per year and one teacher per year. Thus there would be 30% increase in the strength of students i.e. 2600

students strength by 2028 and increase of 30 teachers by 2028. Thus there would by 2400 students and 286 teachers will be there by 2028.

viii) The library is doing fast advancement in computerization and automation of library functioning and services. if it does not allow increased strength of non teaching staff automation and computerization will not solve the problem of manpower

Training

Now a days training to the staff is essential, today all the four libraries having manpower with basic knowledge of computerization. Also other staff is trained to operate computer along with librarians.

Space

There is an average increase of 2% in collection of volumes. At Present each college library is having 400 sq.m. area for stack room, administrative block, periodical, reading rooms, circulation counter and computer terminals etc. Taking into consideration 2% increase by 2028 library may need 2000 sq.mtr. area. But there is reduction in collection @ 1% because of weed out & writing of books and addition of e-books instead of hard copies. Thus, library may need hardly 1% additional space.

Budget

i) As per Analysis there is an average increase of 10% in budget every year, thus there would be 200% increase and library budget will four time by 2028

ii) Though, there is 10% increase in budget this will not be sufficient to cope-up with the cost required in the begging for computerization & automation. Therefore as per analysis there is need of 20% increase in budgetary provision at least for next five year. So that further cost may have little increase @ 4% only, 8% of the budgetary provision will be needed for advance training to the present staff and 5% for infrastructure requirements and 4 % for regular expenses i.e. collection of volumes. Hard copies as well as e-form publication.

Software

i) Right now library is using SOUL And DELNET software and has completed 25% work of data entries. It is good that the records enter in this software are as per standards maintained by AICTE norms and it is possible to impart this data in any other DELPLUS/LIBMAN software.

ii) The proposal to purchase library software is on the anvil and by end of this academic year library staff will use software.

iii) It is confirmed by software expert team that it the software will take care of all library functions in the coming next ten years. If proper and skilled computer operators are maintained

iv) The Library for compatible data base development will need further revised version of the library software.

Computerization

The library has completed 20% of data base creation & 80% is still pending. It is analyzing that it will take at least next 3 years to computerized the whole data at present speed. Also to automate all function of library need further three more years. Thus library need next seven years span for computerization of library.

i) Right now library is having only four advanced systems.

ii) Library would need a separate sever of suitable capacity to cope – up with a future requirements.

iii) **INTRANET :** The INTRANET work is under progress. Each department is having a separate system. It is projected that at least two systems will be needed by each development.

iv) **Broadband Connectivity :** Taking in to consideration the projected requirements. there is need of 100 mbps. Capacity of separate broadband connectivity.

CONCLUSION

There is considerable growth in digitization of Libraries. The academicians use its resources and services for latest information to enhance and speed up research activities. The availability of huge information, resources and services. The digitized access is used by academicians of various faculties of i.e. civil, Mechanical, Electronics, Electrical and other such facilities. To do the positive and optimum utilisations of library digitization and networking is the requirement of time.

After verification of the importance of this process digitization and networking. There is need to provide sufficient funds for this process to make its best use, and make it easily available free of charge to the students and teachers to the optimum utilization of rich information flow, particularly in the field of applied sciences and social science for the development of human beings. The findings of this study explorate positive trend and considerable contribution of digitization and networking. There is justification to provide more funds for digitization and networking of all the college libraries.

REFERENCES

1. Ali Amjad, (2007).Digital Libraries and Information Networks, Ess-Ess Publication, New Delhi.
2. Ali A. Ed., (2006) An Encyclopedic Dictionary of Library and information Science 3 Vols. Ane Book of India, New Delhi.
3. Bal Krishnan S. and Paliwal P.K., (2001), Library Digital Technology, Anmol Publication, New Delhi.
4. Chaus A.S., (2008), Chaus Marathi-English Dictionary, Ultimate Publishers, Nagpur.
5. Clure Charles R.Mc. and Berlot Johncarlo, (2008), Evaluating Networked Information Services, Ess-Ess Publication, New Delhi.
6. Gupta Santosh, (1993), Research Methodology and Statistical Techniques, Deep and Deep Publication.
7. Jeevan V.K.J., (2004), Digital Libraries, Ess-Ess Publication, New Delhi.
8. Krishan Kumar, (1996), Research Methods in Library and Information Science, Beacon Publication, Delhi.

9. Kumar P.S.G., (1987), Computerization of Indian Libraries, B.R. Publication, Delhi.

10. Mallaiah T.Y., and Badami K.K., (1993), Library and information Service Facilities in Mangalore University Library; from research scholars Point of View: A Survey: Annual Of Library Science and Documentation.

11. Nair R.Raman, (1992). Computer Application to Library and Information Services, Ess-Ess Publication, New Delhi,

12. Pandey S.K., (1993) Library Computerization: Theory and Practice, Ess-Ess Publications, New Delhi.

13. Sing P.K., (2004). Digitised Methods of Library Services, Shree Publishers, New Delhi.

14. Tiwari Purushotham, (2006) Digital Library, APH Pub, New Delhi. http/su.digitaluniversity.org

15. www.bigce.org.in

16. www.bmit.ac.in

17. www.coep.ac.in

18. www.govt.maha.co.in - Solapur District at a glance.

19

Some Best Practices adopted in the College Libraries and Information Centres: *An Overview*

Umesh kumar Y

Senior librarian, Hasanath College for Women, Bangalore-42

Manjunath M

Librarian, Govt FGC, Hesaraghatta. Bangalore-88

Vijayaraj Kumar U S

Librarian, Govt FGC, Rajajinagar, Bangalore-10

ABSTRACT

The Paper throws light with the introduction to the role of libraries in the present context, and the impact of ICT on libraries. Also the article stresses on the current challenges faced by the college libraries, and how it can be overcome by using the best practices. The paper also highlights the broad areas under which the best practices are classified, along with the list of best practices under each category. Some of the best practices that are adopted in the college libraries are discussed and concludes that with the adoption of the best practices in college libraries there will be a continuous improvement and overall performance in the institution or the organization.

Key Words. Academic libraries, College libraries, Best practices, Information literacy, user education, library services.

INTRODUCTION

The Present Information and communication technologies (ICT) have made a tremendous impact on the functions of the academic libraries specially the college libraries. The developments and changes in the ICT have changed the user's expectations from the academic libraries in different ways. The ways to build a college library collection and offer services to the end users vary from the recent to past exercises. Thus to effectively meet the demands of the end users, the academic libraries /college libraries need to identify and adopt good and best practices and benchmarks which will ultimately enhance the value based services of the college libraries in an academic environment.

In the present day scenario of the fast- paced educational innovations the best practices become necessary for continuous review and improvement of the overall functions of the college library and information centers. At times there is hesitation on the part of some institutions/colleges to share their best practices data. In the present age of information explosion the college libraries and information centre play not just an important learning-support function, but the library itself has been emerging as a site of learning, sometimes more important than even the class – room. In the huge and heterogeneous higher education system, there are numerous best practices, but only a few have been considered /discussed for this presentation and for the enhancement of the institutional effectiveness.

ROLE OF THE COLLEGE LIBRARIES

The Role of the Library and information Centre in a college is aimed at realizing the educational goals of the College or the Parent Organization. The College libraries not only provides stimulus to reading by Procuring materials for study and research, by introducing open Access system, by providing Long hours of open, by organizing the library resources in a systematic way, but also feeds the Intellect of the student, encourage the Researches of the faculty and thus serve the teaching and research needs of the faculty.

The College Library and Information Centre Acts as a vehicle for Disseminating Information and the related computer technologies through the best practices for Utilization by its community of users and also for the exchange of information among its users.

Current Challenges faced by College Libraries are as Follows:

1. Explosive growth of information and documents
2. Increased cost of the Documents and information Materials
3. Increase in users information needs
4. New role of the Librarian and greater responsibilities.
5. Latest techniques and concepts in handling of Information.
6. New electronic Information environment.
7. Creation of Databases and its Security.
8. Marketing of library and Information services.

The college library and information centre of an institution play a central role in facilitating dissemination and creation of new knowledge. In the present learning environment, the library and information centre as learning resource has taken up increasingly more academic space and time in the life of the user, thus it is time to identify and adopt the best practices that will lead library and information centre to improve their process and activities, thereby optimizing the resource utilization and delivering high quality, and value added services to their users.

A Best Practice may be innovative and be a philosophy, policy, strategy, program, process or practice that solves a problem or create new opportunities and positively impacts on the organization. Institutional excellence is the aggregate of the best practices followed in different areas of institutional activities. In general, the use of technology and innovative ideas lead to evolve best practices evolving in the library and information environment.

Thus A '**Best practice** ' in library in simple terms is known as that practice which makes the way for enhancing an existing function or an activity and helps in effective implementation or use of the process thereby leading to a continuous improvement and overall performance of the library. With this information as background an attempt has been made to highlight the best practices that are adopted in the college libraries. The following is an overall view of the best practices that are adopted in college libraries and information centres.

The broad areas under which the best practices are classified are:

a. Management and administration of a library.

b. Collection and services.

c. Extent of use of services.

d. Use of technology in libraries.

Under the area of **Management and Administration of Library** the following are some of the best practices involved:

a. In-service Programmes.

b. Observation of other Library practice.

c. Staff promotional policy.

d. Maintenance of service area.

e. Special deposit scheme.

f. Resource Generation through external membership.

g. Resource generation through internet services.

h. Student participation programme.

Under the area of **Collection and Services** the following are some of the best practices involved:

a. Collection development in different formats.

b. Compact storage of less used collection.

c. Library book exhibition.

d. Extended library opening hours.

e. Extended hours of service.

Under the **Extent of the use of Services** the following are some of the best practices involved:

a. user education (Information Literacy Programme).

b. Initiation to freshers (Information literacy).

c. Preparatory course for students project (Information literacy).

d. User orientation (Information literacy).

e. Information Aids (Information literacy).

f. Library use statistics.

g. Library Best user award.

h. User feedback practice through different formats

i. Suggestion Box and timely response.

Under the **Use of Information technology** the following are some of the best practices involved:

a. On-line information retrieval- Internet access.

b. Free browsing unit –Internet access.

c. Broadband internet centre.

d. Library homepage for information dissemination.

e. A strong and Dynamic Library Website.

f. User feedback through Library Homepage.

g. Access to E-resources.

h. Information retrieval through Web OPAC.

i. Campus-wide local area network- LAN facility.

j. Database creation using international standard formats.

k. Electronic surveillance system - CCTV / cameras.

Some Best Practices adopted in college libraries are as Follows:

1. Book Display programme: to Organize Exhibitions and book Display programme on important dates, and important Occasion on eminent personalities. This helps and provides an opportunity for users to know the various types of information resources available on a particular aspect in the Library and Information Centre.

2. Orientation programme: One of the best practices is to create awareness among the students about the library resources, the library services, good reading habits, creative programmes and activities for maximum utilization of the library. In other words enlighten the fresh students at the beginning of each academic year about the importance of the library, thereby exposing the students to its various sections of the library, the library resources and the various library services.

3. Educating the User: The college libraries have a great role and responsibility in creating awareness among its users which will help to make use of the library resources, facilities, services, more effectively and efficiently. Through 1. User orientation which may be individual or groups. 2. Library Brochures, circulars, Pamphlets and handouts.

4. Staff Users Meet: The college Libraries should organize various programmes including orientation, lectures on related issues, and topics, workshops, seminars, which focuses the issues useful to the users as well as to the staff. The college libraries may organize programmes in information handling in the present digital era, knowledge networking, role of librarians in the electronic era, subject searching, time management, public relations, knowledge based systems, this helps to keep abreast the staff and the users about the latest developments and trends in library principles and practices, thereby bridging the gap between the staff and the users.

5. Developing Virtual Presence: The college Libraries can use web 2.0 applications like social networking, blogging, use of RSS feed, audio and video streaming, wikipedia, etc, and interacting delivery information services.

6. Demonstrations and Exhibitions: The Libraries should organize demonstrations and exhibitions to create awareness about their collection, services. This can be done inside the library separately through displaying the special collection and literary works of specific authors or group of authors thereby creating an awareness about the particular author or literary works among its users, thus attracting even the people

From different sections of the society like parents, management members, relatives of the staff members and the public.

7. Information Brochures: Information brochures and Pamphlets are also one of the important sources for creating awareness about the facilities, services, and the collections of the library, the users can be provided the information brochures at the time of their enrollments as registered members. The Information brochures may be on reprography or Xerox facilities, latest publications, and latest additions to the library. CD/DVD list, Book bank Facilities, library rules and regulations, electronic resources, and online information services list.

8. Web Based Services: The College libraries can provide various web based services through its strong Library Website updated with services such as–

Virtual tour

Ask the Librarian

Help desk

Electronic announcement

Digital Suggestion box

Frequently asked questions

Face book

Virtual reference desk

Full text article

Lecture notes

e- Books

Project reports

Dissertations, etc.

The other best practices involved in college libraries are:

a. Personalized faculty service - which provides the faculty with Research information either in form of document or journal article through the journal related identification process.

b. By establishing a good rapport with the Publishers specimen copies can be sought to the library and copies thus displayed will help in the book selection process along with the faculty.

c. Pending of books to the family members and relatives of the non-teaching staff of the college.

d. Providing internet facilities free for all the students of the college

e. Sending the list of the latest additions of book or the latest arrivals to all the faculty members and the students of the college and also their display in the notice board.

f. Library collection display list – the library can display the total number of books, journals, periodicals, magazines, project reports, dissertations, audio and video cassette, CDs DVDs , number of book banks etc.

g. Display of the services offered at the library like CAS, SDI, Newspaper clipping service, reprographic services etc.

h. Exchange of information between different colleges or institutions can be viewed better with exchange of college magazines and reports.

i. Instituting an award or prize for the best user of the library.

J. The library staff can help the students in training them in their curricular and extra-curricular activities and also help them in participation for different levels of competitions and cultural shows.

k. User education through instructions on use of the internet and web resources.

l. Providing Book Bank facilities to the backward class students of the institution.

m. Creating a pleasant environment in the library for the users to sit and enjoy reading, and doing reference work, like setting up a small water fountain and providing audible light music.

We know that the best practices are evolved through stages of failures and corrections and through the borrowed best practices we can enhance our competitive advantage and also enhance the institutional effectiveness.

CONCLUSION

The College Libraries should take Initiations of the broad activity to enhance the socio-economic position of the books / documents in the library. Also they should create an environment and conditions for keeping abreast of the new and latest knowledge and uses of modern technological achievements in the field, and also in the diffusion of the latest information and lastly the training of professional personnel through a unified system, so that the knowledge from the source to its

Beneficiaries or users can be disseminated in a most efficient and effective way through the adoption of the best practices.

When the library staff work in coordination and with a team spirit under the dynamic leadership of the librarian with the involvement of the best practices they are sure to benefit the user community and thereby contribute to the overall performance in achieving the goals and objectives of the institution. Also by adopting the best practices in the library and through its effective implementation at the appropriate time we can create a friendly environment, thereby bridging the gap between the library and the users, which in total will result in the optimum utilization of the resources, thereby effectively meeting the challenges along with the goals and objectives of the institution we work.

Thus the best Practices adopted should bridge the Gap between the college library and the users for effective and maximum utilization of the resources, which will result in the advancement and promotion of higher educational goals and the Vision and Mission of the college Library.

We hope that the outlined best practices will serve as one of the ways to strengthen the library and information services of college libraries.

REFERENCES

1. Best practice. Available at http://en.wikipedia.org/wiki/Best_practices
2. National Assessment and Accreditation Council. Best practices in library and information services: a case presentation. Available at http:// naacindia.org/Publications/Best%20Practices%20Library%20Science.doc
3. National Assessment and Accreditation Council. Guidelines on quality indicators in library and information services: universities / autonomous colleges. Bangalore, NAAC, 2005.
4. National Assessment and Accreditation Council. Guidelines on quality indicators in library and information services: affiliated / constituent colleges. Bangalore, NAAC, 2005.
5. NAAC- a Profile. Bangalore. National Assessment and Accreditation council, 2006. A brochure.
6. NAAC- Best practices in Library and Information Services, case presentations, Best practices series-2 . NAAC-2006.
7. Kulkarni .S.A. Best practices in College Libraries. National seminar on Library and information services in changing era. 22-23 January 2009.
8. A.J. Davies and A.K.Kochhar: A framework for the selection of Best practices.
9. National Seminar on Best Practices in Library and Information Services 9-12 August 2006, Bangalore University Library, Bangalore.
10. Tikekar .A .C. Best practices in academic libraries: paper presented at "Vision Libraries -2020." Organized by north Maharastra University. Jalgaon .8th April 2009.

20

Information Access in the Environment of Multimedia databases of Digital Library: A Conceptual Schema

Dr. Ramesha
Reader, DLIS, Bangalore University, Bangalore

M.Raghavendra
Librarian, Govt First Grade College, Javanagondanahally, Hiriyur (T), Chitradurga (D)

ABSTRACT

In particular, with the mounting fame of the World Wide Web the main challenge in Information retrieval has become content-based retrieval of multimedia objects. However, in their rush to meet the immediate demands of user's, people are advertently creating solutions for accessing multimedia data in all sectors round the globe. Access to multimedia databases is not much sophisticated; as a result multimedia information access becomes bottleneck for user community. In the present study an attempt has been made to provide content-based retrieval through integrated query processing with an architectural representation, its architecture fully integrates traditional query processing and content-based retrieval techniques in multimedia environment.

Keywords. Multimedia databases, Information Access, Query processing, content based retrieval, Digital Access, Information Seeking.

INTRODUCTION

The term "multimedia" is shaped by combination the two terms "multiple" and "media" collectively. Multimedia data presents straight illustration of the physical world in the digital format. The multimedia data includes photographs, X-ray images, sound, and videos. Other multimedia data include drawings, charts, and animations. Any visible images and audible sound are also fall under multimedia data.[1]

A multimedia database system comprises a large, distributed information space, where the objects carrying the knowledge required by the users, Large-scale multimedia information retrieval is one of the major scientific challenges of this decade. Multimedia information retrieval lies at the intersection of artificial intelligence, information retrieval, human-computer interaction, and multimedia computing. This system enable users to process, summarize, present, interact with, and organize information within and across different media such as text, speech, graphics, imagery and video. These systems go beyond traditional hypermedia and hypertext environments to analyze and generate media as well as support intelligent interaction with or via multiple media.

MULTIMEDIA DATA STORAGE AND DISTRIBUTION

Many data storage and distribution systems have been investigated. These include the centralized system, the storage area network (SAN), the content distribution network (CDN), and the serverless or peer-to-peer (P2P) network. Databases are stored digitally in the form of files with appropriate file extensions, the file extensions denotes the type of digital data contained in them.[2]

The centralized arrangement keeps all the multimedia items

in one place. The storage area network stores the multimedia objects on several servers. These storage servers are associated over a local area network using optical fibres. The content distribution network allocate the multimedia objects on servers that are stretch over a wide area network. Client requests are sent to the nearest server that contains the object to serve the request.

The server less systems or peer-to-peer networks do not everlastingly keeps the objects on the servers. The server enclose the object will only serve the first few requests for the object. Afterwards, the nodes that have the object will become free and serve other clients, thus, the server can become free, and it can be disconnected from the network.[3]

DATA REPRESENTATIONS

Multimedia data type comprises numbers, text, graphics, animations, image, audio, and video. However, a computer can only handle digital data that represents either 0 or 1.

Computer graphics are represented using the coordinates on the displaying screen. Computer animations are performed by updating changes to the frame buffers and these changes are then drawn on the displaying screen. Images are represented as two-dimensional pixels of colours. Each colour pixel can be described using colour representation RGB (Red, Green, and Blue).[3]

Sound waves need to be accepted and digitized into digital signals for computer processing. The digitization of analog waves is done by taking sample values at a fixed sampling rate. The quality of the digitized sound is mainly determined by the number of sample values and the sampling rate.

Videos are represented as an array of image frames. 24 to 30 frames should be displayed per second to show full continuous motions. High definition televisions use a very high frame rate of around 60 frames per second.

MULTIMEDIA DATA ACCESS AS STREAMS

In traditional client/server computer systems, the types of

data being accessed are usually textual and binary data. Binary data are often stored in database files, and textual data are stored in document files. In multimedia systems, multimedia data such as video, audio, and images are stored in data files. These data may be accessed in a pull-based manner or a push-based manner.[4]

Traditional data are usually accessed in a pull-based approach. The client programs send discrete requests to load data from the server after receiving this request, the server accesses the block of data, encloses it in a data packet, and passes it to the client. The client then opens the data packet and accesses the data inside the packet. After serving this request, the server program would wait for another request from the client.

Multimedia data are often accessed in a push-based approach. The client program sends a request to the server asking for the multimedia file starting at a particular block. after receiving this request, the server accesses the data in file, encloses it in a data packet, and passes it to the client. The server then accesses the next block of data in same file and passes it to the client, and so on. The server would continue to access the next block of data in same file and pass it to the client until it receives another request from the client. When the client receives a data packet, it opens the packet and accesses the data inside.

Due to the continuous nature of the multimedia data, many data requests would be sent to the server in the pull-based approach. All the requests and the returned data packets flow continuously like water in a river stream. In the push-based approach, the data packets also flow continuously through the communication path like a stream. Thus, the multimedia objects are accessed via request streams.

CLASSIFICATION OF DATA STREAMS

Depending on the time interval between consecutive packets, a stream can be classified as strongly periodic, weakly periodic or aperiodic streams.[5]

Depending on the variation of data size between consecutive

packets, a stream can be classified as strongly regular, weakly regular, or irregular.

Strongly Periodic Stream: If the time interval between any two consecutive packets is constant, then the stream is called a strongly periodic stream, it has a fixed time interval between consecutive data packets.

Weakly Periodic Stream: If the time intervals between two consecutive packets are not constant but only periodic, then the stream is called a weakly periodic stream in which the time interval between consecutive packets oscillates between one other. When we merge two strongly periodic streams with different periods, the resultant stream is a weakly periodic stream.

Aperiodic Stream: Aperiodic streams are streams such that the time intervals between consecutive packets are neither constant nor periodic. An aperiodic stream with different time intervals between consecutive packets.

Multimedia data can be used in many types of applications. These applications include broadcasting, video-on-demand, communications, monitoring and control, and even information systems. The design of multimedia systems should consider the storage system, delivery network, and the scheduling algorithms. Most of these systems store large multimedia objects in their storage system for future retrievals. Inside the storage system, multimedia objects are stored as large binary data files, and they are accessed and delivered using streams. Multimedia streams can be classified by their periodicity, regularity, and continuity. A stream may be classified according to the time interval between consecutive packets. Second, a stream may be classified according to the data size of the packets. Third, a stream may be classified according to the continuity of the pocket.

In order to process continuous multimedia streams, multimedia computer systems are built with stringent processing time requirements. Each component of the computer system needs to be able to process large amounts of data, process data in parallel, and finish the processing within a guaranteed time frame. Otherwise, undesirable effects would appear to lower the quality of the multimedia streams.[6]

When storage servers are designed to handle multimedia streams, the architecture of the storage servers also needs to handle the processing time requirements. The storage server needs to access data continuously to the clients according to the user's requests.

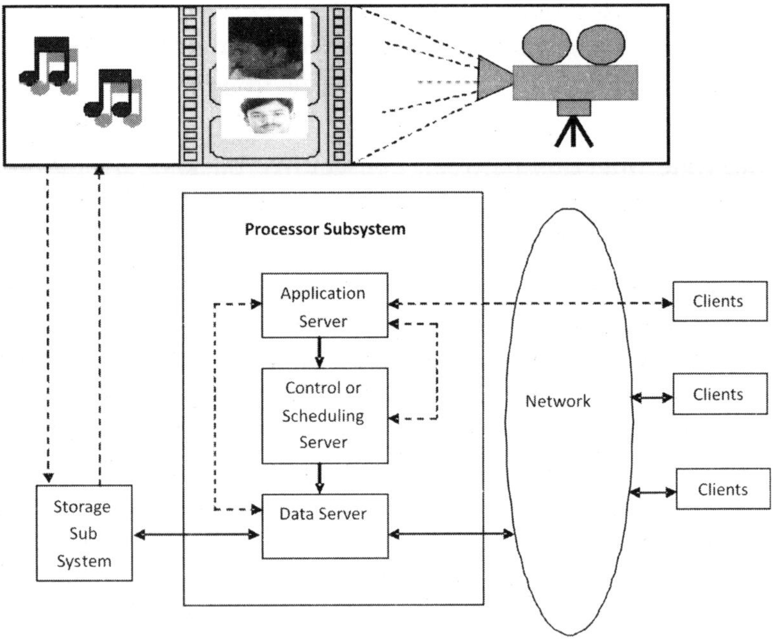

Fig. 1. Architecture of Multimedia database

It composed of a storage subsystem and a processor subsystem. The processor subsystem serves requests from the clients via the network. It maintains the quality of streams that are delivered to the clients. When data are required, it sends requests to the storage subsystem.

The main responsibility of the storage subsystem is to store the multimedia objects. All the multimedia objects are stored on the storage devices in the storage subsystem. The storage subsystem serves data requests from the processor subsystem. The main reason to separate the storage subsystem from the processor subsystem is because of the workload. Since the object is large and the stream is long, it takes a long time to deliver the object to the clients. The workload on the storage subsystem is thus heavy. If the storage subsystem and the processor subsystem are running on the same server, the application server's ability to respond interactively to the users will be adversely affected. The user may need to wait a long time for a very simple mouse click.

The processor subsystem is composed of three servers: the application server, the scheduling server, and the data server. The application server receives requests from the clients and provides a response back to them. The scheduling server divides a request stream into a number of requests. It then schedules the requests in a timely manner. It sends the requests to the data server. The data server searches for the location of the requested object and forwards the requests to the storage subsystem.

When the storage subsystem serves a read request from the data server, reads the object from the storage device, and passes the accessed data to the data server. When the storage subsystem serves a write request, it writes the object to the storage devices. Most multimedia clients only access the objects for viewing purposes only. Since multimedia objects are often read and played to users, most requests would only read the object from the server. Thus, the main concern on the storage subsystem is on the read operations only even though the storage subsystem provides both read and write operations.

When the data server receives data from the storage subsystem, it directly passes the data to the clients via the network. It will then send another data request to the storage subsystem at the time controlled by the scheduling server and so on. By this way users can access the multimedia data round the clock.

In the present context large amount of multimedia information are available electronically in various nontextual forms, such as graphics, images, spoken or music audio, animation and video. The enormously availability of data in the internet leads the problem of accessing.

The growth of information every year goes on stretching round the globe. In the era of information creation and distribution, it is necessary to understand data storage and general information flow over the world. Here are some figures of data storage.

Kilobyte (KB)	1,000 bytes or 10^3 bytes
	100 Kilobytes: A low resolution photograph
Megabyte (MB)	1,000,000 bytes or 10^6 bytes
	I Megabyte: A small novel of 3.5 inch floppy
	2 Megabytes: A high resolution photographs
	5 Megabytes: The complete works of shakesphere
Gigabyte (GB)	1,000,000,000 bytes or 10^9 bytes
	100 Gigabytes: A library floor of Academic journals
Terabyte (TB)	1,000,000,000,000 bytes or 10^{12}
	1 Terabyte: 50,000 trees made in to paper and printed
	10 Terabytes: The print collection of the U.S. Library of Congress
Petabyte (PB)	1,000,000,000,000,000 bytes or 10^{15} bytes
	2 Petabytes: All U.S. Academic research Libraries
	200 Petabytes: All printed material world over
Exabite (EB)	1,000,000,000,000,000,000 or 10^{18} bytes
	2 Exabytes: Total volume of information generated in a year.
	5 Exabytes: All words ever spoken by human beings

Newly created information is stored in four physical media, i.e. print, film, magnetic and optical, and seen or heard in four information flows through electronic channels, telephone, radio, TV, and internet.[7]

The following are the present trends in the growth rate of information:

1. Print, film, magnetic and optical storage media produced about 5 exabytes of new information in one year. Ninety

two percent of the information will store on magnetic media, mostly in hard disks.

2. The amount of new information stored on paper film, magnetic, and optical media has doubled in the last three years.

   Information Explosion: New stored Information grew about 30% a year.

   Paper less Society: the amount of information printed on paper is still increasing, but the vast majority of original information on paper is produced by individuals in office documents and postal mails, not in formally published titles such as books, newspapers and journals.

3. Information flows through electronic channels: Telephone, radio, TV and the internet, contained almost 18 exabytes of new information, three and a half times more than is recorded in storage media.

   Telephone calls: worldwide, on both landline and mobile phones contained 17.3 exabytes of new information is stored in digital form.

4. The World Wide Web: contains about 170 terabytes of information on its surface, in volume this is seventeen times the size of the Library of Congress print collections.[8]

It is clear that the problem of Accessing of multimedia information in this global information junk is really a great challenge and giant problem. Even if it is text we couldn't do it completely. In this consequence many research have already done on the same particular topic, still a lot more works to be done in these areas of multimedia information retrieval and delivery systems.

CONCLUSIONS AND FUTURE WORK

Due to heavy growth in Multimedia information and technology the development of multimedia access has been an interesting research focus. One of the main challenges is to transfer multimedia information to end user based on their needs. Here we proposed architectural solution framework that best fits for the Multimedia data access, which integrates the techniques in all levels of the system, makes it an attractive intermediate model to increase the efficiency of the overall system architecture. This framework can also be implement for a web-based Multimedia Digital Library Access.

REFERENCES

1. Rao, K. R, Bojkovic, Z. S, & Milovanovic, D. A. (2002). Multimedia communication Systems, Techniques, standards, and networks. Prentice hall.
2. Wang, Y, Ostermann, J, & Zhang, Y.Q. (2002). Video processing and communications, Prentice Hall.
3. Faloutsos C. (1996). Searching multimedia databases by content, Kluwer Academic Publishers, Boston/London.
4. Jeon, W. J, & Nahrstedt, K. (2002). Peer-to-peer multimedia streaming and caching service, In *Proceedings of IEEE, ICME,* p57-60.
5. Tse, P. K. C. (1999). Efficient storage and retrieval methods for multimedia information. Doctoral dissertation, Victoria University, Melbourne, Australia.
6. Wactlar H, Kanade T.M, and Stevens S. (1996). Intelligent access to digital video: The Informedia project. *IEEE* Computer, 29(5).
7. Balasubramanian A. (2009). National seminar on open access to textual and multimedia content: Bridging the digital divide, 29th to 30th January, IHC, Newdelhi, Organized by CEC & INFLIBNET of UGC.
8. Tse, P. K. C. & Leung, C. H. C. (2000). Improving multimedia systems performance using constant density recording disks. *ACM Multimedia Systems Journal, 8*(1), 47-56.

21

21st Century Skills in LIS and Related Fields

Prasanna Hanamantarao Hosurakar*

Assistant Librarian, Auden Technology and Management Academy, Bangalore Rural,

ABSTRACT

21st Century Modern libraries are moving towards smaller with rich information potential. In the beginning of the 21st Century, the libraries are undergoing dramatic transformations with strong technological foundations. The library of the recent past was not what the library is today. And the library of the future will obviously be quite different from what it is today. They are changing in tune with time and technology. The present 21st Century generation of libraries and librarians recognize the advent of information communication revolution and realize its potentiality in the field of education and research. Changes in society and demands for information utilization have forced the information professionals have resorted to the applications of modern information technology. This paper highlights the 21st Century Skills in LIS and their related fields.

Keywords: 21st Century, LIS Professionals, Information Technology, Librarian Skills, Information centre, Internet for Library Professionals.

"Proper preparations prevents Poor performances"

INTRODUCTION

Challenges of the 21st century knowledge society impose

collective responsibility on us all to evolve an LIS education system relevant to the emerging education and information needs of the future. Digital economy requires rethinking on education. Changing role of knowledge in society and in economy affects the role, skills and enhances the status of information providers. Free flow of information is a near reality in this highly networked world. The IT has indeed helped in the expansion of human capabilities. Challenges have emerged from the new modes of learning and communication.

In today's environment the **LIS** profession has to change its outlook and methods; learn new tools and retain the dwindling clientele encroached by the imperialist Internet and allied professions. The recent development in science and technology has led to a new alarming situation regarding information created in the world. Today, we are living at the midst of an era of change. The introduction of new technologies in the libraries has brought about sea-change in various services provided by modern libraries. Rapid changes in technology and communication have raised the need for acquiring new skills and knowledge in the present day work environment. Automation of library services is now essential for efficient and effective working of a library system in the changing information environment.

DEFINITIONS

According to **Borko** "Information science is an interdisciplinary science that investigates the properties and behavior of information, the forces that govern the flow and use of information and the techniques, both manual and mechanical of processing information for optimal storage, retrieval and dissemination.

According to **Belkin** "Little progress that has been made in the theory of information science is that its fundamental problem has not yet been stated in its most basic and easily soluble form. This is an important condition, since the statement of a problem defines the methods and approach applied to its solution.

According to B.C.Brooks "The name informatics has a commendable intellectual honesty about it:. That is, it appears to me to be a bit presumptuous to be calling this activity a science as yet".

NEW ROLE OF LIBRARY PROFESSIONALS

21st Century the librarian was merely considered as a custodian of stored books, but now the entire situation has totally changed due to various developments in information technologies and their applications in libraries. Accordingly, a library is now treated as the centre for the creation and recreation of information services and products for academic pursuits.

The nomenclature of librarians has changed to "Documentation Officer", "Knowledge Mangers", "Information Managers", "Information Scientists", "Information Officers", etc. The Libraries are similarly being named as 'Resource Centres', 'Information Centres', and 'Knowledge Resource Centres etc. A number of new products and technologies are being reported which have potential applications for information processing and servicing.

21ST CENTURY OR FUTURE ROLE OF INFORMATION PROFESSIONALS

As the Information Technology has brought in fundamental changes in libraries, therefore, the role of information professionals is continuously changing. The Information Professionals of the future will need:

High level management skills and leadership qualities i.e., he is supposed to be well-versed in planning, execution and marketing principles.

High level information handling skills i.e., to be committed, who is capable of dealing with all types of information technology problems.

- To be flexible and adaptable.
- To be a good communicator

- To be proactive.
- To be innovative and imaginative.
- To have through knowledge in the new methods and technologies.
- To be involved in collaborative work with resource sharing among libraries.
- To be capable of effective exploitation of existing information retrieval services both manual and online.
- To be capable of measuring and evaluating the existing system.

The library and IT professional should work together for continuous refinement in the system and make the system more efficient and convenient.

CHANGING JOB FOR LIBRARIANS

The Library professionals may be distinguished depending on their nature job, subject they serve, or expertise they develop (e.g. Corporate Librarian, Medical Librarian, Engineering Librarian). But the basic skills for being library professional required are almost same irrespective of you work in Educational (School/College/University) or Special (Public/Research/Subject oriented) Library etc.

The Librarian may face dilemma while change in the job due to numerous factors such as:

- Lack of skills required for new position e.g. Using technology for library automation/management.
- Mentally not prepared for new responsibilities in case job change is unexpected.
- New atmosphere for starting all over again as change in users, their requirements, the new library system etc.

In case, the person decides with proper planning with full preparation then it is easy to face new challenges but still one need to do homework for smooth transition. Before applying for a new job, the library professional should be aware and satisfied about the responsibilities, skills required for particular job, the present situation of library or information centre, the parent organization to serve, the nature of users and their requirements etc. & would be expectations from management side & challenges. One needs to study all these aspects and prepare accordingly.

The change in job is must sometimes even in same organization to avoid monotonous routine, to learn something new. In any circumstances one must remain positive and prepare himself/herself as per changing situations in the library professional to face present and future challenges by acquiring new skills whenever required.

BENEFITS OF THE INTERNET FOR LIBRARY PROFESSIONALS

In the context of new electronic environment the role of information professionals is becoming challenging and crucial. The Internet is facilitating collection, organization, Storing, retrieval and dissemination of information in this information era. Access to the internet is becoming easier and is going to be within the reach of most of the libraries and information professionals.

The following are the various benefits of the internet for library personnel:

- The Internet helps in acquiring the right electronic information resources available at various websites.
- The Internet has greatly enhanced both the circulation and inter-library loan services through increased access to online catalogues which allow a user greater convenience in undertaking online searches.
- The reference librarian can provide reference service through the use of the Internet offering greater convenience to users.
- Electronic discussion groups help in professional development and career advancement of professionals.
- Through E-mail service, library professionals can towards

the requests for documents to one or more libraries at any time.

- Orders of books, journals and other reading materials can be sent through e-mail.
- Day to day correspondence could be sent through E-mail, thereby providing effective and fast services to its readers.

21ST CENTURY SOFT SKILLS FOR LIBRARIANS

For today's librarians having professional degrees in library and information science is not sufficient unlike in the past. There is demand for librarians having multidimensional aptitude in the areas of technical work, administrative work and also in providing user oriented services along with soft skills. Like any other profession, the soft skills are required in day-to-day working for carrying out routine jobs more effectively. The librarians working in large organizations like corporate offices are already practicing these skills through by experience or training. One may learn these soft skills easily provided they are aware what these are!!

Following are soft sills required to become a successful library professional.

1. Communications and Collaboration skills

Command on language especially English and also regional one will improve the communication. Good communication skills also require understanding people, self-confidence. With this one can achieve lot and solve problems too.

i) Communicate Clearly

- Articulate thoughts and ideas effectively using oral, written, and nonverbal communication skills in a variety of forms and contexts
- Listen effectively to decipher meaning, including knowledge, values, attitudes, and intentions
- Use communication for a range of purposes (e.g., to inform, instruct, motivate, and persuade) and in diverse

environments (including multi-lingual)

- Utilize multiple media and technologies, and know how to judge their effectiveness a priori as well as assess their impact

ii) Collaborate with Others

- Demonstrate ability to work effectively and respectfully with diverse teams
- Exercise flexibility and willingness to be helpful in making necessary compromises to accomplish a common goal.

2. Customer service Skills

Customer is library user and to satisfy his information needs is customer service. The librarians are always giving attention to their users and providing services through CAS, SDI or other specialized services. The customer service emphasizes the customer satisfaction, which guarantees that user will always come back to library.

3. Leadership skills, Teamwork and Responsibility

Library management especially the big library is team exercise. Hence it is required to have leadership skills to manage and guiding the team time to time, as every subordinate is important for carrying out their work efficiently for smooth running of library.

i) Guide and Lead others

- Use interpersonal and problem-solving skills to influence and guide others toward a goal
- Leverage strengths of others to accomplish a common goal
- Inspire others to reach their very best via example and selflessness
- Demonstrate integrity and ethical behavior in using influence and power

ii) Be Responsible to Others

- Act responsibly with the interests of the larger community in mind

4. Listening skills

The library professionals must have good listening skills as he/she has to interact with different types of users all the time. By carefully listening to users' he/she can identify the exact requirement and then provide the service accordingly.

5. Writing skills

The librarians are sometimes asked to submit/help in writing research proposal/ business proposal/project report, which requires good writing skills. Today there are many library professionals who are contributing to various publications even in-house or even by blogging for sharing their experiences and helping users.

6. Project management skills

In corporate sector many times, librarians are part of some project team and assigned specialized jobs such as knowledge management or digital institutional repository. These require dedication, understanding of the project, time management for completion of work, teamwork and reporting back the results etc.

7. Presentation skills

The presentation skills are required in report writing, library committee meetings and even in daily work which represents the library management overall for users. It not only emphasizes the individual skills but also from library presentation by means of its decoration, user's guides, and library ambience.

8. Teaching skills

This is essential for new user orientations or in case new service is introduced such as online database searching. It also includes motivating reading habits in users.

9. Information Handling Skills

Acquisition, Cataloguing, Indexing, Abstracting, Circulating, General Management and Organization of Information, Organization of Knowledge, Compilation of bibliographies and development of databases.

10. Information Technology Skills

A few other IT Skills which a library professional must know are as follows:

- Basic Computer Skills
- File management Skills
- Disk management Skills
- Bulletin board Skills
- DOS command handling
- Window operations system
- Key Boarding
- Networking Skills
- Scanning, Electronic Journals
- E-mail, Voice-mail, Video conferencing
- CR-ROM, DVD-ROM handling.
- Web page creation and editing skills
- Client-server management Skills
- To create MARC records for the National On-line Network.
- Development of digital libraries

The above operations is not the exhaustive list but only a few basic skills required in order to keep pace with the changing environment, the library professionals need to continuously upgrade their skills and knowledge.

CONCLUSION

21st Century LIS professionals and their related professionals should respond to the opportunities and challenges of the developments in Information Technology with high degree of enthusiasm and professionalism. The information professionals must change and adapt to new electronic information environment and continuously work for providing better and more convenient library and information services to users communities.

REFERENCES

1. Text Book: P.S.G.Kumar, 'A Student's Manual of Library and Information Science, PP.8
2. Journal: M. P. Satija, 'IASLIC-Bulletin', 'Need for revamping the LIS Education in India, Vol.55, No.1, March 2010, Pp.4-5.
3. Journal: Meghna Dhar, 'IASLIC-Bulletin', 'The Changing Role of Library Professionals in the Information Technology Ear', Vol.55, .No.2, June-2010, Pp.119-125.
4. Project: 'Institute of Museum and Library Services', 'Museums, Libraries, and 21st Century Skills', July-2009 (USA), Pp.23-25.
5. Web site Name: http://library-profession.blogspot.com/2008/12/soft-skills-for-librarians.html
6. Web site Name: http://library-profession.blogspot.com/2009/05/changing-job-for-librarians.html
7. Website Name : http://www.imls.gov/assets/1/asset manager/21stcenturyskills.pdf

22

How to Become Traditional Librarian to Digital Librarian: *A Challenge to Library Professionals*

Basavaraja Karapudi

Asst. Librarian, IBS Bangalore

ABSTRACT

Librarians must continuously adapt to new formats for information, such as electronic journals and e-books, which present both challenges and opportunities in providing access and promoting them to library patrons. Due to rapid developments that are taking place in communication and information technologies, there is a need that every librarian need to become digital librarian in spite of constraints, limitations prevailing in the libraries, so library professionals are in need to acquire the relevant skills and expertise to track the world of information and become competent enough to serve in a digital culture. Due to the changes in nature of librarianship resulting from the increasing amount of information available in digital format, educating, and digital librarians has become an important agenda within library and information academic libraries.

Key Words. Traditional Librarian, digital librarian, web knowledge, database skills, internet resources, web design skills, word processing, communication skills, parent organization.

INTRODUCTION

In India, the library and information science profession is still struggling for recognition, reorganization and identity. Since the advent of IT & ICT, users found attraction in library and information centers. Further, the demands from the user community for faster information retrieval have made automation, networking and resource sharing essential for LICs. The field of library science has witnessed tremendous developments during the past few decades. We are on the threshold of a revolution. This revolution will make it possible for information to be made available to the farthest corners of the globe, thanks to the latest information technology. The essence of technology lies in the enormous storage capability of computer, coupled with speed in its retrieval of information, one of the greatest challenges before the library professionals has the management of information.

Digital resources are being built up as self-service centers and librarians continue to pay the role of information provider. Internet has become a boon to the librarians and enabled them to become digital librarians. There is a remarkable and significant shift of reading materials from the open access library shelves to the hands of the end users due to the tremendous growth of information seekers, using web. Users are able to access materials from a computer at their work place or from home in a network environment, both wired and wireless. Libraries started functioning on 24/7 basis. This has forced the traditional librarian to improve his technology skills in order to become a digital librarian. Information and knowledge in today's fast moving world is the key for progress and new developments. For taking steps forward, its imperative the information pertaining to the subject is available and accessible uniformly. Today with the inset of new technology and specialized information connoisseurs, information on any area under discussion can be collected, organized and retrieved without difficulty. Information aficionado; today termed as digital librarian opens out doors of knowledge in an orderly structure.

DEFINITION OF DIGITAL LIBRARIAN

A Digital Librarian can be defined as an Information Specialist, who deals with more of a web-content, in order to reach his targeted user-group. He always updates his knowledge of information resources, information handling tools, and the fast changing needs of users as a result of "Internet Revolution" or "Web Revolution". The traditional libraries are becoming hybrid libraries. And hybrid libraries are becoming digital digital libraries at a rapid speed in case of special, research and academic libraries.

MANAGEMENT OF LIBRARIES IN 21ST CENTURY

Information Explosion

Information explosion is the rapid increase in the amount of published books, periodicals and effects of this abundance of information sources. As the amount of available data grows, the problems of managing the information becomes more difficult, which lead to information overload.

Management Skills

Librarian's job is challenging one. He has to plan, organize, co-ordinate and control the activities of the library. He should be reservoir of certain management skills to be successful in his task. Conceptual skills deal with ideas, technical skills with things and human skill with people. While both conceptual and technical skills are needed for good decision making. Human skills are necessary for a good leader.

Technical Skills

It is an ability to use special special proficiency or expertise relating method process, procedure or techniques of a specific job. Librarians must have to be technically accomplished. Today the librarian functions as a navigator, and updater of information to intellectual reserves with the help of search engines, e-resources and tools such as telnet, UNIX, ms-office, windows and Linux.

Communication Skills

No organize can function effectively without effective communication skill. Communication involves transmission and reception of messages between persons. Librarians act as disseminator of information. There must be free flow of both downward and upward communication.

Human Relation Skills

Human skill is the ability to work with the willing co-operation of other persons. It emerges as spirit of trust, enthusiasm and involvement in the interpersonal relationship. A person with good human skills with has a high degree of self awareness and a capacity to understand others.

Fund Raising Skills

The librarian needs practical knowledge of financial principle, budgeting, maintenance of books of accounts besides rendering service to the reader. Otherwise he may land himself in trouble. A successful librarian is one who adopts the different managerial skills according to changing circumstances.

Focus of Parent Organization

Library & information centre is a center of any academic setting while class-room teaching provides a glimpse of knowledge. Further, the information centers disseminate wide range of knowledge and supplements the instructional work of class-rooms and carry forward the idea of education

Information Collection

"Give me the strength to change the things I can, the grace to accept the things I cannot and great big bag of money"-Jack Handy. The main asset of library is the collection and, provides services; performs activities; delivers products to user community. It is librarian duty to increase the stock of his library, when asked how large a library should be, librarian answered. "Bigger, and with provision for further expansion"

Information Search in the Internet Era

Connecting people with information, some of the examples of tools and processes used in content management are: Taxonomies, thesauri, search engines, portals. Knowledge creation technologies for examples, data mining, information visualization, decision trees and root cause analysis. Document collaboration etc.

Subject Knowledge Skill

To provide the information the librarian must have subject knowledge. It includes awareness of current affairs, awareness of business, awareness of general knowledge, awareness of specific type of information in which the organization is working on.

Barriers to Knowledge Managers

Every library professional who works in academic, public or narrow special library wants to use the techniques of knowledge management to achieve the organizational goal and provide better service to its users, but due to some following barriers they are not able to use that:

- Lack of tool and technologies
- Lack of staff training
- Lack of sufficient budget/funds
- Lack of communication skills
- There is no co-operation between senior and junior staff
- Every library cannot participate in terms of modern technology and its management

Supervision skills

It is an art to guide the subordinates and to observe

everything in according to objectives of organization. It is overseeing the work progress of the subordinates. To supervise the activities of the library the professionals needs self confidence and skills.

Best Practices to adopt

The IT and Knowledge need to work together and focus on getting the right information to right people at the right time. The following points are identified for the better practice in academic libraries:

- Organizing a training programme and inter-change of staff for time being on National level
- To provide special fund for the new technologies
- Staff sharing to develop their professional skills
- To provide sufficient budget
- Inter change of technical staffs among organizations/ libraries

- To equip library with new technologies with network facility

IMPORTANT TECHNOLOGICAL SKILLS THAT EVERY LIBRARIAN SHOULD POSSESS TO BECOME DIGITAL LIBRARIAN

Word Processing Skills

Most of the libraries are using software packages, whether build in house or obtaining a commercially available packages. Every librarian should be an expert by learning the word processing skills, with which they can complete their tasks in the right time. They should be able to do simple to great tasks of customization in the software packages, in order to make it more powerful to reach their end-users.

Database Skills

Its play an important role in creating, maintaining, integrating and with any software package that is installed in a library. It is important for every librarian should have database skills for modification of the different tasks of automation, which are demanded by the end-users. The librarian must have the skills on library software management, database creation programme and script writing.

Electronic Presentation Skills

Libraries should be able to use electronic presentation software to create, power-point of Microsoft are essential for archiving scanned pages, images clippings etc,, for enabling the users to access.

Web Navigation Skills

Irrespective of the role, whether a reference librarian, serial librarian, navigating web is the core activity of the digital librarian. Now, there is a search for better search engine. The librarian is expected to acquire the skills in using search engines like yahoo, Google, Alta vista, Lycos etc., while searching information. Third generation (3G) search engines, next generation semantic web are already underway. Hence digital librarian is expected to update knowledge every minute.

Website Design Skills

Nowadays whether small, medium or large are having their own home pages connecting digital libraries. While designing web site; the skills of the librarian will play major role. Home pages designed for libraries are hyperlinked to the institutional websites. Librarian should enhance their web designing skills and also should acquire newer skills with the changing developments.

E-mail Management Skills

Electronic mail has become a boon to the libraries and acts as a powerful bridge between the library staff and the end-users. Knowledge of how use e-mail, how to subscribe to e-mail discussions, how to participate in discussion lists or news groups is needed. It enable the users to access it quickly.

The inventions of fast networks have made information transfer possible. Now, information is being communicated over e-mail and website. Bulk of information can be transferred from one place to another place and advent of new medium has made their work easier but also has increased the pressure on library professionals.

Computer Network Knowledge

The librarian should have the competency in network technology to access e-journals, consortiums, introduction of local area network. A computer network is a system for communication between computers. These networks may be fixed or temporary, both wired and wireless it is very important that librarian should acquire at least basic competencies in the area of computer networks.

File Management

Since e-books and e-journals are subscribed by the library, lot of downloads need to be organized for archival. This demands various technical skills and competencies for managing various files.

Down Loading Software from the Web

Nowadays there are plenty of software's available free of charge on the web. Librarian should have the knowledge of these software, related to his various activities in the library. Many publishers are allowing the libraries for free downloading of their content at least up to the abstract level.

Knowledge of E-books

Its essential competency for a librarian. Resource of E-books, methods of accessing, different subscription models, archival, organizing usage statistics are some of the areas where a librarian has to master his skills.

Computer Related Skills

In this present era almost all libraries are automated in their housekeeping activities. The library professionals must have adequate skills in computer operations to provide current awareness services, SDI service, resource sharing and referral services, Computer literacy includes windows, operating system, word processing, skills in library software's etc.

Scanning Device

Slowly libraries, switching over to digital libraries. Hence there few techniques for scanning documents or images are to be acquired by the librarian.

Knowledge of PDAs

Due to the revolution in the communication technologies, there is a demand from the end-users that they should be allowed electronic gadgets like PDAs, books readers inside the library.

Deep Web Knowledge

The skills on searching the web, familiarity with webs and open access software are necessary for a Librarian. The web based skills includes creation of library websites, interaction with users through the libraries homepage, creation of blogs etc.

Copy Right Knowledge

As we are aware that librarians are involved in the process of subscribing large number of materials such as books, journals, reports in document as well as in electronic form i.e. CDs interactive multimedia, online databases and library management software. The increase in digital publications has made the copyright issue very hot topics. To deal with above, we need to learn nitty-gritty details of licenses.

Skills & Searching Knowledge

Librarians need to know understand the knowledge resources, technological facilities and resources, financial resources and human resources.

Knowing of e-publishing

It provides wider dissemination. A number of journals have, while retaining their peer review process; electronic publishing has become common in scientific publishing where it has been argued that peer-reviewed paper scientific journals are in the process of being replaced by electronic publishing. Knowledge of e-publishing is it books, or journals are an added advantage for the digital librarian.

Soft Skill

It refers to cluster of personality traits, language skills, personal habits, friendliness and optimism. These skills help the librarian to determine the strength, as a leader, listener, negotiator, teaching, training and teamwork, the ability emphasize with the users. Soft skills are usually demonstrated by individuals with high levels of emotional intelligence.

Internet Resources

There are plenty of resources available on the web. While

some are free and other are free-based. Many publishers are making the information available free of charge up to the abstract level, which can be utilized by the libraries.

DIGITAL LIBRARIANS JOB COMPETENCIES

The literature on job competencies for the technologically oriented librarian consists of two major streams: those that focus on the knowledge base (professional skills) and those that focus on attributes or attitudes (personal characteristics)

Roy Tennat, a leading proponent of developing digital librarians, published a list of skills he considers necessary for those who create and manage digital collection and services. These skills are knowledge of:

- Imaging technologies
- Optical character recognition (OCR)
- Markup languages, including HTML, SGML and XML
- Indexing and D B technology
- User interface design
- Programming
- Web technology and
- Project management

The rapid rate of change in technology meant that certain skills might be obsolete in a short time. To remedy this Tennant recommended that employers seek librarians with the following attributes or personal traits:

- Capacity to learn constantly and quickly
- Flexibility
- Innate skepticism
- Propensity to take risks
- Abiding public service perspective
- Good interpersonal skills
- Skills at enabling and fostering change, and

- Team working skills
- Leadership skills.

CONCLUSION

The present day digital librarian is evolving to network specialist, information broker, systems designer and knowledge manager. In essence, an overall intensification of specialization both in the technological aspects of library and information services, as well as stronger subject-oriented competencies and evaluative abilities are being demanded from the information professionals as well as in in-service continuing education to meet the changing technologies demands at the organization. The transition of traditional collection to digital collections presented the library professionals with new opportunity to play a new dynamic role and serve the information base society in better way than hitherto, especially in the field of science and technology which is very sensitive to the changes.

We are moving a knowledge society, where 70 percent of the work will be based on applying knowledge to problems. Technology has brought about more and more personalization of information transforming libraries from "just-in-case" collection to "just-in-time" and finally to "just-for-you" propositions. The present day librarian is not a librarian as librarians used to be, but a digital librarian- someone who helps to sort through, retrieve and organize the limitless information available in cyberspace, and work out the complex issues that the technology presents.

REFERENCES

1. ABSV Prasad Rao – Why and How to become a Cybrarian, Developing Cyber Libraries:Festchrift in honour of Professonr M.Sankar Reddy, Allied publisher, 2006, P95-103.
2. Nirmala Chigateri – Evolving role of the librarian in virtual library, Indian Academic Libraries 2020: A vision, Karnatka State College library Association publisher, Tumkur 2010, P206-209.
3. Gopal Krishan.S and Pichappan-Emerging thrust areas in Library and Information Sciences, Chennai, Anna university, 2008,

4. http://skyways.lib.ks.us/central/e-book/libraries.html.

5. http://www.learnthenet.com/english/section/email.html

6. Wright Alex, In search of the deep web, 2004. Kurose, J.F.Computer networking, 2004.

7. Rajiv Gupta, Sanjay Kumar Singh and Vijay Kumar-Preservation of Digital Information, IASLIC Bulletin, 48 (4), 2003.

8. Gearrett J and Water D- Preservation of Digital Information: Report of the Task Force on Archiving of Digital Information, may 1996

9. Almnesh, D G and Hasting S K-A metadata approach to preservation of digital resources: the University of North Texas Liberians experience, First Monday, 7(8), August2002.

10. "Competencies for Special Librarians of the 21st Century:" Report Submitted to SLA Board of Directors by the special committee on Competencies for Special Librarians. Joanne Marshall, Chair; Bill Fisher; Lynda Moulton; and Roberta Piccolo: May 1996.

11. Information Literacy Competencies and Criteria for Academic Libraries in Wisconsin. http://www.wla.lib.wi.us/waal/infolit/ilcc.html

12. Moore, Nick. "The future demand for Information Professionals in Europe." Education for Information 16, 1998, p. 191-208.

13. http://www..legal-database.com/internetlaw.htm

14. Rhodes, Helen; and Jaqueline Chelin. "Web-based User Education in UK University Libraries – results of a survey." Program. 34-1 (Jan 2000): .59-73.

23
Information Needs and Sources of Faculty Members in Engineering and Technological Institutes, Affiliated to Solapur University, Maharashtra

Vijay Kumar N Mulimani
Librarian, Sangameshwar College, Solapur
Prashant R Hiremath
Librarian, A.G. Patil Institute of Technology, Solapur

ABSTRACT

The article mainly gives the information needs and sources of faculty members in Engineering and Technological institutes affiliated to Solapur University, Maharashtra state it highlights the importance of Engineering Library resources especially the reading materials provided by the engineering library and its effective use by the faculty.

Keywords: Faculty members, Engineering, Technology, User survey.

INTRODUCTION

This paper has provided a resources to engineering faculty members in by outlining various options for their continuing professional development and providing pointers on how to access them. In addition, it has provided rationale to providers of continuing education in the engineering field. It is hoped that such providers will advertise their offerings to engineering educators in developing countries.

Solapur city is one of the oldest cities the emergence of Solapur city is found way back in 1135 A.D. on copper – plates as "Sonnalagi" Till end of 16the century "Sonnalagi" was transformed in to "Sonnalapur" There after "Sonnalapur" has been transformed into 'Solapur'.

Solapur is a city in Maharashtra India; it is the administrative headquarters of Solapur District. It is situated at the border of Karnataka & Andhra Pradesh. Solapur is famous as a textile town, especially owing to its talented weavers community Solapur District leads in bedding productions. Its great strides in the field of education, literature and culture as well as rural prosperity brought in by the cooperation movement have made Solapur District important segment of modern Maharashtra.

This paper is intended to provide a resources to engineering faculty members in by outlining various options for their continuing professional development and providing pointers on how to access them. In addition, it is intended to call to the attention of providers of continuing education in the engineering field that a potential audience may be being underserved. It is hoped that such providers will advertise their offerings to engineering educators in developing countries, and offer them at prices that are affordable to that audience.

Maharashtra State Gazetteer. The Gazetteer of the district of Solapur, Photozincopress, Mumbai 2003 P.1

THE GOALS OF INFORMATION NEEDS AND SOURCES

In social Research, varies types of purposes. These are knowledge developments, scientific Research in social life, social welfare, fact Analysis, social control and Inference etc., Information needs and sources of faculty members in Engineering and Technological Institutes, Affiliated to Solapur University, Maharashtra in this topic I have covered following elements ____

(1) Faculty members, Reading habits.

(2) Library provides the information, which is basically needed by faculty members.

(3) Internet and other sources used by faculty members.

(4) Which type of Information sources is most popular and used by faculty.

(5) Book's Journal's is personal collection in e-forms and hard form.

(6) Which types of services provided are provided to faculty members.

(7) Research papers presently by faculty members.

OBJECTIVES

Therefore, the objectives set out are:

1. Does the information needs and sources available match in college Library.
2. Does teachers update knowledge with the help Internet.
3. Whether teachers are satisfied with the information, which is the available in the college Library.
4. Does teachers use maps, charts, models and LCD projector while teaching.
5. Does teachers extend guidance to the students to improve their reading habits.

6. Whether teachers prepare notes of the study materials, ready by him.
7. To explore whether teachers provide to the students extra knowledge relating to the subject matters.
8. How many teachers submit Research Papers.
9. Does college Library provide information, needed by the college teachers.

HYPOTHESIS

Therefore, the hypothesis of the research is that:

1. Engineering and Technological institutes teachers are satisfied with the information made available in the college library.
2. Engineering and Technological institutes teachers use maps, charts, models LCD and Projector while teaching.
3. Engineering and Technological Institutes teachers update their knowledge with the use of Internet.
4. Engineering and Technological Institutes teachers give guidance to student for improve reading habits in study.
5. Engineering and Technological Institutes teachers read Tex books & Reference books related to teaching subject.
6. Engineering and Technological institutes teachers make use of information available in Journals for teaching.
7. Engineering and Technological, institutes teachers are satisfied in their job.
8. Engineering and Technological, institutes teachers are prepare notes of the study material read by them.
9. Engineering and Technological, institutes inform students regarding books relating to the subject matter.
10. Engineering and Technological Colleges institute teachers are use Audio cassettes and C.D's.
11. Engineering and Technological, institute teachers present National and International level Research papers.

THE DATA

The Scholar has made a rigors pursuit for collection of relevant data from Libraries and teachers of Engineering Colleges, Affiliated to Solapur University those are

1. Walchand Institutes of Technology, Solapur
2. College of Engineering, Pandharpur.
3. Bramhadeo Mane Institute of Technology, Belati, Solapur.
4. Bharat-Ratna Indira Gandhi College of Engineering, Kegaon, Solapur.

The researcher found the work of collection of data as painful and tedious work. The constant follow-up action yielded best results and collected relevant data from the respondents to fulfill the objectives at this research. It is really found to be different experience of keeping deep patients researcher. To collect relevant data to the problem, the researcher has used a mixed type of questionnaire, with a purpose to collect comprehensive data. Of course, the utmost care has been taken to include specific, minimum and relevant question only. A copy of questionnaire was given to every faculty members and college librarians. All the full time teachers on roll of these four Engineering and Technological Colleges. The primary data collection is an outcome of responses received from 20 teachers. The Primary data collection is found to be a time consuming process also.

There are five HOD's and Professors in Walchand Institutes of Technology, Solapur and responded received from five teachers. Five in College of Engineering, Pandharpur and received from five teachers. Five in Bramhadeo Mane Institute of Technology, Solapur and received from five teachers. Five in Bharat-Ratna Indira Gandhi College of Engineering, Solapur and received from five teachers.

In addition to this scholar has minutely observed all relevant factors for factual data collection to reveal the facts of the problem

PROCEDURE

The scholar has used "questionnaire" (mixed questionnaire) as a tool for gathering data. All aspects are considered while finalizing the questionnaire. The questionnaire is comprehensive in nature. The researcher has used a sample of Head of department before growing a head to this venture. The scholar, at initial stage gave questionnaire of Head of Departments teachers of each college for testing. The response, ignited to the researcher. The findings are discussed with the guide in detail. The guide opined that there is room for research. The scholar also confirmed the opinions of guide while discussing the problem with other research experts in library and information science. The scholar has used, in addition to questionnaire, observation and internal method wherever necessary for collection of data.

Methods used for data gathering

The scholar has used questionnaire as a tool for data gathering for this dissertation. In addition to a comprehensive questionnaire the scholar has used observation and interviews method to support data. The questionnaire has been finalized after through discussion with the guide and it consists major questions relevant to the aspect. To avoid complexities and make it simple. The questionnaire has been minimized to the possible extent without shrinking of the data required for the objectives of this research.

The questionnaires have been formulated in such a way that it focuses on Information needs and sources of faculty members for academic purpose.

To reach the perfection in process of data collection the scholar has used a mixed comprehensive questionnaire, which has given an opportunity to some open ended question. The questionnaire consists coulee ended questions too and some at them after respondent opinions along with multiple choice options also. Though, the questionnaire is very precise it is competent enough to fetch the relevant data required for the research problem in 39 questions given in the Library questionnaire and 37 questions given in the questionnaire of faculty members.

The scholar has carefully remained alien to avoid reflection of scholar's opinion. Therefore, the data collected from the respondents is without prejudice. The collection of data is limited to only four Engineering and Technological colleges, Affiliated to Solapur University, Maharashtra, 1) Walchand Institute of Technology, Solapur 2) College of Engineering, Pandharpur 3) Brahmdeo Mane Institute of technology 4) Bharat-Ratna Indira Gandhi College of Engineering, Solapur having 5 Head of Department in each college.

To obtain efficient response from the respondents the scholar has made a rigorous follow-up action and collected the questionnaire from the scholars.

To reach to the level of standard perfection for data gathering the scholar has recovered data by observation too, from these four colleges. The scholar has observed while remaining alien when the teachers use actually sources Information since, the scholar is working in the Bharat-Ratna Indira Gandhi College of Engineering for last 2 years. The scholar has recorded some facts from the principals while conducting oral interviews. Also scholar has recorded facts from 10 faculty members that is 02, 02, 02, 04 from each college respectively. The scholar has to highlight that the test results are very carefully recovered and received through questionnaire.

ANALYSIS AND INTERPRETATION

There are five Head of Department in each institute, Walchand Institute of Technology, Solapur, College of Engineering, Pandharpur, Bramhadeo Mane Institute of Technology, Solapur and Bhara-Ratna Indira Gandhi College of Engineering, Solapur. This Research is limited to these four Engineering and technological colleges, affiliated to Solapur university, Maharashtra.

The universe of study of the present research is expressed in the following table.

Table 1. Table showing college wise Head of Department in Engineering and Technological Colleges affiliated to Solapur University, Maharashtra.

Sr. No.	Name of College	No. of faculty members
1.	Walchand Institutions of Technology, Solapur	5
2.	College of Engineering, Pandharpur.	5
3.	Bramhadeo Mane Institution of Technology, Solapur	5
4.	Bharat-Ratna Indira Gandhi College of Engineering, Solapur	5

The above Table is showing that there are 5 Head of Department in each Engineering and Technological Institute Affiliated to Solapur University, Maharashtra.

Table 2. Table showing No. of Research papers/articles presented in seminar, workshop and symposia by HODs of Engineering and Technological Institutes affiliated to Solapur University, Maharashtra.

National Level	International Level	National and International Level	Nil Report
7	1	5	6

The Above table is showing that 7 faculty members have presented National Level Research paper / article in seminar, workshops and symposia, 1 faculty members have presented at International Level, 5 faculty members have presented at National and International level and 6 Faculty members have not presented any Research Paper / article in seminar, work shop symposia either at national or International level.

The Table 3 is showing that, 11 faculty members are satisfactory in their job, 04 Faculty members are very satisfactory, and 04 Faculty members are Extremely Satisfactory in the profession.

Table 3. Showing number of Job Satisfaction level of Faculty members in Engineering and Technological Institutes.

Sr. No.	College Name	Satisfactory	Very Satisfactory	Extremely Satisfactory
1	W.I.T., Solapur	02	-	03
2	C.O.E., Pandharpur	01	03	01
3	B.M.I.T., Solapur	03	01	-
4	B.I.G.C.E., Solapur	05	-	-
	Total	**11**	**04**	**04**

Table 4. Table showing numbers of faculty member's sources of information regarding latest books in their subject.

Library	Publisher	Internet	Library & Publisher	Publisher & Internet	Library & Internet
01	02	03	03	03	07

The Above Table is showing that 1 Faculty member get information of latest books of subject from Library, 2 Faculty members get information of latest books in the subject from publisher, 3 Faculty member get information of latest books of subject on Internet, 3 Faculty member get information of latest books of subject from Library and Publisher, 3 Faculty members get it from publisher and internet and 7 Faculty members get it from Library as well as Internet.

Table 5. Table showing teachers extending guidance to student for improvement in reading habits by________

Conduct group discussion	Give Project work	Dictate list of books available in the library
9	6	4

The Above table is showing that, 9 Faculty members conduct group discussion of students for improvement of reading habits, 6 Faculty members Give project work to students for improvement reading habits, and 4 Faculty members Dictate list of books available in the Library to students for improvement of reading habits in study.

Table 6. Table showing that satisfaction level of teachers regarding information made available in the college Library.

Satisfactory	Very Satisfactory	Extremely Satisfactory
12	6	1

The Above table is showing that, 12 Faculty members are satisfactory with the information made available in the College Library, 06 Faculty members are very Satisfactory with the information made available in the college Library and 01 Faculty members is extremely satisfactory with the Information made available in the college Library.

FINDINGS

In this research dissertation, Researcher has come out with following concrete findings.

1. 63.17% Engineering and Technological Institutes Faculty members are Satisfactory, 31.57% Very Satisfactory, 5.26% Extremely Satisfactory for Information, which is available in the College Library.

   It mean's Engineering and Technological Institutes Faculty members are satisfactory with the Information made available in College Library.

2. 84.21% Faculty members of Engineering and Technological Institutes use maps, charts, models and LCD projector frequently while teaching and 15.79%. Faculty members use less frequently.

   It mean's that, Engineering and Technological Institutes Faculty members are using map's, charts, models and LCD Projector frequently while teaching.

3. 84.21% faculty members update their knowledge with the help of Internet and 15.79% use some other sources.

It mean's that, Engineering and Technological Institutes teachers are updating their knowledge with the help of Internet.

4. Engineering and Technological Institutes, Faculty members extend guidance to student for improvement of reading habits to students in study.

5. Engineering and Technological Institutes, 78.94% Faculty members are use text books as well as Reference books related to their subject and 21.06% refer allied material too.

6. 78.94% faculty members make of use Journals very frequently and 21.06% use journals less frequently.

   It's clear that, Engineering and Technological Institutes teachers use Journal's for teaching.

7. 57.88% Faculty members are 'Satisfactory' in the job, 21.06% are very satisfactory & 21.06% are extremely satisfactory in the Job.

   It's found that in Engineering and Technological Institute Faculty members are having 'Satisfaction' in their Job.

8. 94.74% faculty members for development of study material for students prepare notes and 05.26% do not do so.

   It means that, maximum number of teachers of Engineering and Technological Institutes, prepares notes of the development of study material for the students.

9. Engineering and Technological Institutes, Faculty members in 94.74% faculty members inform to students regarding availability of books relating to subject matter and 05.26% teachers do not extend such guidance to the students.

   It's clear that, Engineering and Technological Institutes faculty members intimate students frequently regarding latest books relating to subject matter.

10. Engineering and Technological Institutes, Faculty members in 63.17% teachers frequently use teaching aids like Audio

cassettes and CD'S and 36.83% teachers use some other teaching aids.

It means that majority of Engineering and Technological Institutes Faculty members are using Audio cassettes and CDs along with reading material.

11. 68.42% Faculty members have presented research papers in the national and International Level. Seminars, symposia and workshop.

It means that majority of the staff members are presenting research papers in the national and international level. Seminars, symposia and workshop.

SUGGESTIONS

Information needs and sources of faculty members in Engineering and Technological Institutes Affiliated to Solapur University, Maharashtra. Are made clear in this project, the research scholar has come to the conclusion make some concrete suggestions based on this research study those are:

1. Faculty members should join online discussion group for their subject.
2. Faculty members use of E-Books & E – Journal will enrich subject knowledge.
3. Faculty members should improving their Qualification and enrich knowledge for our Better prospects in the field of research.
4. Faculty members should publish own books for the benefit of others.
5. Faculty members should read other allied books to along with the curriculum books.
6. Faculty members should read research Paper in seminar, work –shop and symposia at all possible access.
7. Faculty members should visit of Books Exhibition and purchase useful Books for development of personal collection.

8. Faculty members should use Non – Book materials very frequently.
9. Faculty members should motivate students to develop reading habit by a separate consultation or action research.
10. Faculty members should involve in the Library development activities.
11. Faculty members should note recorded the Books read by them and recommend for their addition in the institutes library.

CONCLUSION

This is to conclude that the engineering and technical institutes of Solapur are running very efficiently and the faculty members are very much satisfied with information needs and sources in engineering and allied subjects. Faculty members in engineering colleges have advantage of high quality graduate educations, with master's and doctoral degrees from well respected universities. Those who are dedicated to improving the situation in their native countries often return home after graduate study abroad, and take teaching position at local universities. They are then often beset by a multitude of problems – inadequate salaries, forcing them to have an additional job which detracts from their university effectiveness ; lack of financial resources for teaching and research laboratory equipment, and for publications that could keep them abreast of developments in their technical and professional field ; and lack of funds for travel to conference that could keep them technically and professional up to date.

REFERENCES

1. Ary D Lucy, C.Jocobs & Asghav. Introduction to Research In Education, Rinehart Publications, 1972.
2. Bal Krishnan S. and Paliwal P.K., Library Digital Technology, Anmol Publication, New Delhi, 2001.
3. Bal Krishnan S. and Paliwal P.K., Academic Library Automations, Anmol Publication, New Delhi, 2001.

4. Bhandekar P.L., Methodology and Techniques of Social Science Research, Himalaya Publication, Bombay, 1982.

5. Bodhankar P.L., Social Research Methodology, Aurangabad.

6. Bodhankar Sudhir and other, Social Research Methodology, Sainath Publications, Nagpur, 1993.

7. Bose H., Information Science Principals and Practice, Sterling Publishers, New Delhi, 1986.

8. Chandel Sunil Singh, Information Services in AcademicLibraries: Study of ICSSR Institute, Rawat Publications, Jaipur, 2003.

9. Chunekar S.R., Research Structure and Methodology, Shikshan Prasarak sanstha, Sangamner, 1983.

10. Clifford Hawkins and Marcosorgi, Research How to plan speak and writing, Barner and Nobel Inc., New York, 1956.